DISCARDED BY
MEMPHIS PUBLIC LIBRARY

Ellen Davis Rodgers

Heirs Through Hope
The Episcopal Diocese of West Tennessee

by
ELLEN DAVIES-RODGERS

With Illustrations

Published and Sold by
The Plantation Press
Brunswick
Memphis, Tennessee 38134

©Copyright 1983
BY
E. Davies-Rodgers

All rights reserved.
Printed in the United States of America

Library of Congress
Catalog Card Number: 83-50733

Manufactured by
Brandau, Craig, Dickerson Co.
Nashville, Tennessee

Heirs Through Hope
The Episcopal Diocese of West Tennessee

HEIRS THROUGH HOPE
The Episcopal Diocese of West Tennessee

	PAGE
Illustrations	9
Dedication	11
A Message from the Presiding Bishop, The Most Rev. John M. Allin	14
A Message from the Bishop of West Tennessee, The Rt. Rev. Alex Dockery Dickson, Jr.	15
Author's Preface	17

Chapter 1	Time is Prelude	23
	The Episcopal Church in Jamestown, Virginia 1607	23
	The Episcopal Church in America, 1784	25
	The Episcopal Church in Tennessee, 1829, 1834	28
Chapter 2	Heirs in Service	35
	Men of the Cope and Miter (Bishops)	35
	Men of the Cloth	63
	Laymen and Laywomen	66
Chapter 3	The Western District	71
	Twenty-One Counties Formed 1819-1875	71
Chapter 4	The Episcopal Church Comes to West Tennessee, 1832	79
	Map of Counties and Churches, 1983	86
Chapter 5	The Thirty Four Episcopal Churches in West Tennessee, 1983	89
Chapter 6	The Creation of the Diocese of West Tennessee George A. Fox, Archivist, West Tennessee	255
Chapter 7	Election of the First Bishop of the Diocese of West Tennessee, M. Anderson Cobb, Jr., Chairman, Episcopate Committee	259
Chapter 8	A Bishop is Consecrated Gordon Bernard, Vicar, St. Philip Church, Davieshire, Brunswick	265
Chapter 9	Welcoming and Seating of the Bishop in the Cathedral W. Fred Gates, Jr., Retired Suffragan Bishop of Tennessee	277
Chapter 10	Time is Postlude—The Challenge of Tomorrow	281
	Commission on Ministry— The Rev. Robert M. Watson, Jr.	282
	The Tennessee Churchman—Joseph S. T. Alford	284
	Communications—William L. Givens	285
	Development—Glenn N. Holliman	287
	Episcopal Church Home—Mrs. Ralph Scott	289
	Episcopal Churchmen of West Tennessee— George Clarke	291

      Episcopal Churchwomen of West Tennessee—
        Mrs. Charles L. Clarke 292
      Episcopal Young Churchmen—
        Edward T. McNabb, Jr. 293
        James Crumrine 294
      Episcopal Schools—Geoffrey Butler 296
      St. Columba—Lewis K. McKee 298
      Stewardship—Paul A. Calame, Jr. 300
      University of the South (Sewanee)—
        Robert M. Ayers, Jr. 301
      Venture in Mission—David R. Hackett 304
      Youth Service—Donald E. Mowery 304
   The Challenge of Tomorrow 307
Reference Notes by Chapters 308
Bibliography 312
Acknowledgments 313
About the Author 314
Index 315

Illustrations

The Rt. Rev. James Hervey Otey 12
The Rt. Rev. Alex Dockery Dickson, Jr. 13
Bishops of Tennessee 69, 70
Mary Hayes Willis (Mrs. Thomas Benn) Gloster 78
Mrs. Gloster's Earthen Jug 78
Map of Counties and Churches 86
St. James, Bolivar 88
Ravenscroft Chapel, Brighton 92
Christ Church, Brownsville 96
St. Philip, Davieshire, Brunswick 100
St. Andrew's, Collierville 112
St. Matthew's, Covington 120
St. Mary's Church, Dyersburg 126
St. George's, Germantown 132
St. Thomas the Apostle, Humboldt 138
St. Luke's, Jackson 140
Immanuel, LaGrange 146
St. John's, Martin 154
St. Paul's, Mason 158
Trinity, Mason 160
All Saints', Memphis 170
Bishop Otey Memorial, Memphis 172
Calvary Church, Memphis 174
Christ Church, Memphis 180
Emmanuel Church, Memphis 184
Church of the Good Shepherd, Memphis 192
Grace-St. Luke's, Memphis 198
Church of the Holy Apostles, Memphis 200
Church of the Holy Communion, Memphis 202
Holy Trinity, Memphis 206
St. Elisabeth's, Memphis 210
St. James', Memphis 212
St. John's, Memphis 214
St. Mary's Cathedral, Memphis 220
St. Paul's, Memphis 226
St. Anne's, Millington 232

Grace Church, Paris 234
Immanuel, Ripley 242
St. Thomas' Mission, Somerville 244
St. James', Union City 250
Seals of Dioceses of Tennessee and West Tennessee 264
Consecration of the Bishop of West Tennessee 272-275
Seating of the Bishop of West Tennessee 279, 280
Ellen Davies-Rodgers 314

Dedicated to
The Glory of God
in memory of
The Right Reverend James Hervey Otey
the First Bishop of the Episcopal Diocese of Tennessee
January 14, 1834 — April 23, 1863
and
in honor of
The Right Reverend Alex Dockery Dickson, Jr.
First Bishop of the Episcopal Diocese of West Tennessee
April 9, 1983.

"That being justified by his grace, we should be made heirs according to the hope of eternal life."[1]

The Right Reverend James Hervey Otey
First Bishop of the Episcopal Diocese of Tennessee

The Right Reverend Alex Dockery Dickson, Jr.
First Bishop of the Episcopal Diocese of West Tennessee

A Message From The Presiding Bishop
The Most Reverend John Maury Allin

Living history is the continuing review and appreciation of tradition and past events, along with honoring those persons who in special service and significant actions shaped the tradition and shared the events. Such is a renewing experience when the review is focused in the emergence of new expressions and forms of the life and purpose of a people in community, company, common calling or common origin. The review set forth in this book by a concerned and perceptive participant in the tradition and life of the Episcopal Church in Western Tennessee will serve many, both participants in the life of the church and those who may observe from afar, by offering an appreciative insight into the life of the Western Tennessee portion of the church universal.

> "The lot is fallen unto (them) in a fair ground; yea, (they) have a goodly heritage."[1]

One can read with thanksgiving this review of living history. And for the reviewer, the history lives because recorded tradition is manifested in a present continuing community, a faithful community with hope in a loving mission.

Read on. The company is good, the prospects promising!

John Maury Allin
23rd Presiding Bishop

A Message From The Bishop of West Tennessee
The Right Reverend Alex Dockery Dickson, Jr.

The Church in West Tennessee—a Beginning, a Continuation

As we work, pray and serve in the first year of this new diocese of West Tennessee, I am deeply mindful of and thankful for our noble heritage. I am reminded everywhere I turn that we are indebted to all who are a part of the great diocese of Tennessee—laity, nuns, monks, deacons, priests, bishops. I am also confronted everywhere I go with the manifold opportunities for mission and ministry in this great metropolitan area of Memphis and West Tennessee.

I am firmly convinced that God the Holy Spirit has called us, as He called Abraham, to leave behind old relationships and old structures and go forth in faith into these new opportunities to serve our holy and loving God. We are indeed "surrounded by a great cloud of witnesses" who served in our mother diocese. We must be faithful to the vision of mission and ministry they held before us. We must also be open to an even broader and deeper vision to which God the Holy Spirit is now calling us.

We are indebted, also, to our author who serves us all in preparing this history to take with us on our spiritual journey in this new diocese. This book will help us to remember that the Diocese of West Tennessee is indeed a beginning and a continuation.

+Alex Dickson

Alex D. Dickson, Bishop
The Diocese of West Tennessee

Author's Preface

"*HEIRS THROUGH HOPE*, (The Episcopal Diocese of West Tennessee) is a title which is inspiring, challenging and spiritually meaningful. Why was this title chosen? Ever since the inception of a volume related to the creation of the new diocese (1983) the need of an appropriate title became apparent. Much thought and prayer ensued.

At a Sunday morning service at St. Philip, Davieshire, Brunswick, Holy Communion had been partaken by a congregation of worshipful parishioners. At the conclusion the Celebrant, the Reverend Gordon Bernard, beloved Vicar said, "Let us pray." The People joined in praying this Prayer:

> "Almighty and everliving God, we most heartily thank thee for that thou dost feed us, in these holy mysteries, with the spiritual food of the most precious Body and Blood of thy Son our Savior Jesus Christ; and dost assure us thereby of thy favor and goodness toward us; and that we are very members incorporate in the mystical body of thy Son, the blessed company of all faithful people; and are also *HEIRS, THROUGH HOPE*, of thy everlasting kingdom. And we humbly beseech thee, O heavenly Father, so to assist us with thy grace, that we may continue in that holy fellowship, and do all such good works as thou hast prepared for us to walk in; through Jesus Christ our Lord, to whom, with thee and the Holy Ghost, be all honor and glory, world without end."   Amen.[1]

As though some special dispensation had been invoked those three great words resounded—*Heirs Through Hope*—and immediately it was resolved to make them the title of this new volume on Episcopal Church history.

Later, with the decision in mind the Holy Scriptures were searched for passages which seemed to depict best the spirit and meaning of the chosen words of the title. These passages filled with the hope of a glorious inheritance were revealed:

> "And if children, their heirs; *heirs of God*, and *joint-heirs with Christ*; if so be that we suffer with *him*, that we may be also glorified together."[2]
>
> "Wherefore thou art no more a servant, but a son; and if a son, then *an heir of God through Christ*."[3]
>
> "Hearken, my beloved brethren, Hath not God chosen the poor of this world *rich in faith*, and *heirs of the kingdom* which he hath promised to them that love him?"[4]

Many who will read this book will be reminded of the content of three other volumes on Episcopal Church history previously written by the author:[5] "The Romance of the Episcopal Church in West Tennessee," 1964; "Holy Innocents," 1966 and "The Great Book, Calvary Protestant Episcopal Church 1832-1972, Memphis, Tennessee", 1973. In this particular, later volume the privilege has been assumed to quote freely from these volumes passages which deal especially with the history of the American Episcopal Church and other aspects of historical background as deemed wise to be chosen.

Immediately following the election of the Right Reverend Alex Dockery Dickson, Jr., as the first bishop of the newly created Diocese of West Tennessee a volume of "The Romance of the Episcopal Church in West Tennessee," was mailed to his Vicksburg, Mississippi, address. A few weeks later, in conversation he remarked that doubtless few Bishops experienced the gift of a recorded history of the area over which he was to preside so early after becoming the Episcopate![6]

This work, *HEIRS THROUGH HOPE*, The Episcopal Diocese of West Tennessee, is by no means an effort to take the place of "The Romance of the Episcopal Church in West Tennessee" in the annals of the Episcopal Church. "The Romance of the Episcopal Church in West Tennessee" was written at a time during which the full Diocese of Tennessee was functioning. The content of the present book attempts to give an account of the background,—the foundation stone,—from which the new branch evolved, yet, with particular emphasis on the elements pertinent today to the Churches of the Diocese of West Tennessee in 1983.

As few have ferreted the detailed process by which a diocese is created this subject is of importance and is stressed herein. The nomination and election of a bishop to head the flock in West Tennessee, his consecration and enthronement, all these are of timely interest.

Unfortunately circumstances prevented the author's attendance at the sessions during which the Diocese of West Tennessee was in the process of being created. Therefore, not having been present to witness the procedure it seemed unwise to vicariously write of the sessions held. So, several able persons who were present were asked to write covering chapters of the various phases of the proceedings. Their gracious acceptances of this request are reflected in their very accurate and readable contributions incorporated as important phases of this volume. Their assistance is acknowledged with sincere appreciation!

Yes, it is a bit unusual to voluntarily attempt the writing and publication of such a volume. There was no assignment which requested the performance of this task. There has been no committee nor group to advise, to dictate nor to edit the process nor the product! However, many have given most acceptable advice when consulted. Nor have coffers other than an individual purse been used to cover the financial expenditures necessary for the production of such a tome. Please be assured the writing of this book has been truly a labor of love. Yes, a labor of love for the Lord, for His Church with faith in, hope for and love of His people.

Those who were present in the Convention of the Diocese of West Virginia in January 1976 will recall the introduction given by the Bishop of that Diocese, the Right Reverend Robert P. Atkinson as he presented Hillman Philip Rodgers and the author and said: "Miss Ellen writes Episcopal Church histories for missions!" It is true that the motive in writing is for missions—not for (personal) money. Records reveal that from the sale of the three books, before named, written from 1964 to 1973, a substantial sum of more than forty thousand dollars was given toward the building of an Episcopal Mission in Brunswick, Shelby County, Tennessee,—St. Philip, Davieshire.

Doubtless there will be a need whereby the new Diocese of West Tennessee can use all funds which good fortune may provide. Thus, after the cost of production has been met by the sale of this volume—*Heirs Through Hope*—all proceeds will be allocated by the author to The Diocese of West Tennessee Endowment Corporation, chartered January 17, 1983, to be held in trust, the income to be used to support the West Tennessee Mission program.

As this Preface approaches conclusion let us return to the title chosen for this writing—*Heirs Through Hope*. Indeed may attention be given to the meaning of the key words—*heir* and *hope*. Who is an heir? An heir is defined in several ways:

> "A person who succeeds, by the rules of law, to an estate in lands, tenements, or hereditaments, upon the death of his ancestor, by descent and right of relationship."[7]
>
> "One who succeeds or is to succeed another in the possession of property; an inheritor; one who receives any endowment from an ancestor.—Heir apparent, one whose right to inherit is unforfeitable, if he survives the ancestor."[8]

A few passages about *heirs* from literature are recorded:

> "I the heir of all the ages in the foremost files of time."[9]
> "Make us heirs of all eternity."[10]
> "Heirs of God, and joint-heirs with Christ."[11]

> "Children of yesterday,
>   Heirs of to-morrow,
> What are you weaving?
>   Labor and sorrow?
> Look to your looms again,
>   Faster and faster
> Fly the great shuttles
>   Prepared by the Master.
> Life's in the loom,
> Room for it—room!"[12]

The fictitious Uncle Ezra passed from his earthly existence—he died! "Did he leave a will?", the inquisitive family members asked. "Well, what did he leave?," they continued. Uncle Ezra did leave a will. He left, of course, all of his worldly possessions of which his legal descendants, his heirs, were the inheritors. Such ownership he had to leave. Yet, because of the good man's Christian fortitude as a devout soldier of the Cross he also left a clearly recorded legacy of his service to God and man. This legacy was his passport to life eternal as he experienced the heirship so lovingly bestowed by his Lord.

Yes, our Lord left a will, a covering, specific and determining document, biblically recorded and His many bequests are our priceless heritage:

> "In my Father's house are many mansions: if it were not so, I would have told you. I go to prepare a place for you."[13]
> "I will not leave you comfortless: I will come to you."[14]
> "This is my commandment, That ye love one another, as I have loved you."[15]
> "That whosoever believeth in him should not perish, but have eternal life."[16]

These are only a few of our Lord's blessings bestowed on us his heirs.

What shall we say of *Hope?* Hope is defined as a firm belief, trust, self reliance, assurance, courage, an act of anticipation or expectation.

The Holy Bible carries a number of logical and persuasive passages concerning the meaning of *Hope:*

> "And now, Lord, what wait I for? my hope is in thee."[17]
> "For thou art my hope, O Lord God; thou art my trust from my youth."[18]
> "Therefore did my heart rejoice, and my tongue was glad; moreover also my flesh shall rest in hope."[19]
> "For we through the Spirit wait for the hope of righteousness by faith."[20]

And again we pray the Almighty and everliving God dost

assure us of his favor and goodness toward us and that we are the blessed company of all faithful people. Yes, and that we are also Heirs Through Hope of God's everlasting kingdom!

It is a fond wish that this volume, *HEIRS THROUGH HOPE*, may be placed side by side with the author's former volumes on Episcopal Church history as a record for now and for posterity. Through these carefully researched and enthusiastically written passages may many of the innumerable details of the fascinating functioning of the Episcopal Church be cherished in this area of God's kingdom, the new Diocese of West Tennessee, and beyond.

Ellen Davies-Rodgers

Mrs. Hillman Philip Rodgers

Davies Plantation
Brunswick, Tennessee
July 28, 1983[21]

CHAPTER 1

Time is Prelude

The Episcopal Church in Jamestown, Virginia 1607

The founding of Jamestown, Virginia in 1607 marks a period of both historic and religious significance. It was there our nation's history began with the establishment of the first permanent colony. Also, it was to Jamestown that the ancient Church of England, the Episcopal Church, came to the American continent.

Prior to the colonization of Jamestown, it is known that on occasions English clergy had landed on the shores of America. One English minister came with John Cabot in 1497; another sailed with Sir Francis Drake in 1579—both, in reality, were ships' chaplains and held services ashore, while their vessels were anchored nearby.

Significant is the fact that Sir Francis Drake's famous voyage around the world touched the shore of California. Later, in commemoration of this historic event a large Celtic cross, known as the Prayer Book Cross, was erected in Golden Gate Park, San Francisco, on the highest elevation. The chaplain of the fleet, the Reverend Francis Fletcher, held services which marked the first Christian services on America's western shores.

It was in 1587 that a company of English people, sent by Sir Walter Raleigh, sailed to the coast of North Carolina and with them brought the Prayer Book. Virginia Dare, born in August of that year, became the first white child baptized in America.

The whole purpose of religious extension was expressed in the terms of the patent for Virginia in 1606. In the language of King James that "so noble a work may, by Providence of God, hereafter tend to the glorie of his divine majestie, in propagating of Christian religion to such people as sit in darkness and miserable ignorance of the true knowledge and worship of God, and may in time bring the infidels and savages (living in those parts) to human civility and quiet government." King James gave further admonition in his instructions of 1606, that "all persons should kindly treat the savages and heathen people in these parts, and use all proper means to draw them to the true service and knowledge of God."[1]

A group of Englishmen which sailed on December 9, 1606 from Blackwell, England to Virginia shores brought the first minister of the Episcopal Church to James City. He was the Reverend Robert Hunt. The dedicated Captain of the ship was John Smith. Bishop William Meade wrote of the devout minister and the sea captain, "two men who seemed to know no fear, but that of God."

To American shores, in the settlement of the Colony of Virginia, "England's children brought her choicest gifts across the sea." Such gifts were her concepts of civil rights, of English common law and the right of representative government. And one of her greatest gifts, that of the historic faith of her Church—the Church of England. Pertaining specifically to this gift was the contribution of the Book of Common Prayer and, at first, the Bishop's Bible; later, by a few years, the magnificent King James version of the Scriptures.

James City Parish in Virginia was created by the Bishop of London. King James I, Defender of the Faith, gave approval and impetus to this religious progress. Thus the English colonists of 1607 came to America with the full intention of bringing to their new home, in this broad wilderness, their Church! Definitely, this was the opposite purpose of the Pilgrims to Massachusetts in 1620, who came to escape the influence and domination of the Church of England.

So, let us repeat: Jamestown was the first American parish of the Anglican Communion. Virginia had previously not been touched by Christianity. The Reverend Robert Hunt was the first Anglican pastor in the New World. It was on June 21, 1607, that the colonists received Communion from Mr. Hunt and thereby inaugurated the continuity of the Anglican Church in the Western Hemisphere. And from the crude church edifice of the historic Jamestown settlement was to grow the virile American Episcopal Church which has become our heritage of today.[2]

The Jamestown Church completed in 1647 was reconstructed in 1907 as Jamestown Brick Church. It was patterned largely after the Old Brick Church in Isle of Wright County, Virginia.

Old Bruton Parish founded at Williamsburg in 1674 was restored in 1710.

Merchant's Hope Church, built in 1657, in Prince George County, Virginia most admirably "represents the supremely classical of ecclesiastical architecture in Colonial Virginia."

St. Luke's Church, near Smithfield, Virginia, was completed in 1632.

Christ Church, Pennsylvania, was founded in 1695.

The established edifices and dedicated persons of long ago endow anew the present generation with spiritual strength. Having sustained the religious needs of one or more generations during the settlement of the American Colonies they truly make of us of this generation their heirs through hope! Thereby we recognize the Church of today as the product of a most rewarding religious, cultural and legal heritage.[3]

The Episcopal Church in America, 1784-1789

From its beginnings in the Colonies and later in the United States the history of the Episcopal Church is unalterably tied to the history of the constitutional government of this great republic.

On July 4, 1776, within only a few hours after the Declaration of Independence had been made, the Vestry of historic Christ Church in Philadelphia met and passed on this resolution: "Whereas the honorable Continental Congress have resolved to declare the American Colonies to be free and independent states in consequence of which it will be proper to omit those petitions in the Liturgy wherein the King of Great Britain is prayed for, as inconsistent with the said Declaration."

It was from this prayer that Dr. William White deleted, in his handwriting, all references to the King of England and Great Britain. He also made changes in the wording of the prayer in keeping with the spirit of the Declaration of Independence, so recently sighed, and the resolution passed by the Vestry of Christ Church:

A Prayer for the King's Majesty
O Lord our heavenly Father, the high and mighty, Ruler of the universe, who dost from thy throne behold all the dwellers upon earth; Most heartily we beseech thee, with thy favour to behold all in authority, legislative, executive and judicial in these United States and so replenish them with the grace of thy Holy Spirit, that they may alway incline to thy will, and walk in thy way; Endue them plenteously with heavenly gifts; grant them in health and wealth long to live; strengthen them that they may vanquith and overcome all their enemies; and finally after this life, they may attain everlasting joy and felicity, through Jesus Christ our Lord.
Amen[4]

With the Revolutionary War over, the independence of the Colonies was secured and jurisdiction by the See of London was elimated. The principles of freedom invoked by the Declaration of Independence were of common knowledge. Yet, let us not fail to recall that repeated attempts to secure the Episcopte for the Colonies ended in failure. The English Church remained unwilling to arrange for the grasping of such an opportunity by the Church in the American Colonies.

On November 14, 1784, Dr. Samuel Seabury, Presbyter, from the State of Connecticut, in America, was consecrated Bishop at Aberdeen, by Bishop Kilgour, Primus; Bishop Petrie and Bishop Skiller.[5]

On June 20, 1785, Bishop Samuel Seabury landed in America and this item appeared in a Journal in Newport, Rhode Island:

> June 20, 1785. Arrived in town via Halifax, from England. Dr. Samuel Seabury, lately consecrated in Scotland, Bishop of the State of Connecticut. The Sunday following, did the duties of the Church (Trinity Parish) and preached A.M., and P.M., to a crowded audience from Heb. XII, 1st and 2nd verses. Monday proceeded to New London by water, where he is to reside.

In relating the return of Bishop Seabury to America this account from a Boston newspaper is found to be amusing: "Two wonders of the world, a Stamp Act in Boston and a Bishop in Connecticut!"

Therefore, in such manner was elected and consecrated the first Bishop of the Protestant Episcopal Church in America. For the stout-hearted determination of Bishop Seabury and for the broad, vital, ecclesiastical concept conferred by noble Churchmen of Scotland, we of America, should be eternally grateful.

During the time in which Dr. Seabury was in England and Scotland, a very important conference was held in America in May 1784. The conference was attended by clergymen and laymen and steps were taken "to form a continental representation of the Episcopal churches." At this conference it was resolved to hold a general convention of the Episcopal Church in Philadelphia in September 27, 1785.

The 1785 Convention, historically considered the first in America, was held in Christ Church, Philadelphia. Dr. William White presided.[6]

Several years elapsed and the Church moved forward slowly but firmly. The whole effort of those of the Episcopal faith in America, eventually called to the attention of the English Church her duty to those of the same faith in America. How revealing in decision, how consistent, how benevolent—how magnanimous was the action which led to the amendment of English statutes, so that in the future the Episcopate might be "more readily conferred for the benefit of the daughter Church in the new nation across the seas!"

On June 26, 1786, a second Convention convened in Christ Church, Philadelphia. Then on October 10, 1786, in Philadelphia an adjourned Convention was held. Within the interim, from June until October, communications had been received from England. These messages consisted of a letter, forms of testimonials and an Act of Parliament.

So it followed, on February 4, 1787, in Lambeth Palace, London, that Dr. William White and Dr. Samuel Provost were consecrated. Dr. White was consecrated Bishop of Pennsylvania and Dr. Provost as Bishop of New York. Participating in the ceremony of consecration were the Arch bishop of Canterbury, the Archbishop of York, the Bishop of Bath and Wells and the Bishop of Peterborough.[7]

The First House of Bishops in the United States was made possible by the consecration of three Bishops: the Rt. Rev. Samuel Seabury, D.D., Bishop of Connecticut (of the Scotch succession); the Rt. Rev. William White, D.D., Bishop of Pennsylvania (of the English succession) and the Rt. Rev. Samuel Provost, D.D., Bishop of New York (of the English succession). The Protestant Episcopal Church in the United States, by action taken in forming its House of Bishops became free of English domination. Therefore, with its own organization, it could consecrate its own Bishops and ordain its own ministers. Never can the true greatness of these first American Bishops be evaluated.

In 1789 the most important Convention of the Church was held in Christ Church, Philadelphia. It is of interest that the first three sessions were held in the Church. However, the final session, at which the ratification of the Church Constitution took place, was in Independence Hall, where the Declaration of Independence and the Constitution of the United States of America were signed.

The Church was fully organized by the action of the 1789 Convention and became "The Protestant Episcopal Church in the United States of America." A Constitution, a General Convention and a Prayer Book comprised the Church's ecclesiastical equipment and gathered together its liturgical privileges![8]

George Washington expressed the interdependence of religion and prosperity when he said: "Of all dispositions and habits which lead to political prosperity, religion and morality are indispensible supports. Reason and experience both forbid us to expect that national morality can prevail in exclusion of religious principles."

It is true that influences of the church of England are evident in many aspects of Church protocol. Natural and interesting is this background: "The Protestant Episcopal Church in the United States of America came into corporate existence . . . with . . . marks of the Catholic and Apostolic Church and . . . identified therewith by historic continuity." Thus, the Episcopal Church in America today is in organization a free institution in a brave land, where freedom's price was great. Yet, freedom's debt was paid in full measure by the sacrificing of lives and fortunes of innumerable patriots of the American Revolution.

Thomas Jefferson once said: "The God who gave us life, gave us liberty at the same time." "Life, liberty and the pursuit of happiness,"—these three objectives are as much a part of the history of our faith as they are determining principles of the law of the land. These basic precepts, conceived by the Founding Fathers guided by a Supreme Being, were destined to cause to be created that "one nation under God, indivisible, with liberty and justice for all."

The Episcopal Church in Tennessee, 1829-1834

Tennessee admitted on June 1, 1796, by Congress as the sixteenth State, to the great sisterhood of States was comprised of two grand divisions East Tennessee and West Tennessee.[9]

By the State Constitutional Convention of 1834 the grand division of Middle Tennessee was created, thereby legally giving Tennessee three grand divisions—East, Middle and West.

On January 11, 1796, fifty-five delegates had gathered in Knoxville for the purpose of drafting a constitution and seeking admission of the State into the Union. Distinguished indeed was the personnel of this first Constitutional Convention.

The task of drafting Tennessee's first Constitution was concluded on February 6, 1796. The delegates assembled had admirably expressed their purpose, spirit and mutual accomplishment in the preamble of the document:

> We the people of the Territory of the United States, south of the River Ohio, having the right of admission into the General Government as a member State thereof . . . Do ordain and establish the following constitution or form of government and do mutually agree with each other to form ourselves into a free and independent State by the name of the State of Tennessee.[10]

The broad democratic concept that government is ever to be achieved by mutual compact, was fully embodied in Tennessee's first Constitution. Of the document, Thomas Jefferson said that it was "The least imperfect and most republican" of any adopted up to that time.

On April 8, 1796, George Washington submitted Tennessee's Constitution to the Congress. On May 31, following, the bill was passed admitting Tennessee into the Union. On June 1, President Washington affixed his signature and the great seal of his office to the measure and thereby granted full statehood to Tennessee.

The early Tennesseans were largely God-fearing, sturdy, intelligent people. More specifically, they were frontiersmen challenged by the joy of adventure. Among them were many determined characters "who held in no restraint the untamed and turbulent passions which they had inherited from their Scotch-Irish progenitors." Also among the early settlers in Tennessee there were not only the staunch, law-abiding citizens possessed of religious fervor and with a dedicated purpose for better living at any cost, but others who were of questionable character. Such persons were disguised desperadoes, recognized fugitives and those of the pirate class! Of the pirate gang some remained in the Western District as late as 1834 and operated extensively along the Mississippi River and the Natchez Trace.

Dr. Arthur Howard Noll in writing about the coming of the Episcopal Church to Tennessee states: "It is no spirit of arrogance that the body who progress in Tennessee it is the present intention to set forth, is termed, 'The Church.' That it is the body, which is mentioned in the creeds of Christendom as the One, Holy, Catholic and Apsotolic Church."

In recounting the beginnings of the Church in Tennessee consideration must be given to its background and purpose. Deeply rooted is the heritage of the Episcopal Church. Characterized by ritualistic dignity, with qualities of prescribed form, classical content and depth of meaning, the service is religiously and historically distinctive. Its doctrine, ministry, discipline, worship and sacraments have attained for the Church a position in ecclesiastical annals. The Bible, The Book of Common Prayer and The Hymnal constitute its basic literature.

The Diocese of North Carolina organized in 1817, was placed under the care of the Rt. Rev. Richard Channing Moore, Bishop of Virginia. In 1818, the Rev. John Phillips came as a missionary to North Carolina. In 1823, John Stark Ravenscroft, a minister of Virginia—, "Of the same sturdy Scotch-Irish stock as the early settlers of Tennessee,"—was unanimously elected the first Bishop of

North Carolina. "He was nominated by William Mercer Green, later Bishop of Mississippi.[11]

The Consecration of Bishop Ravenscroft marked a very noticeable step in Church history. As a result of this influence the Church was encouraged to venture into the neighboring state of Tennessee. Thus it was from Tennessee's sister state of North Carolina that the Church's first teacher-missionary came to Tennessee in 1821 in the person of James Hervey Otey. Unsuspected indeed was the destiny which centered around Mr. Otey's coming to this State. That he should in future years render such conspicuous service that to future generations he would be known as the "father of the Episcopal Church in Tennessee," was not evident at his coming.

Mr. Otey, a Virginian by birth, came to Tennessee and opened a school for boys near Franklin in Williamson County. He had recently graduated with honors from the University of North Carolina and was married.

Within his family had been churchmen; but he, personally knew very little about church ways. However, as principal of the school he deemed it necessary to begin the day with some type of religious experience. To aid Mr. Otey in meeting this need a gentleman from Columbia, Tennessee, Mr. James H. Piper, gave him a copy of the Book of Common Prayer. The full significance of such a gift was the influence which changed the course of the life-work of James Hervey Otey. "That Prayer Book in God's Providence, made Otey a Christian and a Churchman," wrote Bishop Thomas F. Gailor. He remained in Franklin for eighteen months.

Mr. Otey was offered an appointment as principal of the Warrenton Male Academy, Warrenton, North Carolina. His acceptance of this position in Warrenton was one of the most decisive opportunities of his entire life. In Warrenton, he was to find the abundant encouragement which awaited him. His experience there was to be, in reality, a challenge to light his way toward life anew, with heights undreamed of in the field of religious service.

In Warrenton, Mr. Otey was enabled to renew a friendship with William Mercer Green which had begun at the University of North Carolina several years before. The Rev. Mr. Green had been only recently ordained a deacon and was in charge of Emmanuel Church in Warrenton. Events unfolded rapidly which destined James Hervey Orty's firm and consecrated devotion to the Church of his choice.

On May 8, 1824, Mr. Otey was baptized by his old friend, the Rev. Mr. Green in St. John's Church, Williamsboro, North Carolina, and confirmed by the Rt. Rev. John Stark Ravenscroft. Immediately he began preparation for Holy Orders.

Of all his associates in Warrenton, no one played a more significant role than a devoted churchwoman who acted as Mr. Otey's sponsor in baptism—Mary Hayes Willis (Mrs. Thomas Benn) Gloster. Mrs. Gloster was the wife of a prominent physician in Warrenton. Dr. Gloster and Mary Hayes Willis were married in Orange County, North Carolina, May 30, 1795. Of beloved Mrs. Gloster much of her life and service to her Church will appear in forthcoming pages.[12]

Emmanuel Church, Warrenton, North Carolina, was consecrated to Almighty God on Tuesday, August 1, 1824, by the Rt. Rev. John Stark Ravenscroft, assisted by the Rev. Mr. Green, Rector. Of record in the Parish Register are the names of the Vestry who served Emmanuel Church at that time: Kemp Plummer, George Anderson, John Anderson and James H. Otey. These facts of history are descriptive of the particular environment in which the founders of the Episcopal Church in Tennessee lived and served prior to their coming westward. It was there James Hervey Otey became identified with the Church and held his first official position, a vestryman of Emmanuel Church. It was there "the closely-knit lives during these years of the three men—Ravenscroft, Green and Otey—more than any other one thing, provided the devotion and dynamic force which was to spread the Episcopal Church throughout the whole middle and lower South.

After ordination by Bishop Ravenscroft on October 16, 1825, Deacon Otey returned to Tennessee. In 1827 he went again to North Carolina, where he became a Priest, "on Sunday the seventeenth day of June in St. Matthew's Church, Hillsboro (North Carolina) on testimonials from Christ Church, Nashville, in the State of Tennessee."

In 1825, Mr. Otey reopened his school, Harpeth Academy, near Franklin, Tennessee. Patient, diligent teaching and careful, thorough preaching followed on his return to the State. He gained the distinction of being one of the greatest educators in Tennessee's early history. His success as a minister often seemed futile. He was ever fearless in speaking the truth and many were the times he felt that the was as "a voice crying in the wilderness."[13]

Bishop Ravenscroft, despite his declining health, came to Nashville in June 1829, at the urgent request of Mr. Otey. Many came to hear and to see a Bishop! He explained the doctrine, discipline and worship of the Church.

At this time there were approximately fifty communicants of the Church in Tennessee. Therefore, by reason of the number of delegates present at the first convention the "representation of one delegate for less than every five communicants" was larger than in any succeeding Convention. The meeting was held in the Masonic Hall, Nashville, and Bishop Ravenscroft presided. Three clergymen were in attendance: "The Rev. Mr. Otey, the Rev. Dr. Stephens and the Rev. Mr. Davis and six lay delegates."

At this Convention on July 1 and 2, 1829, the organization of the Protestant Episcopal Church began in Tennessee. A Constitution and canons were adopted. The following parishes were recognized as parts of the newly organized diocese: Christ Church, Nashville; St. Peter's Church, Columbia; St. Paul's Church, Franklin, and St. John's Knoxville (though not fully organized). Not one of these organized congregations had erected a house of worship!

Strengthened spiritually and liturgically, the very young Diocese of Tennessee opened the Convention of 1830. The stalwart Mr. Otey had wrought, with the generous assistance of his dear friend, Bishop Ravenscroft, an organization of the Episcopal Church in Tennessee and it was ready to move forward. Although only three in number—the Reverend Daniel Stephens, St. Peter's, Columbia; the Rev. Mr. Otey, St. Paul's, Franklin and the Reverend George Weller, Christ Church, Nashville—the Clergy of the Diocese assembled, with Lay Delegates from their respective congregations. The meeting convened in the Masonic Hall, Franklin, on July 1. Dr. Stephens was elected President and G. M. Fogg, Secretary.[14]

The third Convention of the Episcopal Church in Tennessee was held in the Masonic Hall, Columbia, from June 30 to July 2, 1831. Again the three clergymen present were Dr. Daniel Stephens, the Reverend George Weller and the Reverend James H. Otey. On the first day, the Right Reverend William Meade, D.D., Assistant Bishop of the Diocese of Virginia, by invitation, had arrived. He took his seat and presided over the deliberations of the Convention. On the next morning the "Convention attended divine service in the Presbyterian Church." The Reverend Mr. Otey read the prayers and the Reverend Mr. Weller preached the convention sermon. The report made by Bishop Meade to the Standing Committee of the Diocese of Tennessee, which set forth the details of his visit, indicated a full and rewarding mission.[15]

On July 6, 1831, Christ Church, Nashville, was consecrated,

the first church edifice to arise in the Diocese of Tennessee, and two church buildings were in progress with cornerstones laid: St. Paul in Franklin and St. Peter in Columbia.[16]

In 1833-1834 Tennessee was one of the twenty states, of the twenty-four then in the American Union, wherein the Episcopal Church had been organized. At the time there were fifteen Bishops, two of whom were assistant Bishops. Therefore, it was quite evident the body had not yet reached full stature as an organized national "unit of ecclesiastical government in the Church of America."

Admitted to the diaconate on June 29, 1832 were John Chilton and Samuel George Litton as the first ordinations in the Diocese of Tennessee. Bishop Levi S. Ives of North Carolina administered the ecclesiastical rites to these two able men who were destined to serve brilliantly in the advancement of the Church within the State.

Eight clergymen were at work in Tennessee in 1833. The great need of a Bishop was keenly felt. To carry forward this effort due notice was given of a convention of the diocese, called to meet in Franklin on June 27, 1833. Nine parishes comprised the organization. The Rev. Dr. Stephens presided at the Convention and Mr. Godfrey M. Fogg served as secretary.

The election of a Bishop was the chief business of the Convention. James Hervey Otey received the votes of all the clergy on the first ballot, except two which were cast for the Rev. William Mercer Green and the Rev. Henry Anthon. By unanimous vote by the nine laymen present, Mr. Otey's election was confirmed. Of interest indeed are the names of the men who signed the testimonial of the Bishop-elect: "The Rev. Daniel Stephens, D.D., the Rev. George Weller, D.D., the Rev. John Chilton, the Rev. Samuel G. Litton; Messrs. John C. Wormley and George C. Skipwith, of Columbia; William G. Dickinson, B. S. Tappan and Thomas Maney, of Franklin; Matthew Watson, Godfrey M. Fogg and Francis B. Fogg, of Nashville, and John Anderson of LaGrange."[17]

Mr. Otey, prior to this time, had travelled only in Virginia, North Carolina and Tennessee. It now became necessary that he go to Philadelphia during very cold weather to receive consecration. In Christ Church, Philadelphia on January 14, 1834, James Hervey Otey was consecrated the first Bishop of the Protestant Episcopal Church in Tennessee. The Presiding Bishop, Dr. William White was assisted in the ceremony by the Bishops of Pennsylvania, New

York and New Jersey. Bishop Doane preached the consecration sermon which was in part:

> There is a common notion that Bishops are stately persons, and that large salaries, noble edifices and splendid equipages are somehow an essential appendage of their office. But here is a Bishop who has never had a Church to preach in, and has never yet had a living at the altar, but has been obliged to labor for his children's bread in the laborious, though most honorable vocation of teaching; spending five days out of seven in a school, and for years has not had a month's relaxation.

At the time of consecration Bishop Otey was almost thirty-four years of age, and with two exceptions the youngest Bishop, up to that time, consecrated in the American Church. "He became the thirtieth in the line of the American Episcopate and raised the number of Bishops then living to sixteen."[18]

A Virginian by birth, a North Carolinian by appointment and a Tennessean by choice, Bishop Otey began with abundant vigor, great physical stamina and dedicated religious precepts his magnificent work for the Church in Tennessee. As he carried the message and gave opportunities "to hear the church" the settings varied. Court houses, community halls, homes and in some towns, Presbyterian or Methodist Churches were graciously loaned as places wherein services were held. He was totally fearless in preaching the truth, based on his keen knowledge of the Bible and of the Book of Common Prayer. Bishop Otey once said "that an amount of prejudice, ignorance and prepossession prevailed in this diocese respecting our communion, unequalled in any other State of the Union."

One form of effort to improve this bespoken ignorance and prejudice was the organization in 1858 of the Diocesan Book Society. The project was an idea of the Rev. Charles Todd Quintard, M.D., destined to succeed Bishop Otey to the Episcopate in Tennessee.

For thirty years the first Bishop of Tennessee "toiled in poverty." Nevertheless, in his time he was gratified by staunch faith in believing that his labors had not been in vain. Bishop Otey had firmly established "the educational character of the diocese" of Tennessee. His leadership was strong in that he was a "Catholic, Prayer-Book Churchman of the old school." Truly he had "laid the foundation of the Church of Apostolic Truth and Order in Tennessee." The foundation which he created a century and a half ago endures as a beacon of hope of which we are today the dutiful heirs and recipients.

CHAPTER 2

Heirs in Service
Men of the Cope and Miter (Bishops)

No history related to the Episcopal Church should be written without covering reference to the dedicated, able men who have served as Bishops of their respective Dioceses. Of course, this account must deal primarily with the Bishops of the Diocese of Tennessee.

Repeated herewith for emphasis is the fact that the first House of Bishops in the United States was made possible by the consecration of the three bishops: the Right Reverend Samuel Seabury, D.D., Bishop of Connecticut (of the Scotch succession); the Right Reverend William White, D.D., Bishop of Pennsylvania (of the English succession) and the Right Reverend Samuel Provost, D.D., Bishop of New York (of the English succession). Thus the Protestant Episcopal Church in the United States became free of English domination and with its own organization could consecrate its own Bishops and ordain its own ministers.[1]

Interesting indeed and perhaps unique in the Church in America was the close personal association of these three distinguished prelates of the South: the Rt. Rev. John Starke Ravenscroft, North Carolina; the Rt. Rev. William Mercer Green, Mississippi and the Rt. Rev. James Hervey Otey, first Bishop of Tennessee.

Much has been recorded concerning the lives and admirable selflessness of the great churchmen—the Bishops of Tennessee. From 1834 through 1982 they carried the torch of faith and spiritual benediction by which the Church's fascinating pathway has been brilliantly and eternally illuminated.

Indeed we must herein make note of their worthy names—names of grace, grandeur and glory—of these beloved gentlemen of the Tennessee Episcopal Church. A page is carried whereon their photographs appear. A brief resume of some of the identifying characteristics and a synopsis of the achievement of each bishop is inscribed.[2]

The Right Reverend James Hervey Otey
First Bishop of the Diocese of Tennessee

At "Mount Prospect," his father's farm home located at the

foot of the Peaks of Otter in Bedford County, Virginia, James Hervey Otey was born on January 27, 1800, the seventh son of twelve children. His parents were of stout-hearted, good English stock who were independent thinkers with courage and convictions, spiritual and otherwise.

On October 18, 1821, James Hervey Otey married Eliza Davis Pannill. Their nine children were: Virginia Maury, born August 5, 1822; Paul Hooke, M.D., born April 3, 1825; Henrietta Coleman, born July 15, 1826; Reginold Heber, born February 26, 1829; Sara McGavock, born June 30, 1830; Mary Fogg, born October 27, 1832; Eliza (Donna) R., born August 7, 1836; Francis J., born September 23, 1838 and William Mercer Otey, born April 15, 1842.[3]

All of the Otey children were born in Franklin, Tennessee except Paul Hooke who was born in Warrenton, North Carolina; Frances J., and William Mercer Otey were born in Columbia, Tennessee.

James Hervey Otey was a brilliant and astute scholar, a distinguished teacher and a noble preacher. Because of the magnitude of the qualities of character which he possessed and of his greatness in the professions which he had chosen, he was a leading citizen of his age. Although he became "the patron saint of Tennessee Episcopalians," because of his long, fruitful ministry to the Church, he continued ever in the hearts of the people as an *Educator,* a position of esteem in which he was held throughout his life.

These schools which he established give evidence of his keen interest in the great needs of education within the borders of his beloved adopted state of Tennessee:

- 1821—Harpeth Academy (for boys) opened December 19, Franklin, Tennessee.
- 1837—Madison College, Madison County, Tennessee. Charter granted. Plans discarded because of financial conditions. (Prior to 1837 Bishop Otey was laying a foundation for an Episcopal University in the South.)
- 1838—Columbia Female Institute, Columbia, Tennessee, founded by Bishop Otey and Bishop Leonidas Polk.

    "Bishop Otey returned from a northern tour on which he solicited funds for Columbia Institute, a school for girls, which he and Leonidas Polk were sponsoring. He brought with him $3,000 in cash and $5,000 in promises. The school had about 130 girls enrolled and was 'very flourishing'." (1840)

1844—Mercer Hall (for boys), Columbia, Tennessee.
1847—Ashwood School (for girls) on Columbia-Mt. Pleasant Pike (nearly opposite Hamilton Place, residence of Lucius J. Polk).
1848—Ravenscroft Male Academy, Columbia-Mt. Pleasant, Tennessee.
1860—University of the South, Sewanee, Tennessee. Cornerstone laid on October 9, 1860, by Bishop Otey, Bishop Polk and others (cornerstone destroyed by Federal troops during Civil War. After War—only a charter and 10,000 acres of land remained!).

Many were the churches organized by Bishop Otey in Tennessee and they were the State's first of the Episcopal faith.

"The following Churches were erected during Bishop Otey's Episcopate, and stand here in the order in which they came into existence:[4]

1. Christ Church — Nashville
2. St. Peter's — Columbia
3. St. Paul's — Franklin
4. Trinity Church — Clarksville
5. Calvary Church — Memphis
6. St. Paul's — Randolph
7. St. Luke's — Jackson
8. Zion Church — Brownsville
9. Immanuel Church — LaGrange
10. St. James — Bolivar
11. St. Thomas — Somerville
12. St. Andrew's — Fayette County
13. St. Mark's — Williamsport
14. St. John's — Knoxville
15. St. John's — Ashwood
16. Trinity Church — Tipton County
17. St. James — Greenville
18. St. Matthew's — Covington
19. Holy Trinity — Nashville
20. St. Andrew's — Riverside
21. St. Paul's — Athens
22. St. Paul's — Chattanooga
23. Grace Church — Memphis
24. Church of Advent — Nashville
25. St. Mary's — Memphis
26. St. Stephen's — Edgefield

27. Immanuel Church   Ripley
28. Church of Redeemer Shelbyville
29. Trinity Church   Winchester"

Before 1860 Bishop Otey had organized the Diocese of Mississippi; had laid foundations for the Diocese of Alabama, Louisiana, Texas, Florida and Arkansas, and had blazed a trail through Indian Territory for other missionaries to follow.

About Bishop Otey there was a singular dignity of character which set him apart from others of his time. By his zeal, piety and learning, he was distinguished among the bishops of the United States. That he was among the first pulpit orators and that he won wide approbation from dignitaries of the Church for his statesmanlike direction of church affairs has long been a matter of record.

The teachings of Bishop Otey were based upon his belief which was founded on broad study, honest, resolute convictions, and definite Christian fortitude. He taught and preached, as he believed, that the Episcopal Church was catholic-universal, ecumenic, heaven-wide, world-wide. He believed the Church offered the Apostles' Creed as the test of Christian fellowship through and as an expression of faith.

Bishop Otey died in Memphis on April 23, 1863.

Today, in 1983, it is thrilling to express anew the devotion and appreciation in which James Hervey Otey continues to be held by all of the Episcopal faith. Therefore, the dedication of this volume to the memory of Bishop Otey seems most appropriate as we continue the attempt to carry His message of faith and fidelity as his "Heirs Through Hope".[5]

The Right Reverend Charles Todd Quintard
Second Bishop of the Diocese of Tennessee

The lineage of Charles Todd Quintard began with Isaac Quintard born in Lusignan in the province of Poitou, France. He was a "Sargettier," a manufacturer of the Sergette, which was a fine-twilled cloth, commonly known as serge. Soon after the revocation of the Edict of Nantes, 1685, Isaac Quintard, his wife and their only child of record, Isaac Quintard II, emigrated from France to Bristol, England.

Charles Todd Quintard was born December 22, 1824, in Stamford, Connecticut. The following chronological listing is of interest in giving consideration to the life and work of this eminent churchman:

1846—M.D. degree, University of the City of New York, Medical College.
1848—To Georgia to practice medicine—Athens, Rome. Met and married Miss Eliza Catherine Hand of Roswell, Georgia on October 19.
1851-1855—Professor of Physiology and Pathological Anatomy, Tennessee Medical College, Memphis, Tennessee.
1852—A friendship was begun with Bishop Otey, Dr. Quintard "made up his mind that a man's soul was worth more than his body."
1853—M.A., Columbia University.
1854—January, admitted as a candidate for Holy Orders.
1855—January 21, Ordained Deacon at Calvary Church, Memphis, Tennessee. Served diaconate on the Alston Plantation at Ravenscroft Chapel and St. Paul's Randolph. Later St. Matthew's Covington, was added to this group and the area was named "Quintard Parish."
1856—January 6, Ordained a Priest.
1857—Rector, Calvary Church, Memphis, Tennessee.
1858—January, Rector, Church of the Advent, also served Church of the Holy Spirit and St. Ann's, Nashville, Tennessee. Diocesan Book Society organized by Dr. Quintard, led to establishment of Episcopal bookshops.
1859—Organized Rock City Guard, a militia company composed largely of young men of Nashville, Dr. Quintard was Chaplain. Afterwards company merged into First Regiment, Dr. Quintard continued as Chaplain of the Regiment in Civil War, 1861.
1860—October 9, cornerstone laid, University of the South, Sewanee, Tennessee.
1861-1865—Chaplain of the Confederate Army during Civil War.
1865—October 11, Consecrated, Second Bishop of the Protestant Episcopal Church, Diocese of Tennessee. Service of consecration held in St. Luke's Church, Philadelphia, Pennsylvania. Tennessee Trustee, University of the South, 1865-1898. Between November 28 and March 22, 1866, traveled over major part of Diocese—confirmed 314 persons. Viewed devastation of churches, homes, and properties wrought by Civil War.

1867—LL.D., Cambridge University, England. Communicants in Tennessee 1,998. In England—attended first Lambeth Conference. He was Chaplain of the Order of the Hospital of the Knights of St. John in Jerusalem, of which the Prince of Wales was the Grand Pryor.

1868—September 8, official re-opening of the University of the South, Sewanee, Tennessee.

1871—January 1, Vestry of St. Mary's Church, Memphis, rendered St. Mary's to the Bishop for a Cathedral Church.

1876—The "Bishop's House," by St. Mary's Cathedral, first occupied by Bishop Otey, had become the property of the Diocese as a permanent Episcopal residence.

1877—March, School of Theology opened, University of the South.

1878—D.D., University of the South, Sewanee, Tennessee. The aid of the Sisters of St. Mary was secured.

1885—In Diocese there were 47 ministers; 4,150 communicants; 32 parishes, several missions.

1887—May, Bishop Quintard reported to Convention of progress made. "Many of the churches have been improved and beautified. There is an evident growth in churchly and religious life . . . We are gradually getting to a better style of ecclesiastical music. In the six or eight parishes in which surpliced choirs have been introduced, they have given great satisfaction to the worshippers."

1888—Attended Lambeth Conference.

1890—Made a trip East to raise money for work in the interest of Negroes.

1891—Hoffman Hall established at Fisk University, Nashville, Tennessee, for the training of Negro clergymen.

1895—April 20, Diocesan Convention voted to elect an Assistant Bishop for the Diocese. The Rev. Thomas F. Gailor was unanimously elected the First Assistant Bishop (Bishop Coadjutor).

1897—May, Diocesan Convention (65th) held at Sewanee, the last attended by Bishop Quintard. In summer, attended Lambeth Conference and was the only bishop present who had taken part in the first conference in 1867.

1898—Over 5,274 communicants in Diocese of Tennessee. More than 230 ministers on roster of clergy during the years of Bishop Quintard.[6]

The five children of Bishop and Mrs. Quintard were Bayard, d.y.; Clara Eliza, d.y.; George William, Edward Augustus and Clara Eliza Quintard.

The steadfast friendship of Bishop James Hervey Otey and Dr. Charles Todd Quintard was of outstanding significance in the history of the Episcopal Church. In 1852, when their friendship began, Bishop Otey was fifty-two years of age and Dr. Quintard was twenty-eight. Doubtless, at the outset, each must have in some degree realized the impelling force of their association. Surely, they must have felt certain forebodings that a friendship such as theirs was destined to impressive achievement!

To this happy meeting of mind and spirit, Bishop Otey brought a knowledge of the abundant power and benevolences of God, an affection for the classics and an enviable backgound in purposeful pedagogy. Dr. Quintard brought his genuine faith in a Heavenly Father, an insatiable desire for knowledge through scientific medical research and a clean-carved positive individuality.

Throughout history few men have united and assimilated such gifts of mind and heart in the cause of God's kingdom as did Bishop Otey and Dr. Quintard.

An attempt to give a summation of the character and achievement of Bishop Quintard cannot be easily accomplished. That he was one of the most colorful personages among the bishops of the State cannot be questioned. Possessed was he with a strong physical nature; he was ever alert, an immense force wherever he appeared, he was the kind of person to be remembered forever. He was generous, dynamic and a man of striking personality.

With boundless energy Bishop Quintard pursued his course with dedicated missionary zeal, fortified by a sympathetic heart, a faith strong and complete, a culture wide and varied and with bouyant humor. Daily he worked for the cause of the kingdom of God. He constantly sought to make his energy contagious, that those about him might also lose themselves in service to others. He was a very outspoken, positive person who had no tolerance for those who suffered from chronic indifference! Someone has said to him, "He was a prince of hospitality."

He ministered his professional medical healing to master and servant alike; he preached the unsearchable riches of Christ, not only from chancel and pulpit on the Lord's Day, but as he went to the bedside of sick men, women and little children; he administered the sacrament of baptism to the newborn infant, white and black, whose advent into the world's arena he had assisted professionally; and when he had done all that medical science could do for the fatally ill, he fed with the Bread of Life and the Cup of Salvation those whose inner eyes would soon look upon the Lamb on His throne in light and join in the heavenly pean of the redeemed.[7]

Bishop Quintard died on February 15, 1898 at Darien, Georgia.

The Right Reverend Thomas Frank Gailor
Third Bishop of the Diocese of Tennessee

"Statesman of the Church, Honored by Oxford University, and friend to humanity was the Rt. Rev. Thomas Frank Gailor, third Bishop of Tennessee, protege of Bishop Quintard. Regarded for years as Tennessee's first citizen. . . ."

The early years of Thomas Frank Gailor were lived closely with his mother, whose great strength of character and devotion gave him courage and abundant inspiration. Coupled with the able guidance given by his mother was the great interest and affection of Bishop Quintard. Early, he took the boy under his protecting care and held him in close association for many years. Bishop Quintard was ever gratified by the achievements of his beloved son-in-faith.[8]

The Reverend Richard Hines, D.D., brought to Memphis by Bishop Otey and placed in charge of St. Mary's Church on Poplar, was also a great influence in the life of young Thomas F. Gailor. In a building on the church grounds, Dr. Hines conducted a school which was attended by the growing boy. There he learned Latin grammar and "began to understand what the Church meant." Later studies under the tutelage of Capt. T.C. Anderson, Principal of the High School in Memphis, led to graduation at the age of fifteen years and nine months. He was the first boy graduate of this institution. During the year 1872, he was employed by a Queensware Company.

After recovery from yellow fever in 1873, Thomas F. Gailor went by boat with his mother to his grandmother's in Cincinnati. In September of that year he entered Racine College, having saved enough of his salary to pay the fees for the first year.

"I was graduated at Racine in June 1876, with the "Centennial" Class. It was my fortune to make the valedictory oration at commencement and to get the Greek Prize of fifty dollars which helped me to pay my way to New York to enter the General Theological Seminary."

Ordered a deacon May 15, 1879, by Bishop Charles Todd

Quintard and ordained a priest, September 17, 1880, Thomas F. Gailor began his ministry in the Episcopal Church.

Friday, September 17, 1880—"On this, my 24th birthday, the Bishop is with me, and Dr. Harris, Beckett, Fitts, Harrison, and Davenport. I was ordained to the priesthood at 11 A.M. Delightful service—Davenport preached an admirable sermon. Tonight the Bishop confirmed 5 persons—I am very happy and hopeful—Oh! the future! What shall I make of it?"

The distinguished clergyman—in embryonic stage—had written in his diary a note of happiness, of hopefulness, yet, with a question of the future, "What shall I make of it?"

In his own words is this account of his first sermon:

> My first sermon was on the evening of Ascension Day. I read the service to a good congregation and just when I had announced the text of my sermon, the fire-bell rang and the entire congregation left the church to see where the fire was. I waited until they returned and then went on with my sermon.

The record of magnanimous service diligently rendered to all mankind by so princely a person cannot be fully written. His question of his future—"What shall I make of it?" These milestones give evidence in part of the manner in which the effort of his lifetime answered his question: Rector, Church of the Messiah, Pulaski, Tennessee, 1879-1882; Professor of English and Literature, Lecturer on Theology, University of the South, Sewanee, 1882-1886 and University Chaplain, 1883-1893.

In 1885, Chaplain Gailor, married Miss Ellen Douglas Cunningham and took her to "The Mountain" to make their home. Their children were: Nancy, Charlotte, Frank Hoyt and Ellen Douglas Gailor.

He was elected Vice Chancellor of the University of the South, 1890-1893; consecrated Bishop Coadjutor, July 25, 1893 and Bishop of Tennessee, February 15, 1898. He was elected Chancellor of the University of the South in 1908, a position in which he served until his death.

Bishop Gailor became the first President of the National Council of the Episcopal Church in America in 1919 and served until 1925.

January 19, 1926 marked the completion of St. Mary's Cathedral, Memphis and Gailor Memorial was added to the name. Hoffman-St. Mary's School for Negroes, near Mason, was changed to Gailor Industrial School about that time. The end of forty years of service as Bishop was celebrated appropriately at Sewanee, July 25, 1933.

Bishop Gailor was the recipient of three degrees, D.D., one conferred by each of these colleges: Trinity College, Hartford, Connecticut, 1892; University of the South, Sewanee, Tennessee, 1893, and Oxford University, England, 1920, Oglethorpe University and the University of Georgia in 1923 conferred the L.L.D.

On Bishop Gailor were bestowed the highest honors of the Protestant Episcopal Church in his beloved Tennessee, in America and in England. He preached several times in Westminster Abbey at the invitation of King Edward VII and King George V.

Great acclaim came to Bishop Gailor by his service as preacher, teacher, administrator, bishop. Through all and to all he was a scholar a spiritual counsellor, an esteemed public citizen, an author, a distinguished ecclesiastic and a loyal friend. He was a *Statesman!*

Outstanding in its simplicity was this advice often spoken by him to one grown faint in well-being; "Don't be afraid, only believe." This thought permeated many of the scholarly addresses made by the Bishop on numerous occasions before many types of organizations, religious meetings, and on college and high school commencement programs.

The Bishop's House in Memphis as well as the Gailor summer home in Sewanee, was ever a mecca for persons from all walks of life.

The life of Bishop Gailor was filled with varied experiences of pathos, great joy and of humor.

Vivid always were his memories of his mother's grief caused by the untimely death of his father, Major Frank M. Gailor, killed in the Battle of Perryville, Kentucky, during the Civil War. Mrs. Gailor had made great effort to learn the location of her husband's grave. On her second journey (1863) to learn what she could, she took her young son, a Mrs. Dudley and a driver for the wagon. Many in Memphis had learned of her going and had prevailed on her to take their letters to husbands, sweethearts, fathers. As such were "contraband" they had to be hidden.

"The most important of them were sewn in the lining of my jacket, which was buttoned up to my throat, and I remember that I felt like a mummy, hardly able to move. . . . I remember the officer coming . . . looking at me as I sat there . . . in my stiff jacket, and he called me 'Buddy,' to my indignation!"

Later, Mrs. Gailor made another attempt to contact officers

who had been friends of her husband, that she might learn the facts concerning her husband's death. She took the train to Chattanooga. Thomas F. Gailor, then six and a half years of age, went with her.

The train was crowded with Confederate soldiers, some were eating raw potatoes, and boy-like- I was glad to eat with them, in spite of my mother's remonstrance.

Major Martin Walt, a friend of ours, was on the train, and just as we were approaching the tunnel, near Sewanee, he brought a satchel to my mother, saying: "We are about to enter a long tunnel and there are no lights. This satchel is full of money for the soldiers, who are to be paid in Chattanooga. There are rough people on the train who may attack me in the tunnel. Please keep the satchel and hold it tight until we get out of the darkness." . . . When we moved into the dark tunnel Mother said to me: "Tom, quick, someone is trying to take this satchel away from me."

"I reached over and felt a hand pulling at the satchel and I bit into it with all the might of my strong young teeth! The hand was hurriedly withdrawn. When we emerged from the tunnel we saw a woman in the seat in front of us nursing her hand!"

The story is told on an occasion, during an evangelistic service conducted by the famous preacher, Billy Sunday, which was attended by Bishop Gailor. The sermon had been long and vibrant. When concluded, the Rev. Mr. Sunday gave an invitation to those present to come forward and make their profession of faith. No one came. In desperation he called out: "Everybody who wants to be saved, stand up!" Everyone in the congregation stood except Bishop Gailor. Billy Sunday, of course, knew Bishop Gailor well. He singled him out by saying; "Bishop Gailor, I see that you are not standing. Do you want to be saved?" To this, the distinguished Episcopal Bishop stood and in full voice replied: "Not today, Mr. Sunday! Not today!"

Once Bishop Gailor had gone to a small town in Mississippi to preach on a very hot August day. His vestments, because of the extreme heat, became wet with perspiration, wrinkled, and in bad condition. Following the service he was invited to a home in the town for the noon-day meal. His hostess knew the condition of the Bishop's vestments and gave them to her cook to wash and iron. While at the table eating the meal, the cook stuck her head inside the door and said: "Miss Jane." "Yes, Sally, what is it?" Said Sally, "I wonder if de arch-angel wants starch in hes shimmy, or no!"

When St. Mary's Cathedral had been completed and a large celebration had been held in commemoration of the occasion—at which time it was named Gailor Memorial—a dinner was given at the Gayoso Hotel in honor of Bishop Gailor. In reporting the meaningfulness of the day the local press had noted:

"It was an expression of the joy of his people in welcoming him back home, in pledging their loyalty, their devotion, their love."

The Bishop sat and listened intently to words of praise and affection as he was lauded, probably as no other living Memphian had been. When the time came for his response he did so in characteristic fashion. "Whatever measure of success he had attained," he said, "he owed to God, his sincere belief in the efficacy of prayer, his mother and Mrs. Gailor."

Totally expressive of Bishop Gailor's numerous experiences abroad, where he was ever associated with the great of Church and State, is this account written by him of June 25, 1930:

"Wore my robes and was in the procession at the great service at the reopening of St. Paul's Cathedral. It was a great occasion. Their Majesties, the King and Queen were present, and many thousands of people, including the great one of the land; but the most interesting thing to me was the procession of carpenters, bricklayers, and stonemasons, who had worked on the building and were given special seats."

On October 3, 1935, Bishop Gailor died at Sewanee, after a short illness.

Fifty-five years as a priest and forty-two years the Bishop of the Protestant Episcopal Church in Tennessee! His fame was not only Tennessee's but the nation's. He was an international figure. Six years as President of the National Council of the Episcopal Church! Twenty-five years as Chancellor of the University of the South! An unexcelled record of rewarding service to God and to his fellowman.

Truly, it may be said of Bishop Gailor: "A great man and the friend of the great, he never lost his simple kindliness."[9]

"The grand old Church is marching
Into the far flung battle line,
Where the voice of God is calling us;
And the task is yours and mine

And Tennessee must answer well
With Hearts both brave and true;
Our Southland dear, with vision clear,
Must learn to think and do.

The short, short days are winding
Into the long, eternal years;
Our lives are only training times
With labor, hopes and fears.

Let us bless our work with service
In the Kingdom, far and nigh,
And save our souls with peace that rolls
Serene from Him on high."

The Right Reverend Troy Beatty
Bishop Coadjutor of the Diocese of Tennessee

The devoted pastoral qualities of Troy Beatty endeared him to churchman and neighbor alike. The remarkable character of his youth lasted through manhood. Total integrity, abundant energy and fervent religious sentiment combined to make him a splendid gentleman and a consecrated, beloved *Pastor*.

Daniel Troy Beatty was born November 12, 1866 in Tuscaloosa, Alabama. When he was three years of age the family moved to Mobile, Alabama. Troy Beatty was sixteen when the family moved to Chattanooga. Soon thereafter, he began a profitable and satisfactory association with the *Chattanooga Times*. Throughout his life, he held in grateful memory the interesting and varied newspaper experiences which he had in this connection.

Young Troy Beatty became a choir boy at St. Paul's Episcopal Church in Chattanooga. The Reverend George William Dumbell, D.D., Rector of St. Paul's (1885-1892), took much interest in the splendid lad and under Dr. Dumbell's influence he became a Lay Reader. Bishop Charles Todd Quintard and Dr. Dumbell encouraged him to enter the ministry. Thereafter, the young man bent all of his efforts toward working and saving the money which he earned with which to further his education.

At the time of the family's move to Birmingham, Alabama, Troy Beatty secured employment with the *Birmingham Age Herald*. He left this position when he matriculated on March 29, 1887, at the University of the South, Sewanee, Tennessee. Full and vital were the years which followed as verified by this chronology of activities and events:

    1889—Entered School of Theology, University of the South, Sewanee.

1891—Ordained a Deacon by Bishop Gregg of Texas and spent nearly a year in Texas assisting the Bishop.

1892—May 18—In Calvary Church, Memphis, ordained to the Priesthood by Bishop Charles Todd Quintard.
November 24, married at Sewanee, Tennessee, Miss Frederika Priest Mayhew. Their children were Troy, Jr., Frederika, Georgiana Mayhew, Mary and Charles Henry Mayhew Beatty.

1893—(-1897) Rector, St. Andrew's Church, Darien, Georgia.

1897—(-1916) Rector, Emmanuel Church, Athens, Georgia. Served on the State Diocesan Council.

1901—Elected Diocesan Deputy of General Convention of the Church.

1908—Delegate to Pan Anglican Congress (all churches in world affiliated with Church of England), London.

1916—(-1919) Rector, Grace Church, Memphis, Tennessee.

1917—D.D., University of Georgia.

1919—May 7—Elected Bishop Coadjutor, Diocese of Tennessee.
Sept. 18—Consecrated Bishop Coadjutor in Grace Church, Memphis; Presiding Bishop Daniel Sylvester Tuttle, Chief Consecrator.

1919—(-1922) Tennessee Trustee, University of the South.

1920—D.D., Honorary degree awarded by University of the South.

1922—April 23—Death came in Nashville, Tennessee.[10]

"His life was an inspiration, one to make any son feel very proud and very humble," wrote Troy Beatty, Jr., in concluding an excellent account of the life history of his distinguished father, Bishop Troy Beatty.

It is felt that to end this sketch of the life of a man so greatly beloved with the words, in part, from the hymn which was his favorite is most appropriate.

> The strife is o'er the battle done,
> The victory of life is won;
> The song of triumph has begun.
> Alleluia!

Lord! by the stripes which wounded thee,
From death's dread sting thy servants free,
That we may live and sing to thee.
Alleluia!

The Right Reverend James M. Maxon
Fourth Bishop of the Diocese of Tennessee

In the passing of Bishop Thomas F. Gailor on October 3, 1935, James Matthew Maxon, Bishop Coadjutor, became the Fourth Bishop of the Protestant Episcopal Church in the Diocese of Tennessee. The first official installation in the history of St. Mary's Cathedral was that of Bishop Maxon.

James Matthew Maxon was born on January 1, 1875, in Bay City Michigan. In 1906, he completed his studies for the ministry at the General Theological Seminary. His ordinations in 1907 were as a deacon and as a priest. He was rector of Grace Church, Galesburg, Illinois, and between 1910-1917 was rector of St. John, Versailles, Kentucky. From 1920 until 1922 he was rector of Christ Church, Nashville, immediately prior to his consecration as Bishop Coadjutor of the Diocese.

Dr. Maxon's association with the University of the South, Sewanee, Tennessee, was in several capacities: 1919-1920, Dr. Maxon was a Kentucky Trustee; 1922-1948, a Tennessee Trustee; 1938-1944, Regent; and between 1942 and 1944 he served as the eleventh Chancellor of the institution.

He was the worthy recipient of three honorary degrees; from Knox College, M.A., 1910; from the University of the South, Sewanee, D.D., 1921; and in 1941 Southwestern University, Memphis, conferred the LL.D.

Dr. Maxon married October 10, 1903, Miss Blanche Morris of Bay City, Michigan the place of his birth. They were the parents of two sons—James Matthew Maxon II and John Burton Maxon.

Entered in his diary by Bishop Thomas F. Gailor was this notation:

> Nashville, October 18, 1922—Christ Church, St. Luke's Day. I acted as consecrator for consecration of James Matthew Maxon as Bishop Coadjutor. Woodcock preached sermon. Burton presented. Great service.

Dr. Maxon became Bishop Coadjutor of the Diocese of Tennessee at a time when his service was fully needed by the Church.

Immediately, he began to give faithful assistance to the inimitable, overworked Bishop Gailor.

Bishop Maxon immediately grasped his duties as he saw them and as he understood the needs of the thriving Diocese. One important item which received his attention was the need of reorganization of practices concerning St. Mary's Cathedral. He stated the Cathedral should be "a great Mother Church in which every communicant in the Diocese will have a real sense of proprietorship. I do not intend to come to the Cathedral and shine awhile and then go elsewhere . . . A Cathedral is not a place to exalt the ego, to win a front seat in heaven. It must be a great spiritual center reaching out with vision, to the people everywhere."[11]

To stress the evangelism of music, through Evensong of all Memphis parishes every Sunday at the Cathedral; to have the Dean visit other churches and to have other ministers fill the Cathedral pulpit at times; to make the Cathedral a center of missionary work, religious education, and social service and to work toward a better understanding of the "Cathedral Idea" on the part of the clergy and laymen alike, all these were among the objectives of Bishop Maxon.

In June 1937, Bishop Maxon and his family moved to Memphis and occupied the new Episcopal Residence. He had felt the Bishop's House on Poplar was too large for his family's needs. Also, it was a part of his plan that the Bishop's House, by the Cathedral, should become the Diocesan House, and therefore, serve as a location for the various offices of the Diocese. All this was accomplished.

The coming of William Evan Sanders to the Cathedral, appointed by Bishop Maxon, first as an assistant on the Cathedral staff and later, in 1946, as Acting Dean, was a beacon light in the Bishop's last years as diocesan.

Bishop Maxon resigned on January 1, 1947, the leadership of the Diocese. His service caused him to be known as a worthy *Administrator* of every facet of the Church's affairs.

Death came to the beloved Bishop on November 8, 1948. He sleeps in the churchyard cemetery of St. John's, Ashwood, a glorious, sacred setting created by the Bishop-General (The Fighting Bishop) Leonidas Polk, and his family, a setting hallowed through the years by the passing of great men who were noble Christians.[12]

The Right Reverend Edmund Pendleton Dandridge
Fifth Bishop of the Diocese of Tennessee

Edmund Pendleton Dandridge was born on September 5, 1881, in Flushing, New York. On October 6, 1909, he married in Alexandria, Virginia, Miss Mary Robertson Lloyd. They were the parents of two children: Edmund Pendleton Jr., and Elizabeth Robertson Dandridge.

Edmund Pendleton Dandridge studied at Woodbury Forest School. From the University of Virginia he received a B.A. degree in 1902, and in 1903, a Master of Arts degree. In 1906, he earned a B.D. from the Virginia Theological Seminary, and in 1921, the Seminary conferred the honorary degree D.D. He received from Oxford University, England, a B.A. degree in Theology in 1908. The University of the South also conferred upon Dr. Dandridge the honorary degree, Doctor of Divinity, in 1938.

Following his ordination as a deacon in June 1906, and as a priest in December 1908, he began his first ministry in Greenbrier Parish, Virginia, where he served from 1908 until 1911. During World War I, he was in France as an Army Chaplain. Between 1911 and 1923, Dr. Dandridge was rector of St. Paul's Church, Petersburg, Virginia. He became rector of Christ Church, Nashville, Tennessee, in 1923.[12]

"The Bower," the ancestral home near Martinsburg, West Virginia, was retained by Dr. and Mrs. Dandridge and was enjoyed by them and their growing children as a pleasant summer home.

At a special convention called by Bishop Maxon on April 20, 1938, Dr. Dandridge was elected Bishop Coadjutor of the Diocese of Tennessee. He was consecrated in Christ Church, Nashville, on September 20, 1938. He continued to make his home in Nashville.

Upon the retirement of Bishop James M. Maxon on December 31, 1946, Dr. Dandridge became the fifth bishop of the Protestant Episcopal Church in Tennessee.[13]

On January 1, 1947, in traditional, solemn ceremony in St. Mary's Cathedral, Memphis, the Right Reverend Edmund Pendleton Dandridge was formally installed as the bishop of the one hundred eighteen year old Diocese. The Cathedral was filled by the more than two thousand persons who came from over the state to witness the impressive service.

The installation was conducted by Dr. Prentice Pugh, rector of the Church of the Advent, Nashville, senior priest in Tennessee, and S. Bartow Strang of Chattanooga, diocesan chancellor.

Bishop Dandridge worked diligently during his time toward the accomplishment of a number of objectives. Significant among these were: the establishment of a closer relationship between parishes within the Diocese; a closer relationship of each parish with the Cathedral parish; planned a graduate training center for religious education; created a greatly needed vault in the Cathedral crypt for the storage of the important records of the Diocese; organized a planning committee for Shelby County and in other urban areas through the state; started a Summer Music Conference at Sewanee and earnestly sought to interest young men to become ministers, to relieve the shortage of clergymen in Tennessee.

Bishop Dandridge experienced the great satisfaction during his regime of the consecration of St. Mary's Cathedral, in 1951.

The positions of national scope in which Dr. Dandridge so worthily served, caused him to become one of the most influential bishops of the Episcopal Church. He was a member of the Episcopal National Council from 1940-1946; a member of the Forward Movement Commission in 1940. He served as chairman of the very important Budget and Program Committee of the General Council. Five times he served as a deputy to the General Convention.

Bishop Dandridge served for three years as Dean of Theology at Sewanee. At the conclusion of this service to the University of the South, this resolution by the Board of Trustees expressed the gratitude and affectionate esteem of its members to Bishop Dandridge:

"Called from a well-earned period of retirement to aid the University of the South in its all important School of Theology, he responded with characteristic alacrity and from a well developed sense of obligation.

His term as Dean of St. Luke's couched between painful controversy and a disastrous fire, he proceeded to rebuild the School of Theology into the likeness of its great days—an undertaking appropriately symbolized in the present expansion of the fabric of St. Luke's.

To this vital task of healing and reconstruction he brought God-given talent for administration, and Spirit-given personal attributes so essential to its successful prosecution. He humored some; others he commanded. Some he drove; others he led—as the Lord's work required. All he respected and encouraged. Rare is the combination of scholarship, pastoral wisdom and administrative gifts that adorn him.

He moves to retirement belatedly, but with the gratitude of a Church happily more enlightened concerning her responsibilities for theological education. He turns over to another remarkably qualified person—as Dean—an institution which, once more, can proudly face its peers."

Significantly and with distinction, the East Window of St. Luke's Chapel, Sewanee, was dedicated in honor of Bishop Dandridge on June 6, 1957.

At his retirement as Bishop of the Diocese of Tennessee, Dr. Dandridge, the Virginia gentleman who had served the ministry of the Episcopal Church for forty-seven years, was saluted as a "Great, Good Man." At a very elaborate testimonial banquet given in his honor early in 1953 at the Richland Country Club, Nashville, and attended by more than three hundred-fifty persons, the beloved minister was paid abundant and deserved tribute. To the homage which came to him, the ever-modest Bishop replied, "These tributes are your accomplishments and I return them to you!"

Brief, indeed, was the retirement of this vital, vigorous man of faith and earnest devotion to the advancement of God's Kingdom among men. On February 6, 1953, Bishop Dandridge was chosen as Dean of the School of Theology, the University of the South, Sewanee, Tennessee.

Death came to Bishop Dandridge on January 28, 1961, in his seventy-ninth year. He suffered a fatal heart attack at the home of his daughter, Mrs. Angus W. McDonald and Mr. McDonald, in Lexington, Kentucky, where he had resided since his final retirement in 1956.

Energetic, scholarly, beloved, Edmund Pendleton Dandridge —a man of grace, full of faith, a man of good deeds, the fifth Bishop of the Episcopal Diocese of Tennessee was called *The Missionary*.

The Right Reverend Theodore Nott Barth
Sixth Bishop of the Diocese of Tennessee

He was a choir boy when he was seven, a bishop at fifty years of age. "I practically grew up in the Church." Bishop Barth once said.

It was in Mount Savage that Theodore Nott Barth was born, July 11, 1898. German, Swiss and Dutch progenitors contributed to his ancestry.

At an early age, the precocious boy showed a distinct talent in music. He studied piano and violin under private instructors in nearby Cumberland, Maryland and became proficient in the art. For quite a while young Theodore Barth was a member of a string quartette. In manhood, he continued to play both violin and piano, an accomplishment which provided for him great personal enjoyment.

After graduation from High School, Cumberland, Maryland, college years and ordination followed:

1918—B.A., University of Virginia; Phi Beta Kappa.
1921—Dec. 17. Ordained to Diaconate in Bishop's Chapel, Baltimore, Maryland.
1922—B.D., Virginia Theological Seminary.
1922—Oct. 18. Ordained, Priest in St. George's Chapel, Mt.

1922-1924—Rector, Deer Creek Parish, Harford County, Darlington, Maryland.
1924-1928—Rector, All Saints' Church, Reisterstown, Maryland.
1928-1940—Rector, St. Bartholomew, Baltimore, Maryland.
1940—March 10-1948, Sept. 21. Rector, Calvary Church, Memphis, Tennessee.
1943—D.D. Honorary Degree awarded by Southwestern, Memphis, Tennessee.
1948—April 21. Elected Bishop Coadjutor, Diocese of Tennessee.
1948—Sept. 21. Consecrated Bishop Coadjutor in Calvary Church, Memphis. Tuesday morning at ten o'clock, St. Matthew's Day—the Apostle and the Evangelist.
1953—Sept. 21. Installed as Bishop of the Diocese, in St. Mary's Cathedral, Monday morning at ten o'clock.

On June 4, 1923, Theodore Nott Barth and Elizabeth Pike Ellicott were married by the Rt. Rev. John Gardner Murray in a beautiful garden setting in Baltimore.

A son and a daughter were their children. Theodore Nott Barth, Jr., married Mary Bayless of Athens, Tennessee. They have one daughter, Melissa Bayless Barth, born August 13, 1961. They make their home in Maryville, Tennessee. Sarah White Barth married Aubrey Tomlin. They have one daughter, Elizabeth Barth

Tomlin, born August 8, 1951, who married David Keith Heller in Birmingham, Alabama on August 28, 1982.

Only a man full of faith, diligent in leadership and capable of distinguishing himself by forceful sermons and dedicated service, could have won the approbation of the communicants of historic Calvary parish. Dr. Barth possessed all of these qualities and during his rectorate of eight years won the sincere and lasting affection of the people of Calvary. These years are recorded among the brightest and most fruitful in the church's history.[14]

Most certainly it may be said that as Bishop Otey preached through his teaching, Bishop Barth taught through his preaching! Fervent in prayer, he sought with perseverance to share with all men the joy which he had found through prayer. The schools of prayer and the retreats conducted by Bishop Barth are recalled as memorable experiences, rich in the abundance of God's grace and in glorious closeness to the Master!

Early in his episcopacy, Bishop Barth became interested in making the Diocesan House a more efficient and comfortable environment for the administration of the affairs of the Diocese. Therefore, a program of renovation was initiated and necessary improvements were made both to the interior and exterior of the large stone building. Concerning the project he had remarked before the 1953 Convention:

> It is a lovely old house . . . I hope to gather around me there the various offices and officers who ought to be near at hand . . . I have asked for enough (money) to keep it in good repair . . . I am going to spend my working hours there. But in a very real sense it is your house . . . We want to look our best when company comes.

The plan of record-keeping started by Bishop Dandridge was earnestly continued by Bishop Barth. The vault in the crypt of St. Mary's Cathedral was completed. At the 1955 Convention the Bishop urged each Parish to assemble its records and to use the vault as a depository for the historical documents of the Church. He felt keenly the great need of preserving all kinds of church records. He said that numerous irreplaceable items of church history had been either lost or destroyed during past years. That he foresaw this important step as just a beginning would seem plausible. He must have foreseen the future inadequacy of the arrangement which he encouraged. That to meet the future needs of the Diocese a larger room might be required—certainly fire proof, accessible, comfortable during all seasons, where the records and objects of church history might be preserved, observed and consulted.

Canon James R. Sharp moved the diocesan records to the vault. In 1956, M. C. Nichols of Chattanooga was appointed to serve as Administrative Assistant to Bishop Barth. He also performed many duties previously carried forward by Canon Sharp.

Far reaching indeed were the objectives and the accomplishments during the days of Bishop Barth. The purchase and renovation of property on which was created the Du Bose Conference Center at Monteagle, Tennessee, was an effort of gigantic proportions and great reward. On eight college campuses in Tennessee new student centers were established, thereby providing representation of the Episcopal Church on every college campus within the State. The organization of All Saints' Mission, Memphis; the creation of a fund with which to aid in the building of churchhouses; the rebuilding of Emmanuel Church, Memphis; participation in a Diocesan Survey sponsored by National Council, and the decided increase in membership during Bishop Barth's constructive years, all were evidences of marked achievement of the Church in Tennessee.

In commemoration of ten years of growth and progress in the Diocese since Bishop Barth's consecration as bishop, special services were held at St. Mary's Cathedral, on Sunday, September 21, 1958. The Festal Evensong, in honor of Bishop Barth, was planned by Tennessee Episcopal clergy.

The well-rounded, versatile personality of Bishop Barth made him popular as an *Evangelist* in the pulpit and as a guest in the home! He was a gifted and pleasing conversationalist. His love of music, his keen appreciation of sculpture and painting; his fondness for travel—all these were among his cultural interests.

He was an enthusiastic sportsman. Fishing was a favorite diversion and he was a baseball enthusiast. He found great pleasure in being at the helm of a sailing yacht! Annually, he made a trip with friends who sailed in Chesapeake Bay. He was a Rotarian.

Death came to distinguished and beloved Bishop Barth on August 22, 1961, Tuesday night, at nine-forty-five, in the Baptist Hospital, Memphis, Tennessee. His illness had been long and arduous. From February until August, while he was hospitalized, he welcomed his friends and remained remarkably active under the circumstances of declining health.

Of the many words of praise which have been so well written, descriptive of the life and work of Bishop Barth, no account has been found which better expresses, than does the following, the fullness of spirit and the abundant goodness which were typical of this dedicated disciple.

Peace, which is held so tenuously by the multitude, was magnified in the lifework of the Rt. Rev. Theodore N. Barth and attained in his death.

The sixth bishop of the Episcopal Diocese of Tennessee was a true disciple of Christianity, leaving its mark of grace on whatever he touched.

Resplendent in the robes of his office, he remained a humble man, a servant happy in the work to which he was dedicated. In the pulpit, he had a mighty ringing voice which he could soften to a dramatic whisper, drawing the minds of his listeners down the paths of his teachings.

In his gentle eyes, one felt he saw and knew the future. Indeed he was a man reaching out to eternity.[15]

The Right Reverend John Vander Horst
Seventh Bishop of the Diocese of Tennessee

The spacious rooms of the Diocesan House rang with musical tones created by one lustily whistling (interspersed by song), and seemingly unaware of having an audience. "Who is that who whistles so joyously," a visitor asked. The pleasant, alert secretary replied, "Oh that is our new Bishop of the Diocese whose office is upstairs—our happy, 'Whistling Bishop'!"—the Right Reverend John Vander Horst, D.D., Tennessee's seventh bishop of the Episcopal Church.

To be possessed of those qualities of character which embody dedication of total personality in deeds of duty and devotion to God; a dignity appropriate to every need in administering the ecclesiastical rites of the Church; a magnetism by which people are fortified in faith and are drawn together in worship, most assuredly denote "the mystery of godliness," concerning which St. Paul wrote. And, when coupled with all these, the heart of the man is found to be grateful and gay, the true qualities of a *Steward* have been achieved.

Faithfully written by Bishop Vander Horst in his journal in August 1961, were the following records, significant in church history:

8/22—"Call from Mrs. O'Kane at home telling me of the death of the Rt. Rev. Theodore Nott Barth, D.D., Father-in-God and Friend of the Diocese of Tennessee. . ."

8/24—"St. Bartholomew's Day—8:30 A.M., celebrated a memorial service of the Holy Eucharist to the Glory of God and for the repose of the soul of Theodore Nott Barth, Sixth Bishop of Tennessee 10 A.M., assisted by Dean Sanders and the Rev. Thorne Sparkman, D.D.

Read the Burial Office for the Bishop. 5 P.M., St. John's Ashwood, the Dean and I read the interment service together. . ."

John Vander Horst was born in Orange, New Jersey, on January 10, 1912. He attended the Gilman School, Baltimore, Maryland. At Stephen's House, Oxford, England, and the Virginia Theological Seminary he pursued the study of Theology.

Ordained a deacon in June 1938, a priest in 1939, he began his first rectorate at St. John's Church, Ellicott City, Maryland, where he was the rector until 1942. Other churches which he served were: St. Paul's Church, Macon, Georgia, 1942-1945; Church of the Good Shepard, Philadelphia, Pennsylvania, 1945-1951, and St. Paul's Church, Chattanooga, Tennessee, 1951-1955.

On April 17, 1940 John Vander Horst married Helen Gray Lawrence. Their four children were Helen, John Jr., Ella, and Allston Vander Horst.

Obviously destined to serve his Church in positions of rank, the Reverened Mr. Vander Horst was elected on March 2, 1955, Suffragan Bishop. On April 19, 1961, he was chosen Bishop Coadjutor and as Bishop.

Bishop Vander Horst has been the recipient of two honorary degrees, D.D. Both degrees were conferred in 1955, by the Virginia Theological Seminary and the University of the South, respectively.

More than a thousand persons crowded St. Mary's (Gailor Memorial) Cathedral on the morning of October 12, 1961. Each had come to witness the solemn, colorful service of installation of the Right Reverend John Vander Horst, seventh bishop of the Protestant Episcopal Church in Tennessee.

At ten-thirty "Bishop Vander Horst rapped soundly on the massive West Door of the Cathedral and requested admission for installation. . . ." Thus began the service of induction, investiture and installation. The Bishop's knock on the door was answered by the Standing Committee of the Diocese and the Cathedral Chapter of St. Mary.

At the foot of the chancel steps the Bishop knelt and there received the blessing of Bishop Louttit. He received at the altar the crozier, a symbol of his office. He was escorted by the Canons of the Cathedral to be seated in the Cathedra, the bishop's chair. Following the service of the Holy Eucharist, Bishop Vander Horst addressed the large assembly.

The magnificient music was a splendid contribution to the memorable service. Truly, the choir, the organ, the trumpets, the drums blended to enhance the solemn beauty and great religious dignity of the historic rites.

On the day of Bishop Vander Horst's installation, a special session of the 129th Convention was held and unanimous approval was obtained of his request that a Bishop Coadjutor be elected. After such action had been taken, he announced the election would be held on January 19, 1962, during the Diocesan Convention.

One of the great objectives of Bishop Vander Horst and his associates was that of expansion. This program included the forward look of purchasing land for church sites in and around the metropolitan areas and in smaller counties, as well, while land is available and no higher in price. Strengthening the student center units, Barth House and Quintard House, Memphis, and others over the state, was recognized as a very important need. The task of giving essential guidance to the work of the Diocese, comprised of one hundred sixteen Parishes and Missions and one hundred forty-eight Priests and Deacons, was unquestionably a broad, magnificent challenge.

Many and varied were the duties in stewardship experienced by Bishop Vander Horst. It was he, this stalwart man-of-God, who with hope, grace, and great joy carried forward the business of his Heavenly Father.

Bishop Vander Horst resigned on January 10, 1977. He died April 19, 1980.[16]

The Right Reverend William Evan Sanders
Eighth Bishop of the Diocese of Tennessee

On appointment by the Right Reverend James M. Maxon a well qualified and thoroughly likeable young priest began to serve as Acting Dean of St. Mary's Cathedral. The date was December 23, 1946. And, of this young man, the Reverend William Evan Sanders, whom he had appointed, Bishop Maxon wrote:

> " He is a cherished son in the Gospel upon whom I lean in my declining years . . . He has ability, in my judgment, equal to that of any Priest in the Diocese."

And, one year later on the very same day, the Acting Dean was appointed Dean, by the Right Reverend Edmund Pendleton Dandridge. Dean Sanders was popular, from the beginning, with the people, both young and old. It was a predecessor, Dean Harold Brown Hoag, who said of him that he would carry forward "the greatest period in Cathedral history." And, most likely he did!

Dean Sanders' period as Dean of the Cathedral stands unsurpassed in scope. This is verified by the fact that he served as Acting Dean or as Dean under four Bishops of the Diocese: Bishop Maxon, Bishop Dandridge, Bishop Barth and Bishop Vander Horst.

William Evan Sanders was born on Christmas Day, 1919, in Natchez, Mississippi.

After graduation from high school, in Nashville, he entered Vanderbilt University, where he received a B.A. degree in 1942. Enrollment in the University of the South followed and in 1945, he earned a B.D. degree. In 1946, the S.T.M. (Master of Sacred Theology) was earned in Union Theological Seminary, New York. The University of the South conferred an honorary degree, D.D., in 1959. His ordinations were as a Deacon in February 1945 and as a Priest in June 1946.

Interesting indeed is a brief account of the time served by Deacon Sanders as Curate to the Reverend Thorne Sparkman at St. Paul's Church, Chattanooga, Tennessee. The Rev. Mr. Sparkman, a Rhodes scholar, a brilliant preacher, easily won the admiration of intelligent young men of the Church. He was recognized by his "ecclesiastical superiors" as being most capable of instructing young deacons in pastoral duties and in procedure. Therefore among the seven young men who served their apprenticeships under Mr. Sparkman were: Eric Sutcliffe Greenwood, 1944-; William Evan Sanders, 1945, and James O. Bodley, 1947-1949. All did well and have served the Episcopal Church with diligence and with dedication.

In a very beautiful service at St. Mary's Cathedral, Dean Sanders married on June 25, 1951, Kathryn Cowan Schaffer. They are parents of Elizabeth Kathryn, Laura and Evan Sanders.

Dr. Sanders was elected on January 19, 1962, to serve as Bishop Coadjutor of Tennessee. By his consecration, on Wednesday, April 4, 1962, he became the five hundred eighty sixth in the American Succession.

On January 10, 1977 he was elected to serve as the Eighth Bishop of the Diocese. Upon the creation of the Diocese of West Tennessee Bishop Sanders was then elected on December 31, 1982 to remain as Bishop of the continuing Diocese of Tennessee (Middle and East Tennessee).

Although several titles indicative of superior ecclesiastical leadership have been bestowed upon William Evan Sanders, it is believed that not one can excel in meaning, made radiant by the sincere appreciation of his followers, than that of the time honored title, "The Dean!"

The Right Reverend William Fred Gates, Jr.
Suffragan Bishop of the Diocese of Tennessee

The Right Reverend William Frederick Gates, Jr., was born in Lexington, Virginia, on March 29, 1912. He attended public schools in Chattanooga, Tennessee. He attended Hobart College in Geneva, New York, and was graduated from the University of Chattanooga in 1934, with the B.A. degree. He attended the Virginia Theological Seminary in Alexandria, Virginia, and was awarded the degree of B.D. in 1937. He was ordained Deacon by the Rt. Rev. James Matthew Maxon, Bishop of Tennessee, on June 7, 1937, and Priest by Bishop Maxon on March 5, 1938.

Bishop Gates served his diaconate as an assistant at Calvary Church, Memphis, Tennessee. From 1938 to 1942, he was priest-in-charge of St. John's Church, Old Hickory, Tennessee. He was rector of St. Peter's Church, Columbia, Tennessee from 1943 to 1966. At a special session of the Convention of the Diocese of Tennessee, held at Christ Church, Nashville, on May 18, 1966, he was elected Suffragan Bishop. Bishop Gates was consecrated Suffragan Bishop of Tennessee in Christ Church, Nashville, Tennessee, on September 9, 1966. The chief consecrator was the Rt. Rev. John Elbridge Hines, Presiding Bishop.

Bishop Gates has been a member of the Standing Committee, and of the Board of Examining Chaplains. He has served several terms as a member of the Bishop and Council. He has been chairman of the Department of Missions and the Department of Christian Education, and the Department of Publicity and Program. He was active in the civic affairs in Columbia when he was rector at St. Peter's.

As the Suffragan Bishop of the Diocese of Tennessee, he was the Diocesan Finance Officer and had under his direction the Department of Ministries in Higher Education and the newly created Department of Youth Work, as well as the Planning Committee of the Bishop and Council. As Vice-President of the Convention of the

Protestant Episcopal Church in the Diocese of Tennessee, he also served on the Episcopal Schools Commission, the Episcopal Services Foundation, the Stewardship Task Force, Tennessee Management Corporation and the Shelby County Episcopal Planning Commission.

In the Memphis area, Bishop Gates has served on the Boards of the following organizations: Episcopal Church Home, Trezevant Manor, Metropolitan Interfaith Association, Memphis Institute of Medicine and Religion. He also served on the Tennessee Association of Churches and on the Board of Trustees of the University of the South, Sewanee, Tennessee.

Bishop Gates was awarded honorary degrees of Doctor of Divinity by the Virginia Theological Seminary and the University of the South in June 1967.

April 25, 1938, he married Jane Gregory Dillard of Chattanooga, Tennessee. They have two daughters, Susan, Mrs. C. H. Edwards, III, and Anne, Mrs. Reginald O. Kincer, Jr. This opportunity is grasped to express appreciation and affection to Jane Dillard Gates who has played an outstanding role as the wife of a Diocesan. Truly she has been worthy of all accolades which can be accorded her. She has been a perfect "Bishop's Wife."

As the sketches about the Bishops of Tennessee are concluded, let us review the titles which have been given through the passing years to best describe the distinctive characteristics of each prelate —James Hervey Otey—The Educator; Charles Todd Quintard—the Churchman; Thomas Frank Gailor—The Statesman; Troy Beatty—The Pastor; James Matthew Maxon—The Administrator; Edmund Pendleton Dandridge—The Missionary; Theodore Nott Barth—The Evangelist; John Vander Horst—The Steward; William Evan Sanders—The Dean-Bishop.

And what shall we say in an attempt to give a title to Bishop Gates—a title sufficiently covering to even in part depict the gentleman and his vast service to his Church and to his fellowman? "Master of the Money"; the "Exchequer"; the "Professor" (his service to young people) the "Promoter" (his vision concerning Missions)? Of all these he has been so much more! May we entitle Bishop Fred simply and affectionately as a *Kind—Caring Friend.*

On December 31, 1982, Bishop Gates retired. He served as the Interim Bishop of the Diocese of West Tennessee, January 1, 1983—May 31, 1983.

Truly their lives, their dedication and their achievement stand as bulwarks of Christian challenge to all faithful people who and written—about the noble bands of clergy who, through the years have achieved by their selfless service to their Lord, a place of respect and lasting felicitation. To attempt to name in this volume each, who left his imprint on the religious life of Tennessee, would be impossible and unnecessary. The Diocesan Journals carry many names of ministers through the years.

Dr. Arthur Howard Noll in the *History of the Diocese of Tennessee* which he published in 1900, listed and gave coverage to the service of many presbyters. One chapter Dr. Noll entitled "Some of the Giants of Earth in Those Days."[23] He listed many whose names are familiar in the annals of the Church. Among these were Thomas Wright, Samuel George Litton, Dr. Daniel Stephens, Dr. George Weller, Leonidas Polk, John Chilton, Thomas West, Dr. William Thomas Leacock, Franklin G. Smith, Philip W. W. Alston, Charles Tomes, William Croes Crane, John Sandels, Dr. David C. Page, Dr. J. W. McCullough, John A. Harrison, William Crane Gray, Charles Francis Collins, Dr. George White, John Thomas Wheat, Dr. David Pise and Dr. Charles Todd Quintard. All these were among the one hundred names which appeared upon the roster of the clergy of Tennessee in the time of Bishop Otey's Episcopate.

These names were prominent during the Episcopate of Bishop Quintard: Dr. Samuel Ringgold, George Henry Hunt, George Carroll Harris, James Junius Vaulx, John A. Harrison, William Fagg, Moses L. Royce, John Miller Schwrar, George Carroll Parsons, Dr. Richard Hines, Dr. Joseph James Ridley, Thomas W. Humes, Dr. Richard N. Newell, Dr. Telfair Hodgson, Dr. George T. Wilmer, Elisha Spruille Burford, Henry Ripley Howard, Dr. Francis A. Shoup, Dr. Davis Sessums (later, Bishop of Louisiana), Charles McIlvaine Gray, G. W. Dumbell, Dr. James R. Winchester, Joseph H. Blacklock, Dr. William Graham, Edward Bradley, George Frederic Degen, Dr. George Beckett, Dr. George Patterson, Dr. Fredrick P. Davenport, Dr. William Montrose Pettis, Dr. Joseph E. Martin, Dr. Thomas Ferdinand Martin.[24]

Numerous names of ministers are recorded as Rectors, Priests-in-Charge, and in other capacities throughout the historical sketches of the Churches of the Diocese of West Tennessee carried in this volume.

Let us close this chapter about Men-of-the-Cloth by quoting from Dr. Noll:

> "It behooves us to speak and to think with all humility of the spiritual growth to which the Church has attained in Tennessee, and as to what has

been the measure of her influence upon the State and upon society. But it is certain that she has been true to the Church's conception of what the Church is, and under her noble Bishops and the noble bands of clergy who have aided them, she has held fast to that which has been committed to her and has striven with both hands earnestly to do her Lord's work in the way of His appointment."[25]

Laymen and Laywomen

A full and informative book about the men and women of Tennessee might well be written wherein significant names historically vital to the Episcopal Church would be recorded. However, the mentioning of the laity in this volume by no means indicates an attempt to give full coverage to the names of men and women, who, have through the years left a trail of loving service through their affiliation with the Episcopal Church.

The names of only a few staunch churchmen of the past are carried here. At the 1829 Diocesan Convention the Lay Delegates present were: from Christ Church, Nashville—Thomas Claiborne, George Wilson and Francis B. Fogg; from St. Peter's, Columbia—James H. Piper; from St. Paul's, Franklin—Thomas Maney, P. N. Smith, B. S. Tappan and William Hardeman, and G. M. Fogg, Nashville (representing Knoxville.[26] For a part of the Convention were also present—William Hardeman, P. N. Smith and B. S. Tappan of Franklin. Interestingly, there were only about fifty communicants in Tennessee at that time which caused the delegates representation to be much higher than in succeeding years.

Mention is made here of the unusual number of men of the Confederacy who settled in Tennessee after the Civil War and were very active in the affairs of the Episcopal Church. Among these were the Honorable Jefferson Davis, General Gideon J. Pillow, Lieutenant-General Richard S. Ewell, Major Gustavus A. Henry, General Josiah Gorgas, General Edmund Kirby Smith, and the Honorable Jacob Thompson. Other faithful laymen in the early days were John Anderson, LaGrange; Dr. John Shelby and Adlai O. Harris.[27]

Those of the laity who signed the testimonials of the election of Bishop Otey in 1833 were John C. Wormley, George C. Skipwith, William G. Dickinson, B. S. Tappan, Thomas Maney, Matthew Watson, Godfrey M. Fogg, Francis B. Fogg and John Anderson.

The Diocesan Journals which carry the proceedings of the Convention of the Episcopal Church in Tennessee provide lists of Lay Delegates for all Parishes and Missions. These volumes are the best source of information relative to the names of the laity of the State. Although it must be stated that many loyal men and women who daily serve the Church with dedication never have their names of record in such volumes. In fact many are not to be found anywhere! For many souls their service to their beloved Church remains a legacy in the hearts of those who knew them and their Christian fortitude is inscribed only on the lasting roll of God's kingdom.

A very creditable book entitled *"The History of the Episcopal Churchwomen in the Diocese of Tennessee,"* was written in 1981 by the Reverend Al Warren Jenkins. The information used was carefully researched and is indeed a most acceptable work. Included in the book is a very covering outline of significant dates in the development of the work of the Episcopal Church Women in the State. A letter from Mrs. John (Hester Louisa) Shortridge, Tennessee's first Diocesan President of Episcopal Church Women, is included. This history is given:

> "The mission of discipleship for Episcopal Churchwomen in the Diocese of Tennessee began in Memphis, Tennessee on April 23, 1888. On that day the Rt. Rev. Charles Todd Quintard signed the first official Constitution of the Tennessee Branch of the Women's Auxiliary. Bishop Quintard appointed Hester Louisa Shortridge the first President."

The first general meeting was held in St. Paul's Church on May 3, 1888.

A list of the women who have served as Presidents of Tennessee's Episcopal Women and the dates of their terms are listed:

> Hester Louisa Clark Shortridge 1888-1891; Mrs. Eloise Wormley 1891-; Mrs. Shortridge 1891-1892; Katherine Polk Gale 1892-1895; Mrs. Shortridge 1895-1920; Ada Maria Loaring-Clark 1920-1923; Anna Martha Wheeler 1924-1929; Evelyn McNeal Peters Burch 1930-1933; Zoe Morass Sehorn Ramsey 1934-1936; Mary Graham Love 1937-1939; Mary Wharton Yeatman 1940-1942; Margaret Hayes Powell 1943-1945; Sarah Perkins Allen 1946-1948; Irene Turley Rogers Beasley 1949-1952; Elizabeth Overnam Nellums 1952-1955; Helen Dyson Wofford 1955-1958; Grace New Goss 1958-1961; Betty Wells Patten 1961-1964; Evelyn Loduska Anderson Oakes 1964-1967; Carroll Cale Howell 1967-1969; Bette Ann Thompson Winchester 1969-1971; Anne Frazier Ragon 1971-1973; Mary Allen Hazen Tucker 1973-1975; Katherine Louise Street Sharp 1975-1977; Barbara Baker Thurmond 1977-1979; Constance Lavonia Stulce Boyle 1979-1981; Jean Ainsworth Miller 1981-1983[28]

The Rev. Mr. Jenkins recorded names of several laywomen under the title *"Some Outstanding Ladies of the Diocese of Tennessee"* as follows: Ellen Davies-Rodgers, Gwen Awsumb, Mrs. Claire H. Kinnard IV, the Rev. Lucy Lee Shetters, the Rev. Mary Christopher Robert, Florence Roberts, Mrs. Barney O'Kane, Marilyn Powell, Sister Superior Christabel, Miss Ellen Correll, Mrs. Allen Harris, Sr., Isabel Baumgartner and the Sisters of St. Mary's, Sewanee.

The subject of Laywomen is concluded by the listing of the officers of the Episcopal Churchwomen of the new Diocese of West Tennessee, 1983. They are:

> Mrs. Charles Clarke, President; Mrs. Harry Ramsay, Vice-President; Mrs. Barth Mueller, Secretary; Mrs. Robert C. Douglas, Corresponding Secretary; Mrs. Edwin P. Paine, Treasurer; Mrs. Henry Craft, Altar Guild Chairman; Mrs. Henry Wilcox, United Thank Offering.[29]

HEIRS IN SERVICE

Bishops of the Diocese of Tennessee

1834   1982

James Hervey Otey

Charles Todd Quintard

Thomas Frank Gailor

Troy Beatty

James M. Maxon

Bishops of the Diocese of Tennessee

Edmund Pendleton Dandridge

Theodore Nott Barth

John Vander Horst

William Evan Sanders

William Fred Gates, Jr.

CHAPTER 3

The Western District
Twenty-One Counties Formed 1819-1875

The vast area, lying between the Tennessee and the Mississippi Rivers, known as the Chickasaw Country contained some of the richest, most desirable land in the great new west. In 1818 the Legislature of Tennessee requested Congress to appoint commissioners to negotiate a treaty with the Chickasaw Indians, whereby the Chickasaw Country might be acquired. Therefore, General Andrew Jackson of Tennessee and Governor Isaac Shelby of Kentucky were appointed by Congress and negotiations began. After twenty days spent in discussions, the treaty was signed on October 19, 1818.[1]

Several titles were accorded this historic action: Jackson-Shelby Treaty, the Jackson Purchase or the Chickasaw Purchase. Whatever the name, the results were that on January 7, 1819, the treaty was proclaimed by President James Monroe. The text of the treaty begins:

> To settle the territorial controversies, and to remove all ground of complaint or dissatisfaction that might arise to interrupt the peace and harmony which have so long and so happily existed between the United States of America and the Chickasaw Nation of Indians, James Monroe, President of the United States, by Isaac Shelby and Andrew Jackson, of the one part, and the whole Chickasaw Nation, by their chiefs, head men, and warriors, in full council assembled, of the other part, have agreed on the following articles, which when ratified, by the President and Senate of the United States of America, shall form a treaty binding on all parties.[2]

Descriptive of the land acquired by the Chickasaw Treaty is the following:

> Art. II. To obtain the object of the foregoing article, the Chickasaw Nation of Indians cede to the United States of America (with the exception of such reservations as shall be hereafter mentioned) all claim or title which the said nation has to the land lying north of the south boundary of the State of Tennessee, which is bounded south by the thirty-fifth degree of north latitude, and which land, hereby ceded, lies within the following boundary, viz: Beginning on the Tennessee River, about thirty-five miles by water; below Colonel George Colbert's ferry, where the thirty-fifth degree of north latitude strikes the same; thence due west,

with said degree of north latitude, to where it cuts the Mississippi River at or near the Chickasaw Bluffs; thence up the Ohio River to the mouth of the Tennessee River to the place of beginning.[3]

It must be noted that by this cession, the Chickasaw Treaty, the tribe of Chickasaw Indians gave to the United States all of West Tennessee as well as their lands in Kentucky and Alabama. So it was, that the stage had been legally set for the coming of the white man to the Western District and the beginning of his settlement in this vast new area.

Early in 1819, the great movement westward began as pioneers from the Carolinas, Virginia, from East Tennessee and elsewhere ventured into the Western District. Of this area—the Western District—John Haywood, an early Tennessee historian wrote:

> In going from Jackson, in the Western District of Tennessee, through the states of Mississippi and Alabama, and thence to Florence, near the Tennessee line, the alluvial land of the Western District cannot fail to attract the attention of the traveller. There are marshes on the banks of every stream, dangerous quicksands, sluggish waters, and a sound made by the hoof of the horse when it strikes the ground. The falling of a tree at some distance will produce a tremulous motion of the earth to the distance of several hundred yards; and here are frequent shocks of earthquakes. In the banks of rivers, and under high bluffs, sticks or logs of wood are found sometimes petrified. And in digging wells through the sand, leaves and sticks of wood are often found; and also fire coals and pieces of pottery. Along the ridges dividing the headwaters of Sandy River from the waters of Hatchie River, immense beds of marine shells on the top of the ground are presented to view. No fossil or mineral substance is found in what may be supposed to have been its primitive state. They all seem to have been acted upon by heat and moisture. The Chickasaw Old Towns furnish a great variety of marine substances. Calcareous limestone is found in that section of country, a few feet underground, and the small streams are soon sunk or absorbed. Springs are scarce.[4]

From the standpoint of travel facilities within the Chickasaw Indian Territory, historians have given varying accounts. It has been written that the Western District at that time was a "pathless wilderness."

> The trails or traces of the Indians extended hundreds of miles in all directions and they crisscrossed each other over the whole continent, and over these the Indians constantly traveled on continuous trips thousands of miles. The Chickasaws were great travelers, and thought nothing of going to the far West, over their trails.[5]
>
> Their trails or traces were far superior to any the white man could locate, and the early use by white pioneers of these Indian trails was a constant source of friction, for the Indians resented that use. As soon as

state governments were organized, roads were laid out over these traces; and the United States government made these trails available. Thus, the Chickasaw had a trail leading from about where Natchez, Mississippi, now is, on to the Cumberland River where Nashville is now situated, and the trail led thence onward to the Atlantic seaboard, over which the Chickasaws traveled.[6]

Over the trails and traces traveled the caravans of those adventurous persons who came as early settlers to the Western District. The trek started in 1818-1819, continued steadily through succeeding years. In 1825 the movement was described in this manner by the editor of the *Jackson Gazette:*[7]

> Few sections invite emigrants equal to the Western District. In many instances of from twelve to fifteen hundred weight of fine quality cotton can be grown. Lands can be bought for less than their value because of the scarcity of money.

Truly no better description of the detailed preparation and intimate perils in travel of the early settlers to West Tennessee can be found than has been recorded by Joseph S. Williams in his *"Old Times in West Tennessee,"* now a rare volume. The wording of the dedication of his work in 1873 gives stamp of meaning of the content covered:

> Respectfully dedicated to the surviving pioneer settlers, whose brave hearts and strong arms subdued the Wilderness of West Tennessee, and made it the fitting abode for refined, civilized enjoyment and their immediate successors.

Early in his account, Mr. Williams writes of "the land of the Chickasaws and Davy Crockett—the Obion, Forked Deer and the Big Hatchie country—when in the cradle of the wilderness."[8]

Glimpses of the eventful journey from Mississippi territory are taken from the colorfully related account.

> The fatigue and peril of moving a large family of white and black, through a savage wilderness, with all the paraphernalia of comfortable living, in those days of rude travel, was an undertaking requiring almost superhuman endurance and inflexible will, but my father proved himself equal to it . . .
> Through the lonely vistas of the pine woods was seen a long train of movers. In front rode my father, on his faithful and sure-footed dapple-gray mare, with heavy bolsters swinging across the pommel of his saddle, with their black bear skin covering . . . Following close behind was a large black carryall, containing mother, grandmother and the young children. The carryall, . . . my father had made in North Carolina, with an eye single to its usefulness as a sleeping apartment, as a traveling vehicle; long and broad, deep sides and high back, with heavy leather curtains, lined

with thick, green baize, when closely buttoned down and bed made up in it, was comfortable enough for an emperor's wife. It was the traveling and sleeping apartment of my mother, grandmother and three young sisters.

Provident in arrangement my father . . . had purchased a year's supply of everything requisite to a comfortable living in the wilds of the Big Hatchie—coffee, tea, rice, sugar, flour, spices and medicines; card, cotton and spinning-wheels; every variety and kind of seeds; implements of husbandry; carpenter and blacksmith tools, and assorted nails, not forgetting an ample stock of powder, lead and shot; selecting twenty head of choice milch cows with their calves and yearlings, and about the same number of stock hogs.

My mother contributed her share in the necessary preparation for the journey; every one, both black and white, were properly and comfortably clad in home-spun clothes—stout overcoats for the men and long jackets for the women. The seats and knees of her boys' pants she padded with dressed buckskin . . .

We made some days as much as ten miles, oftener, however, not more than six or eight . . .

Reaching the Chickasaw territory, the Choctaw guide was relieved, my father making him many presents for his faithful services, sending presents to his chief. A Chickasaw guide was engaged, and the course of travel decided upon . . .

The country through which we traveled was slightly rolling, wood principally oak and hickory, devoid of tangled undergrowth. Traveling for days . . . we reach the thickly settled portion of the nation, . . . the principal village, at which the chief resided. It was on a Friday: man and beast needed to rest, and the order was given that we would lay over till Monday. No travel was done on the Sabbath.

The author continues to relate in full the incidents of the journey and the eventual settling of their new home.

Buried, as it were, in the wilderness, beyond the outskirts of busy civilized life, we lived in Quaker simplicity. The schoolmaster and the preacher had not yet arrived in the land . . .

My father, the Fall of the first year he settled in the wilderness, surveyed out and cut a road through the Hatchie bottom, and established the first ferry on the Hatchie, below McGuire's, in Haywood. There was then a continuous road from Brownsville to Covington, and became the principal road of travel between the two places, and my father's house the only habitation on the road, which of necessity became a "house of entertainment."[9]

Between 1821 and 1840 a network of post and stage routes developed throughout the Western District.

The picturesque, stage coach was destined to enter and continue as a rough but ready mode of early travel. The entire equipage was unique—the cinderella-type carriage set on wheels capable of the greatest speed of the age was drawn by nattily groomed, prancing horses harnessed usually in tandem fashion. And seated over all, an able driver keen of eye and swift in emergencies, equipped with a whip to urge the horses onward and a conch shell to blow in announcement of an approaching stop. Such stops were usually at a wayside inn and were most welcome interludes for passengers and horses alike. There, travelers found food and refreshment and horses were changed for the onward journey.

History records, that in 1829 post roads were established leading from Memphis by way of Raleigh, Morning Sun, Somerville, Bolivar and Jackson; also one from Memphis by way of Randolph, Covington, Brownsville and Jackson was in operation.

Prior to the post-roads of 1829 numerous ideas had been proposed concerning the need of improved travel facilities for the District. The first concern was that of making navigable the rivers, along which settlement had begun.

The keel-boat was the type of water-craft best suited to survive the hazards of the undredged, narrow rivers of that time. Down the Tennessee, the Cumberland and Ohio Rivers came such boats and into the navigable streams of the Western District. In 1821 three keel-boats came down the Forked Deer River. Up the Hatchie River supplies were carried to the first stores in Brownsville by boat. The Hatchie was navigable to Bolivar and the Obion River was a waterway in the northwest section of the District. Groceries, dry goods, flour, wheat, cotton, corn and whiskey were usual items of the cargoes transported to or from the area.

As the result of a request to the Legislature, of 1825, for improvement of all rivers, a Navigation Board was appointed for the Western District. A lottery was authorized by the Assembly for the benefit of the Forked Deer River, although there is no record that it was ever held. Effort was made to get a canal cut from the Tennessee River to the Hatchie, which did not materialize. However, in 1834, Memphis operated the first steamboat on the Mississippi River and in 1837 a steamboat was on the Hatchie at Bolivar.

Internal improvements were keenly needed by all, yet were sought diligently by only a few public-spirited citizens. Attention became diverted from rivers as waterways to improved roads, with bridges, as a more nearly desirable means of general travel. Therefore, the wilderness trail, no more than a bridle-path, became a road and in many cases an eventual turnpike.

The Western District was settled by people of energy, courage and ingenuity. They experienced, unquestionably, great hazards and decided inconvenience in travel. After treacherous mountain passes, they crossed fordable streams and throughout the wilderness territory these early travelers were subjected to the danger of lurking wild animals.

During the succeeding years, the Western District began to assume the character of a stimulated, thriving civilization. Obscure trading posts became settlements and remote, sparsely inhabited villages developed into towns of trade and culture. Indeed, many of the populated centers were seemingly destined from their beginning to become patterns of growth and influence in the settlement of the vast new area—*West Tennessee.*

It is of interest to note that by 1830, facilities of travel had both increased and improved. Steamboats and bridged roads—over which stage coaches traveled—contributed immeasurably to the general well-being of the early settlers of the vast west of Tennessee.

Counties were rapidly organized and settled in West Tennessee. The formation of counties, their dates and creation by the Legislature and the chief towns which are their county seats, are of historical value in providing a background for the organization and advancement of the Episcopal Church within their borders. The names of the counties which comprise West Tennessee follow:[10]

Counties of the Western District

Name	Date Formed	Parent County	County Seat
Hardin	11/13/1819	Western District	Savannah
Shelby	11/24/1819	Hardin	Memphis
Madison	11/ 7/1821	Western District	Jackson
Henderson	11/ 7/1821	Western District	Lexington
Henry	11/ 7/1821	Western District	Paris
Carroll	11/ 7/1821	Western District	Huntingdon
McNairy	10/ 8/1823	Hardin	Selmer
Hardeman	10/16/1823	Western District	Bolivar
Dyer	10/16/1823	Western District	Dyersburg
Weakley	10/21/1823	Western District	Dresden
Gibson	10/23/1823	Western District	Trenton
Obion	10/24/1823	Western District	Union City
Tipton	10/29/1823	Western District	Covington
Haywood	11/ 3/1823	Western District	Brownsville
Fayette	9/24/1824	Shelby, Hardeman	Somerville
Benton	11/24/1835	Henry, Humphreys	Camden
Lauderdale	11/24/1835	Dyer, Tipton, Haywood	Ripley
Decatur	11/ /1845	Perry	Decaturville
Lake	6/ 9/1870	Obion	Tiptonville
Crockett	3/ 9/1872	Dyer, Madison, Gibson, Haywood	Alamo
Chester	3/ 1/1875	McNairy, Hardeman, Madison, Henderson	Henderson

Mary Hayes Willis Gloster
(Mrs. Thomas Benn Gloster)

Earthen jug filled with peach brandy carried by Mary Hayes Willis Gloster tied to her side-saddle when she rode from LaGrange to see Mr. Otey, 1832.

Photograph, courtesy of Dorothy Seymour (Mrs. R. C.) Harnden, Memphis, Tennessee.

CHAPTER 4

The Episcopal Church Comes to West Tennessee, 1832.
Map of Counties and Churches, 1983

The settlement of the Western District of the great State of Tennessee and the Church's coming to this section, typify a movement of extensive proportions, in fact and in deed—a story of life and religious endeavor to be carefully and enthusiastically related.

A look at the history of the Episcopal Church in America all the way from Jamestown, 1607, to the Western District, 1832, fails to reveal a more dramatic or more romantic episode than the one which characterized the coming of the Church to West Tennessee.[1]

Innumerable circumstances of livelihood and travel characterized the period dating from the Chickasaw Treaty, of 1818, and the coming of the Episcopal Church to the Western District in 1832. One of the most widespread migrations at the time was from the neighboring state of North Carolina.

The "Raleigh Register," Raleigh, North Carolina, on December 10, 1825, carried the following:

> There are nearly a hundred families in Orange, Chatham, Davidson and Rowan who are moving to the Chickasaw Purchase this fall. The emigration is astonishing.

It is said that a severe drought in North Carolina in 1826 almost caused near famine. Logs were burned that were obstructions in streams or waterways.

> In 1827 a correspondent from North Carolina stated that during the last four months the flow of emigration through Asheville has surpassed anything of the kind the writer has ever witnessed. It was not uncommon to see 8, 10 or 15 wagons and carts passing in a single day . . . wending their way to the more highly favored climes of the West.

Among the many families who came to the Western District, during this period from several of the states, not one came inbued with greater zeal and affection for the cause of the Episcopal Church than did the Gloster-Anderson family from Warrenton, North Carolina. Thrilling and of historic value is the story of their coming!

"We removed to Fayette County in the Western District of the State of Tennessee from North Carolina in the Fall of the year 1827," wrote Elizabeth Willis Gloster (Mrs. John) Anderson. The group of Church people which came from Warrenton to LaGrange consisted of Mary Hayes Willis (Mrs. Thomas Benn) Gloster, widow of Dr. Gloster; her son, Arthur Brehon Gloster; her daughter, Elizabeth Willis Gloster and husband, John Anderson and their five children, and George Anderson, John Anderson's brother. Truly, they were a family of stout-hearted Christians and staunch supporters of the Episcopal faith.[2]

An unusual record of the departure of Mrs. Gloster and her family from Warrenton and from Emmanuel Church, Warrenton, follows:

> The public ordinances were as well attended as on former occasions. In the Warrenton congregation the administration of the Lord's Supper was rendered peculiarly affected by the circumstances, that the appointment was requested at this particular time to meet the desire of the most numerous and influential family belonging to the Church in that place for the last time to unite with their brethren in that Holy Ordinance previous to their removal to the Western Country. This family, Mr. and Mrs. John Anderson and five children moved to Fayette County, Tennessee.

"Sketches of Old Warrenton, North Carolina" written by a communicant of Emmanuel Church, Warrenton, Mrs. Lizzie Wilson Montgomery, relates the story of the removal of the Gloster-Anderson family to the West. The account is quoted by Mrs. Montgomery from a letter dictated by Mrs. Ellen Mordecai at the age of ninety-five to her daughter:

> "I could not have been more than seven years old when the family moved to the Western Country, the vague name for what then seemed the remote region, now Tennessee. I can never forget the starting, when the whole village came to say good-bye. The looks of the big covered wagon, loaded with all their belongings. The stamping of the big-footed horses and all the bustle incident to such an occasion. The vehicle for the family was made strong for the needs of a long journey, which took weeks to accomplish. Warrenton was a friendly, unconventional little place then."

So, it was in the Fall in 1827, that the widow, Mrs. Gloster, with her son, Arthur B. Gloster; her daughter, Elizabeth Willis Gloster (Mrs. John) Anderson; her son-in-law John Anderson; her Anderson grandchildren and George Anderson, a brother of her son-in-law, arrived in LaGrange, Fayette County, Tennessee. The town was at that time a growing community characterized by wealth, education and culture.

At the time of LaGrange's incorporation, in 1828, there were 240 inhabitants, 60 houses, 4 stores, 2 taverns and a dozen mechanics! Yet, not one church had been established within the borders of the town!

The absence of a house of worship in LaGrange greatly disturbed Mrs. Gloster and the members of her family, who had brought with them lasting memories of their devout religious experiences while communicants of Emmanuel Church and residents of Warrenton, North Carolina. They were church people who sorely felt the absence of church privileges. Seemingly, to these newcomers, LaGrange had everything to offer as a desirable place of abode, except a house of worship. Therefore, Mrs. Gloster and her family determined to do all within their power to supply the community's greatest need![3]

Several accounts have been written descriptive of Mrs. Gloster's dramatic and inspiring service in behalf of the bringing of the Episcopal Church to the Western District. However, no research has revealed a more interesting, and it is felt more accurate, account than the following written by the late Miss Mae Anderson, a great-granddaughter of Mrs. Gloster:

> All of my life I have been told that the little church Immanuel, a picture of which hangs on my wall, was Grandfather's church and that his negroes made the bricks from which it was built. He, Uncle George and Grandma and Grandma Gloster were so lonely for the church service and dear Mr. Green, the first permanent rector in Warrenton and his good helpful sermons. They decided to have a church service at the Anderson home, asking those citizens who might like to join them. This they did and in a short time had a good congregation. Since Grandfather John Anderson always had prayer morning and evening in his home, I'm sure he read the service. This was the first service of the Episcopal Church held in the District of West Tennessee.
>
> In 1832, Grandma Gloster decided to go and see the Rev. Otey, her godson and Episcopal missionary in Tennessee. She rode on horseback with one of Grandfather John Anderson's good reliable old family negroes. The Rev. Otey, at once wrote to New York for a missionary—the Rev. Wright came.

At the time Mrs. Gloster made the eventful ride to see Mr. Otey she was fifty-two years of age. Family tradition has related that in one arm, as she rode her horse, she held a grandchild, and that below her other arm, tied to her side-saddle, was an earthen jug filled with peach brandy. Mrs. Gloster's reasons were—the grandchild's presence would protect her from any advance by males and the brandy would ward off chills and fever! The stone jug remains today a prized possession of Mrs. Gloster's descendants.

No other woman has made a more significant journey in behalf of the extension of the Episcopal Church in Tennessee than did dedicated, energetic, determined Mrs. Gloster. Her memorable horse-ride deserves to be fully recorded in the annals of Church history as a selfless act wherein a sincere Christian Lay-woman was busy about the business of her Heavenly Father.

Due to the fact the Rev. Thomas Wright was the first minister—missionary organizer—to spread the Word and establish churches of the Episcopal faith in West Tennessee, it seems most appropriate that a brief account of Mr. Wright be recorded in this volume.

In St. James Church, Wilmington, North Carolina, on April 22, 1819, the North Carolina Diocesan Convention was held. For the first time in the proceedings of an official gathering of Episcopalians the name of Thomas Wright appeared.

His presence as a lay delegate was the first step toward a full and rewarding missionary journey to be made as he preached the Gospel and organized churches, during the next thirteen years, across the states of North Carolina and Tennessee.[4]

Again in 1820, Thomas Wright served as a lay delegate from St. James Church, Wilmington when the Convention met in St. Paul's Church, Edenton, on April 29. During the Convention, on Sunday, April 20, he was "admitted to the Holy Order of Deacons." Bishop Moore had confirmed Thomas Wright in 1819 and in 1820 admitted him to the diaconate. On April 28, 1822 he was ordained a Priest by the Rt. Rev. Richard Channing Moore in St. James Church, Wilmington. On May 1, 1820, Thomas Wright was engaged by the *Domestic and Foreign Missionary Society of the Protestant Episcopal Church in the United States of America* as a Missionary.

Let us complete the summary of the work of the Reverend Thomas Wright in North Carolina as best we can prior to his coming to Tennessee in 1832. In 1826, he was one of the ten clergymen in North Carolina—the Reverend Adam Empie, the Reverend John Avery, the Reverend William Mercer Green, the Reverend Richard S. Mason, the Reverend Henry M. Mason, the Reverend Robert J. Miller, the Reverend Elijah Brainerd, *the Reverend Thomas Wright*, Presbyters; and the Reverend George W. Freeman and the Reverend Philip B. Wiley, Deacons. In 1830 and 1831, Mr. Wright was elected a delegate from the Diocese of North Carolina to the General Convention.

On June 3, 1832 Bishop Levi Silliman Ives wrote in his record:

"The changes which . . . have taken place among our clergy are: *The Reverend Thomas Wright has been transferred by me to the Diocese of Tennessee.*"

Gird up now thy loins like a man: for I will demand of thee, . . .

The challenge of waiting people to hear the Word came across the almost pathless wilderness. The relentless heat of late June was o'er the earth. Mountains stood in bold resistance and streams presented handicaps. A steady steed, sure-footed and well shod was required that the missionary journey might be continued from North Carolina to Tennessee's Western District.[5]

Of old, God had spoken to Job and challenged him to gird his loins,—meaning, to strengthen his back, prepare himself,—that He would demand of him. And, as recorded by St. Matthew, Jesus spoke to his disciples—"If any man will come after me, let him deny himself, and take up his cross and follow me." Thomas Wright, a dedicated minister of the Gospel was imbued with deep sympathies firmly grounded in stalwart Christian faith. He accepted as God directed him, he took up his cross and followed as a disciple of his Lord and Savior Jesus Christ. Alone he rode his horse from North Carolina to Tennessee bringing his message of the Master! What a trek![6]

Only by careful scrutiny of the maps of North Carolina and Tennessee can be conceived the length and travel hazards of such a horse-ride in the year of 1832. Fortunately, the *Travelogue* kept by the Reverend Thomas Wright, in his own handwriting, as he rode his horse from Salisbury, North Carolina to Memphis, Tennessee is at hand. Therefore, we shall let the detailed record, which Mr. Wright kept, give in his own words the facts of his magnificent missionary pilgrimage. The itinerary as kept by Mr. Wright began:

"_____ 12 miles; 9 miles to Stevenson; 8 miles to David's Forge; 16 miles to Mr. Miller's; 12 to 14 to Morganton; 14 by rocky road to Finlay; 18 to Greenlee; 12 to 14 to Carson's; 10 to Alexander's (Mills); 18 to Asheville; 13 to . . .; 10 to Collins; 21 miles to Warm Springs . . . This patch of road is better . . .

"The little rivers between Mr. Mills and Mr. Miller are very bad, particularly if the water is high. The Catawba between Cannon and Greenlee is good and muddy.

"From the Warm Spring to Newport (Tenn.) 25 miles—miserable place—and the French Broad which you find rapid though not very rocky.

"From Newport to Dandridge is 18 miles, but there is a tolerable house at Schorn's ferry. 4 on this . . .

> "From Dandridge to Chapel Hill a good house. 12 miles to Monterey —a miserable establishment.
>
> "10 to Dr. Ramsay's. 4½ to Knoxville. 4. A few miles from Dandridge is Pigeon River which is a safe ford ordinarily."

By June 12, 1832, Thomas Wright had reached Knoxville, Tennessee.

Thomas Wright continued to ride his horse from Knoxville to Nashville, where he would be a part of the 1832 Diocesan Convention. His *Travelogue* noted:

> "From Knoxville to Coxes 10 miles; thence to Campbell's Station. Bells Tavern 6 miles; thence to Meredith's where I stayed at night, 6 miles. This is a good house. From Meredith's to Huists (?) is 6 miles; thence to Eskridge, 8; to Clarke at the ferry over the Tennessee 5 miles."[7]

The Fourth Convention of the Clergy and Laity of the Protestant Episcopal Church in the State of Tennessee was held in Christ Church, Nashville, on June 28, 29 and 30, 1832. The Reverend Thomas Wright was present and was listed among the clergy who attended the sittings of the Convention by invitation.

On the first day of the Convention, by motion unanimously resolved,

> "That the Reverend Thomas Wright of North Carolina, be admitted to the sittings of this Convention."[8]

On July 28, Thomas Wright arrived in LaGrange and was a guest in the Gloster-Anderson household. His arrival there was an event which he had longed for as he rode along from North Carolina. There were his dear friends, old friends, in this little town in the Western District who had so eagerly awaited his coming.[9]

The selfless, determined missionary journey of Thomas Wright in behalf of the Episcopal Church continued. He rode his horse alone! A small Bible, a Prayer Book, a Hymnal, and a minimum of garments for his personal attire, comprised the contents of his saddle bags, flung across his horse. Mountains had been traversed. Rivers,—the Catawba, French Broad, the Tennessee,—had been ferried and minor streams had been forded. He had been the recipient of a hearty welcome by a Diocesan Convention in Tennessee, the state whose people of the Western District awaited his presence, his prayers and his preaching. Numerous had been the stops as the journey had progressed through the District, both in company with John Chilton and later. Towns, homes and wayside stops—all who gathered heard the message. In the towns of Clarksville, Paris,

Huntingdon, McLemoresville, Jackson, Brownsville, Bolivar, Somerville and LaGrange, the people assembled and heard attentively.

As enduring evidence of the religious fruitfulness of Mrs. Gloster's journey and the far-reaching movement created by her effort, five churches were organized in the Western District during the year 1832. St. Luke's, Jackson, was organized by the Rev. Thomas Wright on July 23, 1832. Zion (Christ) Church, Brownsville, came into being on August 25, 1832 as a result of the efforts of the Rev. Mr. Wright and the Rev. John Chilton. Immanuel Church, LaGrange, was constituted under the guidance of Mr. Wright and the Rev. Samuel George Litton. Also organized by the Rev. Mr. Wright was Calvary Church, Memphis, and St. Paul's at Randolph. In reality, the founding of these churches became a record of the journey of the pioneer missionary-organizer, the Rev. Thomas Wright, "through the counties of Madison, Hardeman, Haywood, Fayette, Lauderdale, Tipton and Shelby." Truly, the history of every parish and of every mission in West Tennessee is traceable to the consecrated determination of Mrs. Gloster, the influential vision of James Hervey Otey and the conscientious labors in the broad, challenging field by the Rev. Thomas Wright and his associates, the Rev. John Chilton and the Rev. Samuel George Litton.

To her—Mary Hayes Willis Gloster—must be accorded the title, "Mother of the Episcopal Church in West Tennessee." Resounding through one hundred and fifty-six years, her children in the faith and her children of the flesh rise up and call her "blessed."[10]

The crowning, gloriously justified reward to the dedicated, vigorous effort in 1832 by these extraordinary saints of the Episcopal Church was the creation of the *Episcopal Diocese of West Tennessee in 1983!* Only in their fondest hopes and dreams could there ever have been such an achievement! The boundaries of the Diocese of West Tennessee, as prescribed for the new Diocese were those of the original Western District:

> "The new Diocese of West Tennessee will be composed of that portion of the State of Tennessee, lying west of the Tennessee River and including all of Hardin County."[11]

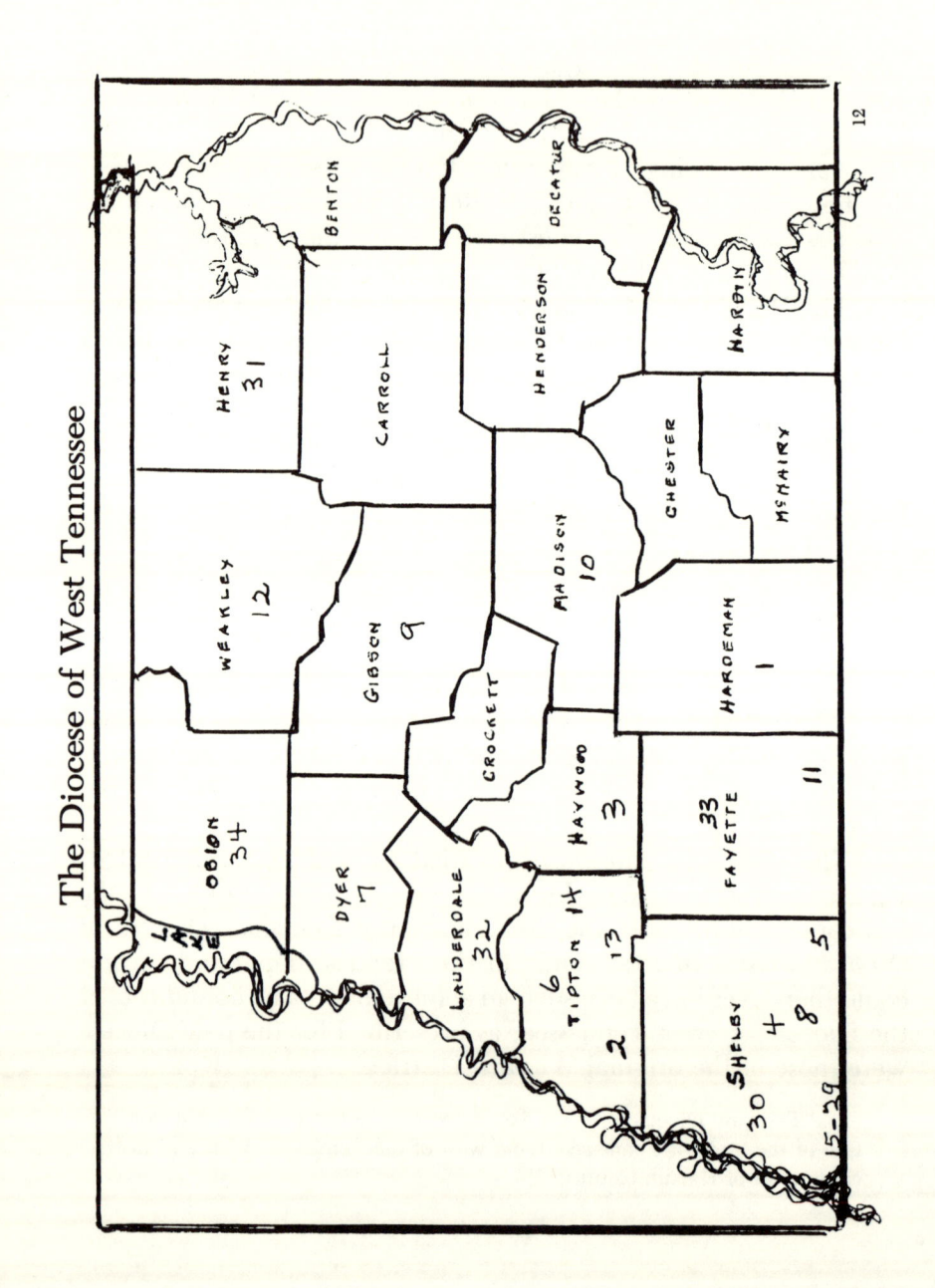

The Diocese of West Tennessee

Twenty-Two Parishes, Twelve Organized Missions

	LOCATION	CHURCH	COUNTY	DIOCESAN STATUS	ADMITTED
1.	Bolivar, Tenn.	St. James' Church	Hardeman	Organized Mission	1834
2.	Brighton, Tenn.	Ravenscroft Chapel	Tipton	Organized Mission	1836
3.	Brownsville, Tenn.	Christ Church	Haywood	Organized Mission	1833
4.	Brunswick, Tenn.	St. Philip, Davieshire	Shelby	Organized Mission	1976
5.	Collierville, Tenn.	St. Andrew's Church	Shelby	Parish	1978
6.	Covington, Tenn.	St. Matthew's Church	Tipton	Parish	1959
7.	Dyersburg, Tenn.	St. Mary's Church	Dyer	Parish	1954
8.	Germantown, Tenn.	St. George's Church	Shelby	Parish	1944
9.	Humboldt, Tenn.	St. Thomas The Apostle	Gibson	Organized Mission	1960
10.	Jackson, Tenn.	St. Luke's Church	Madison	Parish	1833
11.	LaGrange, Tenn.	Immanuel Church	Fayette	Organized Mission	1833
12.	Martin, Tenn.	St. John's Church	Weakley	Organized Mission	1957
13.	Mason, Tenn.	St. Paul's Church	Tipton	Organized Mission	1873
14.	Mason, Tenn.	Trinity Church	Tipton	Organized Mission	1871
15.	Memphis, Tenn.	All Saints'	Shelby	Parish	1960
16.	Memphis, Tenn.	Bishop Otey Memorial	Shelby	Organized Mission	1962
17.	Memphis, Tenn.	Calvary Church	Shelby	Parish	1833
18.	Memphis, Tenn.	Christ Church (Whitehaven)	Shelby	Parish	1958
19.	Memphis, Tenn.	Church Of The Good Shepherd	Shelby	Parish	1872
20.	Memphis, Tenn.	Emmanuel Church	Shelby	Parish	1977
21.	Memphis, Tenn.	Grace-St. Luke's Church	Shelby	Parish	1858-1898-1942
22.	Memphis, Tenn.	Holy Apostles Church	Shelby	Parish	1981
23.	Memphis, Tenn.	Holy Communion	Shelby	Parish	1951
24.	Memphis, Tenn.	Holy Trinity Church	Shelby	Parish	1909
25.	Memphis, Tenn.	St. Elisabeth's Church	Shelby	Parish	1966
26.	Memphis, Tenn.	St. James' Church	Shelby	Parish	1939
27.	Memphis, Tenn.	St. John's Church	Shelby	Parish	1928
28.	Memphis, Tenn.	St. Mary's Cathedral	Shelby	Parish	1858
29.	Memphis, Tenn.	St. Paul's Church (Frayser)	Shelby	Parish	1979
30.	Millington, Tenn.	St. Anne's Church	Shelby	Parish	1979
31.	Paris, Tenn.	Grace Episcopal Church	Henry	Parish	1973
32.	Ripley, Tenn.	Immanuel Church	Lauderdale	Organized Mission	Prior to 1860
33.	Somerville, Tenn.	St. Thomas	Fayette	Organized Mission	1835
34.	Union City, Tenn.	St. James' Church	Obion	Parish	1965

St. James, Bolivar

CHAPTER 5

The Thirty Four Episcopal Churches in West Tennessee, 1983

St. James Church, Bolivar

St. James Parish came into being early in 1834 through the efforts of the missionary, Dr. Daniel Stephens, and was organized on April 17th of that year by the Right Rev. James H. Otey, Bishop of Tennessee. Thirty-seven persons signed the Articles of Association.

Services were held in the Courthouse, the only "preaching place" in the town, until 1840 when a lot was purchased at the corner of Washington and Lafayette Streets for $175.00. A contract was made July 27th between John Shepherd and the building committee, McNeal, Polk and Goodrich. A brick building, 32 x 44 feet, was erected and consecrated in 1845 at a cost of $375.00.

The comments of the Rev. Mr. Stephens, in his report to the Bishop, are interesting and amusing. "Our population in this place is of a singular case, though intelligent. They have heretofore not been in the habit of going to hear any kind of preaching, neither men nor women, and on a certain occasion some ladies said they would rather go to the ball than go hear 'old Stephens' read."

The first vestrymen were: William B. Turley, Calvin Jones, James J. Williams, John H. Bills, Allen Hill, David F. Brown and Thomas C. Jones.

With the coming of the Civil War churches were used as barracks, hospitals, stables and storehouses. They were greatly despoiled and damaged, services were suspended, and many of the clergy served as chaplains in the Army of the Confederacy. Among these was the Rev. William Crane Gray who served the Church in Tennessee most faithfully as a zealous missionary. He was rector of St. James Church from December 25, 1860 to April 24, 1881 and later became Bishop of Florida.

In May, 1869, E. P. McNeal, Leonidas Bills and A. T. McNeal were appointed a building committee for the erection of a new church. Additional grounds were purchased and a contract was made with Willis and Sloan for the erection of the present church at a cost of $11,000.00. The building is of brick, of the Gothic architecture and is 48 x 70 feet. The architect was Mr. Fletcher Sloan, father of the late Mrs. James Foster of Bolivar. He was a designer of many southern churches, courthouses and many of the old buildings of the University of Alabama. There are memorial windows to the Rev. Daniel Stephens, to Ann McNeal, to Pitser Miller and to General Otho French Strahl and Lieutenant John Henry Marsh. Regarding the Strahl-Marsh window, we quote from Bishop Quintard's memoirs of the war: "Just before moving toward Franklin, General Strahl came to me and said 'I want to make you a present' and presented me with a splendid horse named Lady Polk. I used the horse through the remainder of the war and at its close sold her and with the money erected in St. James Church, Bolivar, a memorial window to General Strahl and his adjutant, Lieutenant John H. Marsh. Both of these men I had baptised, but a few months previously, and both were confirmed by Bishop Elliott."

In 1894, the Rev. Charles Scott Ware came to St. James Church and served as Rector until 1902. He returned in 1910 and was Rector until his retirement in 1923. Mr. Ware contributed much to the cultural and literary life of Bolivar as well as the spiritual. Although he was in the ministry over fifty years, he always considered Bolivar his main work and asked to have on his tombstone simply "For Twenty Years Rector of St. James Parish."

Another beloved Rector was the Rev. Charles A. T. Woodward who came to St. James in 1940 and served for 10 years. An altar for the chapel was presented by the Women of the Church in his memory.

The Vicar in 1959 was the Rev. George Elton Sauls. Under his leadership the beautiful stained glass windows were restored and the church re-roofed.

The present Vicar is the Rev. T. D. Roberts, who not only serves his mission families, but the needs of many patients at Western State Hospital. Due to unseasonable weather and continued dampness, St. James Church suffered a collapse of the parapet wall in March of 1973. However, with the help of the Diocese of Tennessee, friends and the excellent workmanship of Mr. Kermit Buck, the wall has been replaced and other brick work restored.

The Rectors and Vicars of St. James, Bolivar

	Beginning	Ending
The Rev. Daniel Stephens	1833	1849
The Rev. L. Jansen	1849	not known
The Rev. Jacocks	not known	not known
The Rev. L. J. Pickett	1857	1859
The Rev. William Crane Gray	Dec. 25, 1860	April 25, 1881
The Rev. W. G. Davenport	Jan. 1, 1882	July 1, 1885
The Rev. Edward Wootten	June 8, 1887	Dec. 1891
The Rev. C. S. Ware	April 6, 1894	1902
The Rev. Neville Joyner	Sept. 1, 1902	June 1, 1908
The Rev. C. S. Mullikin	Sept. 1908	Feb. 1910
The Rev. C. S. Ware	June 1, 1910	1923
The Rev. James B. Sill	Sept. 1, 1923	Dec. 31, 1924
The Rev. Henry Spears	July 1, 1925	July 10, 1928
The Rev. Grant Knauff	Dec. 22, 1928	Feb. 28, 1934
The Rev. James Fitts Plummer	Sept. 1934	Dec. 31, 1939
The Rev. Charles A. T. Woodward	Oct. 1940	Mar. 1950
The Rev. Edwin Dale Baker	June 15, 1951	Jan. 1953
The Rev. S. Wesley Toal	June 15, 1953	June 12, 1955
The Rev. George Elton Sauls	July 15, 1956	June 15, 1961
The Rev. W. Joe Moore	July 1, 1961	June 12, 1966
The Rev. E. S. Ballentine	1967	Mar. 1970
The Rev. Thomas D. Roberts	Oct. 1970	

Thomas D. Roberts, Rector

Ravenscroft Chapel, Brighton

Ravenscroft Chapel, Brighton

Sometime between 1825 and 1830, a widow, Mrs. Elizabeth Whitmel Williams Johnston Alston, with four of her children came to Tipton County, Tennessee from Warren County, North Carolina. They left her youngest son, Philip, at Shocco Spring Academy, Warrenton, North Carolina.

The family settled five miles east of Randolph on a 3,000 acre grant from the Governor of North Carolina, on the stage coach road, and in a wooded area built a palatial home. A few hundred yards from their home they built a small chapel, established a family burying ground. In loving memory of their Bishop, in North Carolina. They consecrated the Chapel—"Ravenscroft", on October 23, 1836, and it was the first church building erected in the Western District. Later Bishop Quintard spent three years in the Alston home and in charge of the Chapel.

During the Civil War a brother of Rev. Philip W. Alston stored the furnishings of the Chapel in a cache in a cane-brake and burned the Chapel to prevent the Federal Forces from destroying it. After the war an old granary was fitted as a place of worship and was used until about 1880.

About 1845 other families began moving onto this same road but two miles farther east, so it was decided to build two miles farther east to be nearer its members. One acre of land was deeded to the Diocese of Tennessee by Miss Betty Alston, the daughter of Samuel W. Alston. Miss Betty and Mrs. Philip W. Alston taught the first school paid by County Funds and gave the proceeds to the building of the new Ravenscroft Chapel. All the furnishings were put in the new building.

In 1907, when things looked dark for the church, Mr. George H. Batchlor came to the rescue and gave his time and services until ill health forced him to retire.

About 1930, Archdeacon Charles Weller began holding services. In 1934, the place of recreation for Ravenscroft Chapel was Batchlor Memorial Room in the home of Miss Hennie Watkins. It was decided to build a Community House as a memorial to the late Rev. George H. Batchlor.

Archdeacon Weller retired January 1, 1937. In February of that year, Rev. Paul E. Sloan came to the churches of Tipton County. On August 7, 1938, the gound breaking service for the Community House was held. Work began the following day.

The Chapel burned on Tuesday, December 6, 1938, burning

all the furnishings including the old Bible that had been used in St. Paul's, Randolph and the marble-topped Altar and Font. These had been in the original Ravenscroft Chapel. About four years before the fire, the original Ravenscroft bell had been stolen and later pieces of it were found nearby—apparently the thieves had heard about the silver dollars that had been melted to line the bell.

The Batchlor Memorial Room was put to use as a place of worship since the Community House had not been finished. The first service was held on December 25, 1938 in the Community House, although it still wasn't finished.

The three churches of Tipton County became Quintard Memorial Parish under the leadership of the Rev. Paul Sloan and he remained with the parish until his death in December 1949.

The parish was served by a number of Supply Priests until July 1952 when the Rev. John Sively became rector. With his guidance the Community House which was still being used, was remodeled into a church. Bishop Theodore N. Barth dedicated it on October 10, 1954. Mr. Sively trained two men at Ravenscroft as Lay-Leaders. One, Mr. Tom Morris, is still holding Morning Prayer Services.

In 1956, the Rev. Sheldon Davis became Rector of Quintard parish. When the parish was dissolved Ravenscroft again became a mission. During this time a baptismal Font was purchased. Mr. Davis remained priest-in-charge until August 1963 when the Rev. Peter Reese took charge. Under his guidance further remodeling was done. A new pulpit and lectern were added. The Rev. Reese served until February 1, 1966.

July 1, 1966, the Rev. Curtis T. Allen became priest-in-charge of Ravenscroft where he is still guiding the small "flock" of faithful worshippers.

Mary Ellen Watkins

The Day's Demand

"God give us men! A time like this demands
Strong minds, great hearts, true faith and ready hands;
Men whom the lust of office does not kill;
    Men whom the spoils of office cannot buy;
Men who possess opinions and a will;
    Men who have honor—men who will not lie;
Men who can stand before a menagogue
    And damn his treacherous flatteries without winking,
Tall men, sun-crowned, who live above the fog
    In public duty and in private thinking;
For while the rabble, with their thumb-worn creeds,
Their large professions and their little deeds,
Mingle in selfish strife, lo! Freedom weeps,
Wrong rules the land, and waiting Justice sleeps."

                                      —Josiah Gilbert Holland

Christ Church, Brownsville

Christ Church, Brownsville

The Rev. Thomas Wright kept a well documented Travelogue as he journeyed from Salisbury, North Carolina to the West District of Tennessee in 1832. Most fortunate indeed has been the possession of this document. The Rev. John Chilton who accompanied Mr. Wright also kept a record of their missionary journey.

Mr. Wright wrote in the account of his journey:

> "Next morning the 17th of (July) we reached Brownsville where I met with several old friends and preached in the morning of the next day to a large number of persons. Here are a few zealous people and the church by God's blessings will succeed."

In his Travelogue Mr. Wright made clear the date on which Zion Church, Brownsville was founded:[1]

> "August 25, 1832 . . . preached in the morning and in the afternoon, assisted Mr. Chilton in organizing a church under the title of Zion."

There were five communicants when Zion Church was organized on August 25, 1832: Egbert H. Sheppard, Mary T. Sheppard, Jane D. Johnson, Eliza Perkins and Sarah Grove. The church was admitted to the Diocese in 1833.

The Rev. John Chilton, the first minister ordained in the Diocese of Tennessee, was the first rector of Zion Church, Brownsville, Haywood County. Zion Church became Christ Church in 1898 following the canonical consent of Bishop Gailor to change the name.

In his report of the parish to the 1833 Diocesan Convention, Mr. Chilton stated, "The congregation worshipped in an upper room of the Court House, comfortably fitted up for the purpose." He also spoke of, "The pious zeal manifested for the cause of God." On March 29, 1834, Bishop Otey visited the church and reported his visit in his message to the Diocesan Convention.

Early clergymen who served the church: the founder-missionary organizer—the Rev. Thomas Wright; John Chilton 1832-1840; Louis Jansen; Thomas West 1842-1843; James W. Rogers, 1852; Cyrus Waters (from Maryland); John Alexander Wheelock; Charles Francis Collins, 1857; Robert A. Cobbs, 1867; Joseph James Ridley, 1868; Mr. Collins, 1878; Matthew Henry; Irenaeus Trout, Nevill Joyner, 1898. The Rev. Charles A. T. Woodward was rector during and after World War II. He began the midnight service on Christmas Eve. He retired in 1950.

In 1962 the Rev. Robert Rickard served as rector and the Rev. Wayne Kinyon in 1963.

Prior to 1956 the first Lay Readers were chosen: E. de S. Juny, Robert Johnson, George D. Arnold, George B. Burgess and Ridley Wills.

The church building was erected in 1846, there were twelve communicants at that time.[2] The parish house was built in 1969. An unusual feature in the church is the Trinity Windows, over the inner doors.

Among the women of Christ Church whose names deserve a place in its history are: Mrs. Margaret Bond; Mrs. Mary Moore; Mrs. Graham Boyd; Mrs. John Owen; Mrs. J. W. E. Moore, who served as chairman of the Building Committee for the Parish Hall.

Miss Minna Wendel served as organist for many years. She is remembered as the most faithful member the church ever had. She was born before the Civil War and died in 1946. She was the first diocesan president of the Daughters of the King in Tennessee.

A very fine cook book has been published by the Women of Christ Church. The volume has had vast distribution.

The present rector of Christ Church is the Rev. Richard M. Flynn who also serves Immanuel Church, Ripley.

> Compiled by
> Mrs. J. O. (Doris) Burgess, Sr.
> (and the Author)

Your Place

"Is your place a small place?
   Tend it with care;—
     He set you there.

Is your place a large place?
   Guard it with care!—
     He set you there.

Whate'er your place, it is
Not yours alone, but his
        Who set you there."

—John Qxenham
The Treasure Chest, p. 164

St. Philip, Davieshire, Brunswick

Saint Philip Church, Davieshire, Brunswick

Of the sketches of history about the other thirty-three churches in the Diocese of West Tennessee, which the Author has either edited, compiled or written, the piece found most difficult to create is the one about the church nearest and dearest to the heart—St. Philip, Davieshire, Brunswick! To have given the land as the site for the church; to have given the church-house and to have aided in superintending its construction; to have kept the records of the Mission Council from January 2, 1977-December 12, 1982 and now to attempt to write a brief history of all this (and to keep it brief!) seems overwhelming and almost incredible.

Not to delay, as venerable Calvary Church, Memphis did in recording its distinguished history of 140 years, (founded 1832), which the Author wrote in *The Great Book* in 1972, the record of St. Philip has already begun. Copious notes have been kept since the first service and earlier. A volume is in progress to tell the complete story which has been entitled, *Four Years and Before, St. Philip Episcopal Church, Davieshire, 1984.* So much for a future covering volume on the organization, activities and achievement of a mission seemingly destined for commitment by creation.

The first service of St. Philip was held on the afternoon of Sunday, December 8, 1974 in the J. B. Griffin Memorial Chapel in Pleasant Hill Cemetery, Brunswick, Shelby County, Tennessee, with the Rt. Rev. W. Fred Gates, Jr., Suffragan Bishop of Tennessee who conducted the service. The Rev. W. Bowlyne Fisher assisted.

A deed for the ten acres of land from Davies Plantation was given on December 30, 1974 to the Diocese of Tennessee as a site for St. Philip Episcopal Church, Davieshire, Brunswick. The site had been chosen by the Episcopal Shelby County Planning Commission in June 1965. Later the Donor was advised by Bishop John Vander Horst: "The Planning Commission felt the tract north of I40 would be more profitable for the purpose of establishing a church." (Acreage south of I40 had been offered also as a site,—where Stonebridge Country Club is now located). The value of the land was placed at $135,000.00.[3]

From the first service on December 8, 1974 to the date of the consecration of the finished church, November 1, 1981, services continued to be held in the Griffin Memorial Chapel. With the coming of Rev. Gordon Bernard on July 11, 1980, to be Vicar of St. Philip, Davieshire, two services were held each Sunday morning,—at eight o'clock in the Stonebridge Center, 3049 Davies Plantation Road, also Sunday School was held there, and the eleven o'clock service continued in the Chapel. The first regular worship service in the new church was held on November 8, 1981.

Of the clergy and lay readers who provided services during the beginning years were: The Rev. W. Bowlyne Fisher, April 1975-May 30, 1976. Lay Readers came from St. Elisabeth with the cooperation of Jack Culpepper; Dr. James Pope McKnight; Joseph Gohn, 1977; M. Clark Baker, 1977; Paul C. Dickenson, 1979; David Leech; Dr. Frank N. Butler, 1980; and then Gordon Bernard, August 10, 1980, the first resident minister.

On June 24, 1976 upon recommendation of Bishops Vander Horst, Sanders and Gates, St. Philip was accepted as an Organized Mission by the 144th Convention of the Episcopal Church, Diocese of Tennessee, held in Chattanooga. "The Chair then recognized Mr. Hillman Philip Rodgers of St. Philip Mission, Brunswick, Tennessee as the first delegate from the Mission to a Diocesan Convention." (Diocesan Journal 1976, p. 44.)

The names of the fifteen Organizing Members whose signatures appeared on the application by St. Philip, dated December 15, 1975, to the Diocese seeking the status of an Organized Mission were: Hiram Tyre Adair; Mrs. H. T. (Lotta Lee Yancey) Adair; Mrs. M. K. (Rella H.) Banholzer; Mrs. Augusta Hooper Brough; Miss Katherine Edgerton; Keith Edgerton; Lt. Comm. Robert Edgerton; Mrs. Robert (Ruth Tarver) Edgerton; William Gage Fleming; Mrs. Rudolph (Susan Hiss) Jones, Jr.; Mrs. Hillman Philip (Ellen Davies) Rodgers; Andrea Matthews Benson; Miss Marian Turner; Mrs. T. Ribers (Katherine McGinnis) Young and T. Rivers Young.[4] Other Convention delegates in following years have been: 1977—T. Rivers Young, William Gage Fleming; 1978—M. Clark Baker; 1979—Mrs. Hillman Philip Rodgers, Mrs. M. K. Banholzer, Paul C. Dickenson; 1980—Luther Marlar, Judge Morgan C. Fowler; 1981—Luther Marlar, Judge Fowler; 1982—Jayne Lewis (Mrs. Gordon) Bernard, Gordon Bernard, Vicar; 1983—Dr. Frank Adcock, Judge Morgan Fowler, Alternate serving as delegate, James Ferguson.

The first issue of the publication of St. Philip, *The Evangel*, appeared on July 20, 1975, Vol. 1, No. 1.

The official service of the breaking of ground as a site for the building of the church of St. Philip, Davieshire was held on September 14, 1980. In about 103° temperature a crowd of more than three hundred assembled on the ground and experienced the very significant occasion. Participants on the program were: The Rt. Rev. W. Fred Gates, Jr., Suffragan Bishop of Tennessee; the Rev. Gordon Bernard, Vicar, St. Philip, Davieshire; Luther W. Marlar, the Senior Warden; Wells Awsumb, the Architect, Mrs. Hillman Philip (Ellen Davies) Rodgers, the Clerk of the Mission Council; Dale Salley, a Lay Reader of St. Philip, Davieshire and Ian Jones, Crucifer.

In speaking as the donor of the land, of which the ground was being broken with appropriate ceremony, Mrs. Rodgers said:

> "In 1974 my husband, Hillman Philip Rodgers, and I gave this 10 acres of land to the Diocese of Tennessee as the site for Saint Philip Protestant Episcopal Church, Davieshire.
> Today the Diocese and I give the land to you, the people.
> Many types of rewarding crops have been planted on this good land for more than a century by my family.
> Today we plant the Cross and by the grace of faith, pray for an abundant harvest!"[5]

On All Saints' Day, November 1, 1981, Sunday afternoon at four o'clock, the Church of St. Philip, Davieshire, was consecrated to the Glory of God in a memorable ceremony. The Order of Procession was: Crucifer, Flag Bearers, The Wardens—Luther W. Marlar, Judge Morgan C. Fowler; Benefactors—Mrs. Hillman Philip Rodgers, Alfred Millikan, Jr.; Crucifer—Rodney Nash; President of the Churchwomen of Saint Philip and Lector—Mrs. Allan W. Applegate; Epistoler—Judge Morgan C. Fowler; Gospeler—The Rev. James Cubine; Litanist—The Rev. James Boyd; Vicar—The Rev. Gordon Bernard; The Bishop's Chaplain—The Rev. Robert Allen; The Suffragan Bishop—The Rt. Rev. W. Fred Gates, Jr., D.D.; The Bishop of the Diocese—The Rt. Rev. William E. Sanders, D.D.

When the Procession reached the door, Bishop Sanders, standing at the door said: "Let the door be opened." The door was opened by the Donor of the land and of the church.

The consecration was meaningfully recorded by a bronze tablet erected on one of the large brick gate posts at the entrance to the church grounds. The inscription follows:

"SAINT PHILIP EPISCOPAL CHURCH, DAVIESHIRE
CONSECRATED NOVEMBER 1, 1981
BY THE BISHOPS OF
THE EPISCOPAL DIOCESE OF TENNESSEE
THE RT. REV. WILLIAM E. SANDERS
THE RT. REV. W. FRED GATES, JR."

The Bell for St. Philip, Davieshire, was cast by the Petit-Fritsen Royal Bell Foundry, Helmon, Holland, near Aarle-Rixtell and about seventy miles from Amsterdam. The old, reputable company was started in 1660. The casting of the bell was done on Friday, June 12, 1981. (Bells are cast on Friday and left in a vault to cool over the week end!). The cast bronze bell, musical note B, 31½" in diameter, weight 704 pounds. The inscription on the bell:

"SAINT PHILIP EPISCOPAL CHURCH, DAVIESHIRE
Given to the Glory of God
and in loving memory
of
HILLMAN PHILIP RODGERS
1899-1976
by
Alfred G. Millikan, Jr.
November 1, 1981"

A bronze tablet in the Narthex marks this very special memorial gift:

"SAINT PHILIP
EPISCOPAL CHURCH, DAVIESHIRE
Bell
Given to the Glory of God
and in loving memory of
"Uncle"
Hillman Philip Rodgers
November 28, 1899-Janaury 30, 1976

By
Alfred G. Millikan, Jr.
Placed November 1, 1981"

Quoted from the Saint Philip *Evangel* of August 1981, carried under Council Notes, was the following:

"The Mission Council met at "The Oaks" on July 14. Alfred Millikan, Jr., the donor of the bell for St. Philip, Davieshire, reported most interestingly on his trip to Holland to see the casting of the bell on June 12. Alfred is giving the bell as a memorial to his godfather, Mr. Hillman P. Rodgers. The bell, which is bronze, weighing 720 pounds and properly inscribed, will be installed by the Verdin Company of Cincinnati when it has properly cooled, been tuned and sent to this country. Alfred's report was enhanced by the pictures which he made of the casting and other highlights of his trip."

A. G. Millikan, Sr., accompanied Alfred, his fifteen year old son, on this most memorable journey.

Since the beginning of services at St. Philip, Davieshire, there has been an excellent musician to serve as organist. The first organist was Miss Elba Gandy, whose service has been recorded on a bronze tablet which marks the fine Möller organ in the Church. The inscription follows:

>Organ
>"SAINT PHILIP EPISCOPAL CHURCH, DAVIESHIRE
>consecrated to the Glory of God and
>placed by her Family and Friends in
>loving memory of
>ELBA GANDY
>the first organist of St. Philip, Davieshire from December 8, 1974 until her death on May 19, 1979. Born in Gandy House, Davies Plantation, February 13, 1923, and died at her home, The Oaks, on the Plantation. She held two degrees in music: Bachelor of Music Education, Louisiana State University, and Master of Music Education, Northwestern University. She was confirmed by the Rt. Rev. W. Fred Gates, Jr., on January 6, 1977, and became the first confirmand of St. Philip, Davieshire.
>Placed November 1, 1981."[6]

The second organist was Miss Catherine Stehl, from 1979 to December 26, 1982, who resigned and married Steve Lawton of Chattanooga. Mrs. Anita Lofton has served since January 1, 1983 as the very able organist at St. Philip, Davieshire.

St. Philip, Davieshire, did not have a choir until services began in the new church. Mrs. Gordon (Jayne Lewis) Bernard was the first director and was succeeded by Mrs. Lofton. Faithful choir members have been Mr. and Mrs. Kenneth Nash, Miss Marian Turner, Mrs. Augusta H. Brough, Mrs. Chessley H. Hulsey, Miss Kimberly White and Mrs. Bernard.

In November 1982 the Vicar requested Bishop Sanders to license as Lay Readers and Chalice Bearers for a three year term, Dr. Frank Adcock, George Leever, Carl Olsen and Ken Robertson. Each serves most efficiently and is of great help to the Vicar.

After the plans for the church had been completed and construction had begun, the Mission Council reached the decision to erect an addition to the church which was seen as greatly needed. Therefore, the addition known as the Education Building was constructed. A bronze tablet in the hall near the addition is explanatory:

"SAINT PHILIP EPISCOPAL CHURCH, DAVIESHIRE
EDUCATION BUILDING
consecrated to the Glory of God
and in thanksgiving
for the dedication and generosity of the
congregation of St. Philip, Davieshire
and to Venture in Mission, Diocese of Tennessee, in
making possible the erection of this wing of the Church.
November 1, 1981"

The first plans for St. Philip, Davieshire, were drawn by Wells Awsumb, architect, Upon his retirement his brother, Richard N. Awsumb, assumed responsibility and supervised the project to its completion.

The beautiful, sturdy church-house is truly the handiwork of an artisan, a master creator with timbers and brick. To the builder, Bernie R. Langston, his three sons and associates, St. Philip, Davieshire will be forever indebted.

Several organizations play a very vital role as contributing factors to the life and activities of St. Philip, Davieshire. The Women of the Church met, November 9, 1980, at three o'clock in the home of Mrs. Allan W. (Dorothy) Applegate with twenty or more in attendance and organized under the name of "The Women of St. Philip, Davieshire." The group elected Mrs. Applegate as president. Other officers elected were: Mrs. Morgan C. (Betty Joe Campbell) Fowler, Vice-president; Mrs. F. J. (Eleanor Guthrie) Bertorelli, Secretary-Treasurer; Mrs. Peter (Linda Lea Sparks) Ferron, Devotional Chairman (served nine months) and Mrs. Freeman (Nelda Pauline McClamroch) Marr, United Thank Offering. Mrs. George (Barbara) Leever served as Devotional Chairman when Mrs. Ferron resigned.

The first officers served 1980-1982. From 1982-83, Mrs. James E. (Laqueta) Ferguson served as president and the other officers were: Mrs. Creed R. (Linda Carol Lehman) Taylor, Vice-president; Mrs. Thornley (Elizabeth Peters) Greaves, Secretary; Mrs. F. J. (Eleanor Guthrie) Bertorelli, Treasurer; Mrs. Robert (Jacqueline Chalman) White, Devotional Chairman and Mrs. Freeman (Nelda) Marr, United Thank Offering.

With Mrs. Creed R. (Linda) Taylor, president 1983, the officers are: Mrs. Kenneth (Barbara) Robertson, Vice President; Mrs. Richard (Mary Ellen) Phillips, Secretary; Mrs. Michael (Cynthia)

Sims, Treasurer; Mrs. Kenneth (Vi) Flanagan, Devotional Chairman and Mrs. Morgan C. (Betty) Fowler, United Thank Offering, Chairman.

On August 22, 1982 a committee comprised of the Vicar, the Wardens—Judge Fowler and Dan Wagner, agreed to contact the men of the Church and interest them in organizing. On Wednesday, September 8, 1982, seventeen men gathered in Davies Hall for a dinner meeting. Mrs. Allan W. Applegate planned and prepared the delicious meal with several of the ladies of the church assisting by serving. A large silver bowl of roses from The Oaks, Davies Plantation, centered the table.

The name *"The Philippians"* was chosen. Those present were: Dr. Frank Adcock, III, the Rev. Gordon Bernard, Craig Clemmensen, James E. Ferguson, Ken Flanagan, Chip Groner, Ed Hargrave, Ken Nash, Carl R. Olsen, Robert O. Phelps, Chuck Reece, Ken Robertson, Mike Sims, Ric Taylor, Dan F. Wagner and Charles Wilburn.

During the years when services were held in the Chapel, flowers and candles were always on the altar and the communion linens properly taken care of by faithful communicants. Miss Marian Turner, Mrs. Hiram T. Adair and Mrs. T. Rivers Young served well.

Officially the Altar Guild was established to begin its work at the time of the consecration of the church on November 1, 1981. Mrs. W. Joe Moore was the first president of the Guild. She was succeeded by Mrs. Creed Taylor and Mrs. Ken Robertson, co-chairman, 1983.

In October 1981 all families of St. Philip, Davieshire, were invited to Tea at Davies Manor, guests of Mrs. Rodgers. Truly, it was a delightful party in that members got to know each other by visiting in this historic home,—hard by the Church! Inspired by the occasion, several, led by Mr. and Mrs. Glen Craig Clemmensen and Mr. and Mrs. James Ferguson, decided that St. Philip, Davieshire, needed an organization, purely social in purpose. Therefore, "The Young at Heart" often enjoy abundant fellowship at covered dish suppers in Davies Hall with a hostess committee in charge.

Under the leadership of the able adult advisers, Mr. and Mrs. James E. Ferguson and Mr. and Mrs. Robert Phelps, the Episcopal Young Churchmen of St. Philip, Davieshire, was organized in the Spring of 1982. Rufus Jones served as president from May to September, 1982. Upon his resignation Lorraine Phillips was elected and continues to serve as the leader of the group in 1983.

The able men parishioners who have served as Senior Wardens at St. Philip are: Thomas Rivers Young, January 2, 1977 to January 21, 1979; William K. Henderson, Jr., January 21, 1979 to August 10, 1980; Luther W. Marlar, August 10, 1980 to December 6, 1981; Judge Morgan C. Fowler, December 6, 1981 to December, 1982; Daniel F. Wagner, December 12, 1982—.

A bronze plaque in the Narthex memoralizes the service of Thomas Rivers Young, first Warden of St. Philip, Davieshire:

> "Dedicated to the Glory of God
> and in Memory of
> Thomas Rivers Young
> 1915-1979
> The First Warden of
> St. Philip Episcopal Church, Davieshire
> January 2, 1977 to January 21, 1979"[7]

The first Mission Council of St. Philip, Davieshire, was organized on January 2, 1977 with the Rev. Joseph Gohn, Priest-in-Charge. T. Rivers Young was elected Warden-Treasurer and Ellen Davies (Mrs. Hillman Philip) Rodgers was elected Clerk. Other Mission Council officers elected have been:[8]

- 1979—January 21—William K. Henderson, Jr., Warden; Mrs. Hiram T. (Lotta Yancey) Adair, Junior Warden; Miss Marian Turner, Treasurer; Mrs. Hillman Philip Rodgers, re-elected Clerk.
- 1980—March 9—Same officers re-elected.
- 1980—August 10—Mr. Henderson resigned. Luther W. Marlar appointed Senior Warden by the Vicar.
- 1980—December 14—Luther W. Marlar, Mrs. Hillman Philip Rodgers, Miss Marian Turner, Mrs. Allan W. Applegate, Judge Morgan C. Fowler, Dale Salley.
- 1981—January 11—Luther W. Marlar, Warden; Judge Morgan C. Fowler, Junior Warden; Mrs. Rodgers, Clerk; Miss Turner, Treasurer. Mrs. Applegate, President of the Women of St. Philip, Davieshire.
- 1982—December 6—Judge Morgan C. Fowler, Senior Warden; Daniel F. Wagner, Junior Warden; James E. Ferguson, Treasurer; Mrs. Hillman Philip Rodgers, Clerk. Other Council members: Mrs. Applegate, Craig Clemmensen, Luther W. Marlar, Kenneth Nash, Miss Marian Turner.
- 1982—December 12—Three new Council members were elected: Dr. Frank Adcock, III, Creed R. Taylor and Mrs. Robert Phelps.
- 1983—Daniel F. Wagner, Senior Warden; Kenneth Nash, Junior Warden; Craig Clemmensen, Clerk; James E. Ferguson, Treasurer, Harley Gylfe, Parish Keyman. Other members: Dr. Frank Adcock, III, Mrs. Allan W. (Dorothy) Applegate, Judge Morgan C. Fowler, Mrs. Robert (Rolli) Phelps and Creed R. Taylor.

The Bazaars held by St. Philip, Davieshire, have been splendid projects the first of which was a Christmas Sale held in Davieshire Library on December 10, 1977. The first sales were sponsored by the Mission Council with men and women participating. The pop-corn balls made and contributed to the sale by the Warden, T. Rivers Young remain a happy memory! Mrs. Augusta H. Brough served as Project Chairman. After the women of the church organized the sales have been sponsored by them. To date, bazaars continue to be held annually prior to the seasons of Easter and of Christmas.

In 1904 a Font was placed in the Church of the Holy Cross at Mount Pleasant, Tennessee, by Mrs. Johnson (Olivia Harris) Long in memory of her daughter, Aimee Ware Long Cotton, 1871-1902; her son-in-law, Henry Austin Cotton and her grandson, Henry Austin Cotton, Jr., 1902-1923. The top of the Font was given later in memory of her husband, Johnson Long, 1833-1913.

The Church of the Holy Cross was desconsecrated in 1943 and the properties removed from the building. The Font was stored at St. Peter's, Columbia, Tennessee. In 1981, Bishop W. Fred Gates, Jr. authorized the placing of the Font in St. Philip Episcopal Church, Davieshire, Brunswick, Tennessee, where it is indeed a cherished object of adornment and service.

Much appreciation was expressed by St. Philip, Davieshire, to Mrs. Curtis Luck who replaced a few broken marble flowers, thoroughly cleaned and restored the entire piece.

On August 8, 1982 many gathered at St. Philip, Davieshire, for a rather unique occasion. On April 4, 1982 the Vicar had introduced the subject to the Mission Council. The Minutes read:

> "Vicar told of the offer by William Dallas Fisher of Dundee, Mississippi, to commission John Clark to paint a portrait of Mrs. Hillman Philip Rodgers to be hung in St. Philip Church, Davieshire. A lively discussion followed with such details as to what color in costume the subject should wear to the place of final hanging!"

The portrait was hung in Davies Hall of St. Philip, Davieshire.[9]

Another gift by Mr. Fisher to St. Philip was the brass railings at the steps to the chancel. A bronze tablet marks the gift:

> "Given to the Glory of God
> by
> William Dallas Fisher
> in Loving Memory of His Wife
> Vernon Hill Fisher
> 1901-1978"

Many types of gifts have been made to St. Philip, Davieshire, memorial gifts and otherwise. Among these are a piano given by Mr. and Mrs. Kenneth Nash and a small electric organ given by Miss Margaret Blount. Ten acres of land beautifully located on Brunswick Road, north of Pleasant Hill Cemetery, were given by Abie Earle and Clara Beaty, Jr., June 4, 1982.

Among substantial gifts of cash received have been those from: Mr. and Mrs. A. G. Millikan; Dr. and Mrs. James L. Vaden; Thomas M. Keese; Mrs. Edward King; Mrs. Henry F. Lipford; Mrs. Jere L. Crook; the Rev. and Mrs. Paul C. Dickenson, Miss Sarah B Gandy; Miss Frances Gandy; Mrs. Robert W. Creech; Dr. and Mrs. Henry B. Gotten; William R. Holden; Samuel B. Hollis; William Dallas Fisher; Mrs. Merritt H. Crenshaw; William J. Armstrong and Mrs. J. B. Griffin.

These marriages have been solemnized at St. Philip, Davieshire:

    June 20, 1981—Richard MacAlpine Lyon and Dorothy Sheeley (Stonebridge Center)
    August 1, 1981—George Edward Hargraves and Jo Campbell Fowler (Griffin Chapel)
    October 3, 1981—Louis Wayne Porter and Martha Elizabeth Moore (Griffin Chapel)
    November 14, 1981—James Edward Magness and Pamela Ann Wilburn (First in St. Philip, Davieshire)
    March 26, 1983—James Edward McBride, Jr. and Laura Ellen Berlin
    July 23, 1983—Dennett Rogers Hansell and Susan Lane Hilliard

The congregation of St. Philip, Davieshire, steadily grows under the outstanding leadership of the Reverend Gordon Bernard, Vicar, who held his first service on July 27, 1980. In 1977, there were 10 families, 16 communicants; in 1978, 14 families, 22 communicants; in 1979, 15 families and 21 communicants. In 1983 there are 68 families with 171 adults and children. There are a number of young couples in the church and their children are a great asset. The goodly number of adolescents is significant. Usually there are several "babies on the way." At a service of baptism recently the Vicar commented: "We do not have to proselyte by drawing members from other churches, we grow our own!" The Nursery is crowded every Sunday morning. Mrs. Daniel (Polly) Wagner is in charge.

The Vicar's great concern for all is ever appreciated. His manner, his great affection extended faithfully to each member of the congregation, his visits to the sick, his approach to those with whom he wishes to share the message of the Church, all these qualities of character are so abundantly depicted by this most acceptable gentleman. After a service one Sunday morning a member of the congregation commented to the Vicar: "My, that was a fine Baptist sermon." The Vicar replied, "It wasn't a Baptist, nor a

Presbyterian, nor a Methodist, it wasn't even an Episcopal sermon, it was the Gospel."

Prior to Vicar Bernard's coming to St. Philip, Davieshire, the Bishops Sanders and Gates had been advised as to the needs of St. Philip, Davieshire, if growth was to be anticipated. There were two needs expressed—a church-house of its own and a "door-knocking preacher!" Praise the Lord and in thanks to His gracious goodness, St. Philip has both!

A bronze tablet placed on the wall of the Narthex denotes appreciation to the Vicar and Mrs. Bernard as expressed by a devoted congregation.

> "SAINT PHILIP EPISCOPAL CHURCH, DAVIESHIRE
> BRUNSWICK, TENNESSEE
> ERECTED TO THE GLORY OF GOD
> BY A DEVOTED CONGREGATION
> WITH SINCERE GRATEFULNESS TO
> AND IN HONOR OF
> THE FIRST VICAR OF SAINT PHILIP
> GORDON BERNARD
> AND HIS GRACIOUS WIFE
> JAYNE LEWIS BERNARD
> NOVEMBER 1, 1981"

One busy day the telephone rang. A woman's voice stated, " I am making a church survey and would like to ask you a few questions." My reply, "I am too busy to answer your questions." Then the woman asked, "Will you answer just one question?" The reply was "Yes." She asked, "Do you know Jesus?" To this I replied, "Yes, I feel that I know him rather well. It so happens that last year I built a Church in honor of Him and His Father! Thank you for calling."

The building of a church-house is a venture in love of the Lord and his people. St. Philip, Davieshire—a mission venture, dedicated in hope to all God's children for now and for all the years.

> Ellen Davies-Rodgers
> Historiographer,
> St. Philip, Davieshire

St. Andrew's, Collierville

St. Andrew's Church, Collierville

St. Andrew's Church stands on the corner of Mulberry and Walnut in Collierville, in the southeast corner of Shelby County, about twenty-five miles east of Memphis, Tennessee. It began with only a few members meeting together after the Civil War in 1865. These meetings were held in the homes until a house of worship could be erected. The family of J.H. Mangum, Sr., was prominent in securing the services of nearby visiting clergymen of the area.

In 1875, Miss Anna Holden, a graduate of the LaGrange Female Institute, came to Collierville as a teacher in the Bellevue Female College. In this same year the Diocesan Convention met in Memphis and there she met the Reverend William Crane Gray, Rector of St. James Episcopal Church, Bolivar, Tennessee. She succeeded in enlisting his interest in the little flock "without a shepherd" at Collierville. A short time later he visited the town and arranged for regular monthly services. "People were very kind," he reported, "and by attendance, assistance with music, etc., encouraged the movement." Services were held in various places, including the homes of Mr. and Mrs. Joseph H. Mangum and Mr. W.H. Holden. Later, in 1881, services were held in Miss Holden's Seminary by Bishop Thomas F. Gailor and other clergy from West Tennessee. Dr. George White, Calvary Church, Memphis also held services in the home of Mrs. J.H. Mangum and in the Christian Church.

A movement was started to erect an Episcopal Church building. With the few members this hardly seemed possible. Behind this inspired desire, however, were seven unselfish, earnest and faithful women: Mrs. Mary Louisa Mangum, Miss Anna Holden, Mrs. Emma Wilson, Mrs. Emma Bailey, Mrs. Laura Baird, Mrs. Eloise Holden, and Mrs. C.W. Priddy. Full cooperation was given these women to reach their goal by the men: J.J. Bailey, William Holden, R.N.J. Wilson, John H. Holden, Walter Stith, C.W. Priddy, and Joseph Mangum, Sr.

Thousands of little "brick cards" of fifty bricks at ten cents each were mailed to Episcopal Churches and friends in towns and cities. The response came from all over the United States. Bazaars, with historical tableaux, were also held. These were attended by many who came over muddy and dusty roads from Memphis, Holly Springs, LaGrange, and other nearby towns.

On Tuesday, April 22, 1890, Bishop Charles Todd Quintard officiated at the laying of the cornerstone of the new building, assisted by the Rev. Messrs. Spruille Burford, Calvary Church, and J.B. McGlohon, The Rev. William Klein, the Rev. George Patterson, Grace Church, and the Rev. Henry R. Sargent were also present. The new structure was named "St. Andrew's," as the congregation in Collierville has since been known. The Vestry was composed of J.J. Bailey, Senior Warden; R.N.J. Wilson, Junior Warden; William Holden, Secretary-Treasurer; Walter Stith and C.W. Priddy. Dr. Arthur Howard Noll was the resident minister, 1895-1897.

The new Church Building of warm red brick, built in the quiet Victorian style of the day, was lovingly cared for by the small flock. Beautiful memorials were given. Bishop Quintard gave the side windows, which he obtained while attending Lambeth Conference in England. The West Window over the twelve-foot doors was given by Mrs. Laura Baird. The East Window was given as a memorial to the Stith family.

Using the little reed organ, Mrs. Helen Mangum Bedford was the first organist; she, with Miss Louisa Mangum, Mr. Joseph H. Mangum and Mr. Bourdon Holden, were very faithful and efficient in rendering the church music. St. Andrew's was consecrated by Bishop Quintard in 1891. The original copy of the handsome Certificate of Consecration is framed and hangs today in the Parish Hall.

From 1890 to 1941, a Sunday School was maintained for children of the congregation. The staff for this activity was under the direction of Miss Anna Holden. During these years Altar preparations were under the care of the Women of the Church. Often the Altar flowers were obtained from the gardens of the Mangum home.

Credit must be given to the many dedicated men who, by their prayers and labor, helped assure the life of St. Andrew's over this period: Bishops Quintard, Gailor, Maxon, and Dandridge of Tennessee; Bishop Pierce of Arkansas; Bishop Green of Mississippi; Bishop Carruthers of South Carolina; the Rev. Messrs. William Crane Gray, Dr. Lee, J B. McClohon, and Juny; Messrs. Gill, Tupper, A.H. Noll, C.S. Ware, J.M. Trout, Alexander Crawford, and Tichnor. Recognition must also be given to Archdeacons Weller, Root, and Plummer; the Rev. Messrs. Prentice Pugh and Guy Usher; and to Mr. Thomas P. Simpson. Lay Readers who served during this time included James Hunt and Robert Allen.

From 1941 to 1952, the Rev. C.L. Widney, Rector of St. George's, Germantown, held two services a month at St. Andrew's.

There was a resultant growth in Church activities and of confirmations. While the Rev. Mr. Widney was serving St. Andrew's, the Church welcomed a visit from the Rt. Rev. Thomas N. Carruthers, D.D., Bishop of South Carolina, Chancellor of the University of the South, and author of many books. The Bishop was visiting his mother, Mrs. Lennie Carruthers, and family when he made this visit to the Church of his boyhood.

It would be impossible to list all the women who have left a record of loving service at St. Andrew's: but such a list would include Mrs. Helen Mangum Bedford, Mrs. Kate Holden, and Mrs. J.K. (Lucille) Swoope.

Mrs. Henry Hazlip cared for the Altar for many years and was noted for her needlework. She also was responsible for the installation of gas heating for the comfort of the congregation. Mrs. Ed Camp was the Church organist while living in Collierville.

Mrs. Russell Carrington, her mother Mrs. Hazier, and her two sisters Mrs. Butler and Miss Hazier were among the faithful Communicants.

It was Mr. Carrington, with a crew of skilled construction workers from Memphis, who replaced the beams in the original Church Building and made other repairs while serving as Chairman of Buildings and Grounds.

While St. Andrew's had no Priest-in-Residence, Mr. Charles Burnley of Jackson, Tennessee, brought the Rev. Dr. Loaring-Clark, Rector of the Church there, to conduct services for St. Andrew's. Mr. Burnley also served as organist.

St. Andrew's rejoiced to receive its first Priest-in-Residence, the Rev. William Carson Fraser, July 1, 1961. During his tenure work was begun on the Church's first Parish House. This construction was under the supervision of Mr. Stanley Carruthers, nephew of Bishop Carruthers, and a lifelong member of St. Andrew's. In addition to serving as a meeting place for the Church School and other Church groups, the building was used extensively for meetings by several civic organizations of the town. The Church's Vicarage at 208 Andrew Way was purchased for the Rev. Mr. Fraser and his family.

In January of 1965 the Rev. Dr. and Mrs. E. Dargan Butt came to Collierville, and Dr. Butt became the second Priest-in-Residence.

That year the old Parish House was sold to the City of Collierville for use as its City Hall. In 1966 a new Parish Hall, east of the Church, was constructed. It was designed by Gen. Robert Charles

Dean of Boston, United States Army, Retired. General Dean is a native of Collierville and a recognized architect of merit, particularly in the field of restoration. He drew the plans for the Parish Hall in such a manner that the Hall when completed would seem a part of the original structure. Again, the construction work was under the supervision of Mr. Stanley Carruthers. The Parish Hall contains the Sacristy, Church office, classrooms, and large meeting area and kitchen.

Dr. Butt's active ministry at St. Andrew's was completed at his retirement in 1970. On Sunday, July 19, the Church congregation gathered in the Parish Hall following the regular morning service, for a Reception honoring Dr. and Mrs. Butt.

Dr. Butt had come to Collierville from Evanston, Indiana, where he had been a member of the faculty at Seabury-Western Theological Seminary since 1946. He was formerly connected with the University of the South at Sewanee, Tennessee. Dr. Butt was author of the book "PREACH THERE ALSO", and he was a recognized authority of the Town and Country Ministry. Active in community life, Dr. Butt served as Chairman of the Collierville Human Relations Committee. Mrs. Butt, nee Neville Landstreet, was also active in community affairs, and during Dr. Butt's ministry served the Church as teacher and Altar Guild member.

Dr. Butt was succeeded by the Rev. LeRoy M. Carter, who came to St. Andrew's from Trinity Church, Gatlinburg, Tennessee. He assumed his duties as Vicar on July 26, 1970. Father Carter was graduated from the University of Chattanooga in 1950 and from St. Luke's Seminary of the University of the South in 1964. He married the former Martha Marie Dettor, and they had three sons, LeRoy, Jr., Rex, and Reid. Mrs. Carter was active in Church affairs and served on the Altar Guild and as a choir member. She was a watercolor artist of regional note.

The first choir at St. Andrew's was organized in 1970 and first assisted the congregation's worship at the Christmas Eve Celebration of the Holy Communion that year. In 1972 the Church purchased a pipe organ to replace its old electronic instrument. The four-rank organ with Kilgen console was originally in the Chapel of St. Joseph's Hospital, Memphis, Mrs. Irene Saunders, of Rossville was the Church's organist.

The Congregation of St. Andrew's holds its annual Parish Meeting on the Feast Day of St. Andrew, November 30. At these meetings the members elect their Mission Council for the following year. Serving on the Council for 1972 were: Milton Schaeffer,

Warden; Walter Dunn, Clerk; Brinkley Snowden, Treasurer; Stanley Carruthers, James Dempster, Mrs. Beth Lewis, Col. William Milnor, Dr. William Outlan and Turner Wingo.

Mrs. Dorothy Brode Mangum, has given many years of faithful love and devotion of her tasks as Chairman of the Altar Guild. The flowers still come primarily from the Mangum gardens, and Mrs. Mangum is assisted by the Women of the Church.

Father Carter was assisted at the Altar by a corps of Acolytes, which included Senior Acolyte Harrell Schaeffer, his brothers Milton, Jr., and Joseph III, and Mr. Carter's three sons.

St. Andrew's Church, after much effort and sacrifice on the part of the communicants and of the Rev. Lee Carter, finally became a parish at the 146th Convention of the Diocese of Tennessee in February, 1978. Everyone who could made the trip to Nashville to participate in the service. About 50 people from St. Andrew's marched in the procession behind a beautiful St. Andrew's banner made by Mrs. Martha Carter for the occasion. Each person wore a wooden cross necklace (cross of St. Andrew) and sang the St. Andrew's hymn "Jesus Calls Us".

This triumph for St. Andrew's was followed by a year of tragedy and sadness. Father Carter contracted cancer that same year and died on July 14, 1978 at the age of 50. On June 14, 1979, Father Dargan Butt, former priest and beloved member of the congregation at St. Andrew's died at his home in Collierville. In November of 1979 Brinkley Snowden, longtime treasurer and devoted church member died of a heart attack. Memorial windows at the altar were dedicated to Dargan Butt and Lee Carter and a ciborium in memory of the service of Brinkley Snowden.

During Father Carter's tenure at St. Andrew's he had conceived the idea of the "Order of St. Andrew"—an honorary society into which one member is inducted every year on St. Andrew's day—in appreciation for service to the church. Members include Dargan Butt, Louise (Mrs. Elden C.) Cooper, Dorothy Mangum, Elizabeth Carruthers Lewis, Dr. William Parr, Milton Schaeffer, Brinkley Snowden, Stanley Carruthers, Mabel Wilson and Lucia Chandler Outlan and Lee Carter himself who was inducted just a few weeks before his death.

In August 1979 the Rev. Davidson T. Landers came to St. Andrew's from Grace-St. Luke's in Memphis. He had graduated from the School of Theology at the University of the South in 1970,—he, his wife, Carol, and three young daughters.

Many new young couples with children have moved to Collierville and St. Andrew's has been growing at a steady rate. There are in 1983, 150 communicants in good standing and 217 baptized persons.

In 1982 a successful capital fund drive was held so that the entire interior and exterior of the nearly 100 year old church could be renovated. Much needed plaster and brick work has been done in 1983. St. Andrew's has co-sponsored community Advent and Lenten series in Collierville and has been active in the local Community Chest fund. Eight licensed lay readers from St. Andrew's assist at services at St. Thomas in Somerville.

"St. Andrew's bears its years with grace and beauty."

Jill Schaeffer (Mrs. Richard C.) Broer

My World

"My world is not so very large
  But large enough for me:
It does not span a mountain top
  Nor touch upon the sea.
And yet, because I walk with God
  I cross, eternity!"

—Mae Winkler Goodman.

The Ministry

Q. Who are the ministers of the Church?
A. The ministers of the Church are lay persons, bishops, priests, and deacons.
Q. What is the ministry of the laity?
A. The ministry of lay persons is to represent Christ and his Church; to bear witness to him wherever they may be; and, according to the gifts given them, to carry on Christ's work of reconciliation in the world; and to take their place in the life, worship, and governance of the Church.
Q. What is the ministry of a bishop?
A. The ministry of a bishop is to represent Christ and his Church, particularly as apostle, chief priest, and pastor of a diocese; to guard the faith, unity, and discipline of the whole Church; to proclaim the Word of God; to act in Christ's name for the reconciliation of the world and the building up of the Church; and to ordain others to continue Christ's ministry.
Q. What is the ministry of a priest or presbyter?
A. The ministry of a priest is to represent Christ and his Church, particularly as pastor to the people; to share with the bishop in the overseeing of the Church; to proclaim the Gospel; to administer the sacraments; and to bless and declare pardon in the name of God.
Q. What is the ministry of a deacon?
A. The ministry of a deacon is to represent Christ and his Church, particularly as a servant of those in need; and to assist bishops and priests in the proclamation of the Gospel and the administration of the sacraments.
Q. What is the duty of all Christians?
A. The duty of all Christians is to follow Christ; to come together week by week for corporate worship; and to work, pray, and give for the spread of the kingdom of God.

The Book of Common Prayer, 1977
Catechism, pages 855 and 856

St. Matthew's, Covington

St. Matthew's Church, Covington

A pamphlet printed on the occasion of the 100th Anniversary of the Church Building, St. Matthew's Episcopal Church, Covington, provided the only available historical sketch of the Church for this writing. Therefore, this account has been copied largely from this printed folder. The introduction to the program (June 22, 1958), was signed "The Rector and Vestry of St. Matthew's."

"The early records of St. Matthew's Episcopal Church have been misplaced; and we are unable to give a complete account of the history of the Church, from the time of the first settlers of Covington and the early 1850's.

At the time of the settlement of Covington, in the early 1820's, the names of persons appearing on the County records, were those whose descendants were Episcopalians according to our oldest Church record. We can well assume that Episcopal services were held in Covington prior to 1850.

St. Paul's Episcopal Church, Randolph, which was organized in 1832 by the Rev. Thomas Wright, burned, and was not rebuilt, and some of the Church families settled in Covington in the 1850's. Among these families were Mrs. Elizabeth Baker Jones, with her four sons and five daughters; Dr. Hugh Rose and family; Joseph Green and family and F. M. Green.

The old building west of the present Church and which had been the old opera house, was used for about two or three years.

A small Church on the opposite corner was built about the year 1855 or 1856.

Robert I. Mitchell deeded to the Protestant Episcopal Church in the Diocese of Tennessee, Lot No. 88, of the original plan of Covington. Deed dated June 28, 1858, reciting: for an in consideration of a deed to me to the lot on which the Old Episcopal Church now stands (the building excepted) and $50.00 cash, Lot No. 88, being 124 feet square.

The Church is of Gothic architecture, designed and built by J.J. Malone and Wm. P. Malone. The corner stone bears the date 1858. Mrs. Sophia Malone, wife of J.J. Malone, was present when the corner stone was laid and it has been said many articles of interest were placed therein.

The lumber used in the construction was yellow poplar and red gum, morticed and pegged.

Old Uncle Shirley Fisher, told that he with the other Fisher slaves, sawed all the lumber for the Church by hand, with a Pit

Saw Mill, using a cross cut saw with two men at each end. All the framing was in the rough, but flooring and siding and shingles were dressed by hand. The plaster lathes were split out of oak. In later years the gallery was closed, plaster was removed and replaced by wood beaded ceiling by Alex D. Paine.

In 1956, the transept was extended, the entire Church renovated and redecorated. Central heating and air conditioning was installed. Otherwise, the building is preserved in its original state. The Rev. John Ambrose Wheelock, former Rector of St. Paul's Church, Randolph, was the first Rector of St. Matthew's Church. The chancel windows given by the Rt. Rev. Charles Todd Quintard, Bishop of the Diocese of Tennessee, bear this inscription, "To the blessed memory of the Rev. John Ambrose Wheelock, who entered rest A.D. 1866."

An interesting historical fact was told many times by Ebenezer Paine, concerning these windows. Bishop Quintard was visiting in England, and while there extensive repairs were being made on Canterbury Cathedral. The three fine stained glass windows, two or three centuries old, were being discarded. They were given to Bishop Quintard, for St. Matthew's Church. The windows were shipped by sailing vessel to New Orleans and up the Mississippi River to Randolph, and overland to Covington, in all, six months to complete the journey. (Alex D. Paine)."

Among the charter members were: Dr. Charles G. Fisher, son and daughter, Charles G. Fisher, Jr. and Mrs. Annie Fisher Hamilton and James Baker Hamilton; Mrs. Jacob Tipton, Judge James Byars, Joseph Green and brother, F. M. Green, Mrs. Elizabeth Baker Jones and four sons and five daughters; Dr. Hugh Rose and family; W. P. Malone, J. J. Malone, the Lauderdale family; the Newman family and the McGregor family.

1869-1879, additional members were: J. B. Hills and family; Miss Susan Fisher, William Hamilton and Andrew Hamilton, William V. Byars, Dr. Hugh Byars, Charlie Collins Jr., and his two sisters Laudie and Blanche; Susan Slaughter, Mrs. Pattie Rose Hall, Mrs. Annie Rose Bell, Mr. and Mrs. Richard Jackett, Mr. Robert Malone and family; the family of W. J. Malone; Col. and Mrs. Wood, Mr. and Mrs. John R. Sloan, Mr. and Mrs. J. W. Lemmon, Mr. and Mrs. Ben Adams, Mr. and Mrs. Sam Mitchell, Horace Davie, Mrs. Bettie Bell, Joseph A. Green, Malcolm F. Green, Mr. and Mrs. Ebenezer Paine and their sons, William P., Ed and John; a Mr. Heintz, H. M. Moore, Yank Smith, Robert Smith, Mr. and Mrs. Will Adams, Dr. John I. Sherrod, Nat Elcan and family, Dr.

A. L. Elcan, John A. Tipton, the Claybrook family, the Carraway family; John W. Harris, Burt Mayo, Thomas Barron, Arthur Smith.

Bishop Quintard came annually for a week's visit, and gave great sermons. People of all denominations, saints and sinners like, came to hear him.

According to Mr. Stanley Hamilton, his father, Mr. William P. Hamilton, always entertained the Bishop during his visitations here. Seated at the head of the table, carving the roast, Bishop Quintard addressed all of us children as "Peter," and would say to my father, "Billy, I will serve the children first, because of their impatience, and Billy, I am going to carve this roast as thin as charity."

During the 1890's, Church life was at low ebb, due to very irregular services. Through the efforts of Mrs. Maria Baker Lemmon in maintaining a regular Church School the doors of the Church were kept open. She prevailed upon Mr. J. Allie Green to act as Superintendent in which capacity he served for over a decade. In the late 1890's under the ministry of the Rev. J. M. Northrop, the Church was greatly revived, and was active for a number of years. Miss Sara Lemmon and Mrs. Bessie Lemmon McQuiston served as organists, and there was a splendid vested choir, and acolytes. It was during this era under the ministry of the Rev. J. M. Northrop, followed by the Rev. W. P. Brown, that St. Matthew's was a Parish.

After 1900, many communicants moved from the county. A number married into families of other denominations; and for a decade the Church had irregular services, under numerous ministers who served additional Churches in other towns.

The Church School was steadfastly maintained, through the efforts of the laymen of the Church. During this period, Mrs. Agnes Paine Barret was faithful organist.

1924-1926: A young clergyman, Rev. Paul Williams, came to St. Matthew's and the Church enjoyed regular services, along with the other Churches under his ministry. An active Youth work was organized, and greater interest was taken in the life of the Church.

1926-1936: Services were held intermittently, by various clergymen; and Troy Beaty McCall enthusiastically served as Church School Superintendent for a small group of children. It was under his faithful leadership until his death in 1955, the work thrived and grew.

February, 1937, the Rev. Paul Earle Sloan came to Covington to live and serve as priest-in-charge of St. Matthew's, Covington; Trinity, Mason; Ravenscroft Chapel, Brighton; and Emmanual Church, Ripley.

This was the beginning of a new era for St. Matthew's Church. Under the capable direction of Peyton J. Smith, organist, a vested choir was organized, which service contributes much to the Church.

February of 1945, the Rev. Mr. Sloan was instituted as Rector of the newly formed parish comprised of Trinity Church, St. Matthew's Church and Ravenscroft Chapel, and known as Quintard Memorial Parish. Due to the growth of St. Matthew's Church School and the interest of the membership, Mr. Sloan led his people in building a brick Parish House, adequately furnished by gifts and memorials, for the many purposes it serves. Through Mr. Sloan's devoted service, and until his death December 6, 1949, the Church slowly, but steadily made progress.

From 1949 to 1953, there was no regular minister. Services were held by supply ministers until 1953, when the Rev. John H. Sivley was called, and served as rector until October 1955, assisted by the Rev. Curtis B. Luck, Perpetual Deacon.

June, 1956, the Rev. Sheldon Davis, Canon of Saint Mary's Cathedral, accepted the call to become Rector of Quintard Memorial Parish. The Rev. Curtis B. Luck continued to assist in the work of St. Matthew's. Continued interest and growth enabled St. Matthew's congregation, in January, 1958, to adopt measures to become a Parish in 1959.

Through the efforts of the Woman's Auxiliary, active through the years, altar hangings and other contributions have been made to beautify the Church.

The Church School is in service every Sunday morning.

A well organized Men's Club is alert to the Church's many needs, and is busy with various projects.

St. Matthew's Church sponsors Boy Scout Troop No. 62.

Among the clergymen who have served St. Matthew's were: The Reverends John Ambrose Wheelock, Dencie Drummond, James Rogers, Lawton, Weakley, Charles E. Collins, Father Matthews, F. A. Juny, Calder R. Young, Charles Steele, Howard Dumbell, Troy Beatty, Charles Wright, Ira Trout, J. W. Northrop, Neville Joyner, W. P. Brown, S. R. McAlpin, Oscar Lindstrom, George O. Watts, Arch Deacon A. C. McCabe, Paul Williams, Arch Deacon B. F. Root, Alfred Loaring-Clark, Arch Deacon

Charles F. Weller, Paul E. Sloan, Sterling Tracey, Alfred D. Snively, E. M. Beardon, John Sivley, Curtis B. Luck, Sheldon Davis, Curtis B. Luck.

Faithful organists who have served St. Matthew's are Peyton Smith and Thirza Sloan.

In 1983 communicants number eighty-six, in good standing. The present rector is the Rev. Morris K. Wilson III.

Compiled by the Author

"Faith . . . . . . makes all things possible.
Hope . . . . . . makes all things bright.
Love . . . . . . makes all things easy."

—Unknown.

"To do nothing is tiresome because you cannot stop and take a rest."

—Anon

"Whether therefore ye eat or drink, or whatsoever ye do, do all to the glory of God."

—1 Corinthians 10:31

"A man's reach should exceed his grasp or what's a heaven for."

—Robert Browning

St. Mary's Church, Dyersburg

Saint Mary's Church, Dyersburg

The first Episcopal service was held in Dyersburg in 1889, when Bishop Charles Todd Quintard, with some clergy and a few communicants, held a Convocation in the Methodist Church. There was a baptism and a guild was organized. Mrs. Kerr was chosen president of the guild and Mrs. Coker, secretary.

A lot was given by Mr. Charley Clark on which to build the church.

Before a building was erected, however, Episcopal services were held in the Calcutt residence and later in the Y.M.C.A. hall. Legend also tells of Sunday School being held in the John H. Reed residence in those early days.

The first mention of an Episcopal Church in Dyersburg in the Diocesan records is in the Journal, 1896, when the church is listed as "Dyersburg"—without a church name—and was assessed $5.00.

In 1897 the Bishop Coadjutor, the late Bishop Thomas F. Gailor, was authorized to sell the lot, but for some reason it was not sold. The Report of the Dean for the Memphis Convocation for 1897 includes the following: "In Dyersburg we own a lot and have several hundred dollars in hand. Services are held once a month. The Rev. Mr. J. M. Northrup is in charge of Dyersburg, Ripley and Ravenscroft, residing at Covington. (He was also in charge of the parish at Covington). There was one baptism and two confirmations. Value of property $600.00."

In 1898 the name "Saint Mary's" was chosen. The reason for this choice was that there were an uncommonly number of ladies in the church named Mary—and this pleased them all!

In 1899 the Report of the Dean was as follows: "Baptisms 1, Confirmations 10, church valuation, 1 lot $600.00. For some time the Mission at Dyersburg has been too weak to support even monthly services, people having moved away or suffering financial losses. They have done very well by laying money by constantly for a church building. Besides the lot they have about $500.00 out in notes, drawing interest. My ministry ended April 9—J. M. Northrup, Missionary."

May 1, 1901, the Reverend W. P. Browne became minister-in-charge. That year 20 communicants were reported: 2 baptisms, 4 confirmations, the building fund grew to $815.00.

In 1903, the church building was completed. It was a modest frame building, built in the shape of a crucifix with vaulted ceiling.

Although just a Mission, the members were very proud to at last have their own church building.

The officers at this time were Dr. Lewis Harrison, Warden; Theodore Frazier, Clerk; N. W. Calcutt, Treasurer. The Dean of the Convocation wrote concerning Saint Mary's, "The church at Dyersburg has been completed, and great credit is due this faithful band for the work they have done without help from abroad."

When Bishop Gailor came to consecrate the new church building he found there was one unpaid bill for lumber used of $1400.00. He said the church could not be consecrated until that bill was paid. Mr. N. W. Calcutt personally paid the $1400.00 and the consecration went on as scheduled. The year was 1904.

The Guild, after a hard struggle, managed to provide the furnishings.

In 1904, the Rev. S. R. McAlpin, Deacon, was in charge of Saint Mary's, with residence in Covington. That year 26 communicants, 6 baptisms, 3 confirmations, were reported. Mr. McAlpin was ordained Priest in 1905 and left early in the year for Knoxville. Thirty communicants, 5 baptisms and "numerous improvements" were reported. An organ was given as a gift to the church by C. Hall—a friend of the church.

In 1906-1907, the Rev. Oscar Livingston was in charge of Saint Mary's. No reports were made.

In 1908, the Rev. Emile S. Harper was in charge of Saint Mary's and in Covington, Saint Matthew's, with residence in Dyersburg.

From 1910 to 1927, Saint Mary's was under the leadership of Archdeacon A. C. McCabe, who lived in Dyersburg. Officers in 1910 were N. W. Calcutt, Warden; Champ Simpson, Clerk; and Mrs. J. E. Horton, Treasurer. A church school was mentioned in this report with a membership of ten.

In 1928, the Rev. Paul Williams took over Saint Mary's with residence in Covington. From June 1929 until October 1930, the Rev. George L. Whitmeyer of Union City was in charge, with services held irregularly at various hours.

From November 23, 1930 to October 12, 1941, the Rev. George W. Goodson was Priest-in-charge of Saint Mary's, with residence in Union City. In addition he had the care of Paris and Trenton.

February 13, 1942, the Rev. Leslie A. Wilson took over. He lived in Union City until February 11, 1945, when he moved into Saint Mary's brand new rectory. Reported that year from Saint

Mary's: "Communicants 37, church school 10, teachers 3; Mission Council: Edward M. King, Jr., Warden; R. L. Bird, Clerk; Everett Reed and Mrs. Everett Reed, Treasurer."

June 23, 1946, the new church, the one standing today, was consecrated by Bishop Dandridge. Mr. Wilson left in August of 1947 and Saint Mary's was again without clergy. The Rev. Ernest M. Hoyt arrived in Dyersburg in December 1948. He stayed but a short time, leaving in September 1949. In November 1949, the Rev. Jackson Martin came to Saint Mary's from New York. He served 22 months, during which progress was actually made by Saint Mary's, rather in spite of much dissension and argumentation. After Mr. Martin left, the Rev. William C. Taylor, professor at the University of Tennessee, Martin, provided communion for Saint Mary's for several months.

The Rev. Alfred D. Snively, retired priest from Western Massachusetts, served Saint Mary's from November 1952 until May 1953. Mr. Snively labored faithfully and lovingly and left a united and fine church.

During the months after Mr. Snively left, and they had no priest, the lay readers served faithfully. Mr. R. L. Bird, especially gave unstintingly of his time and services.

On July 15, 1953, the Rev. G. Cecil Woods came to Dyersburg. He was an energetic and forceful young man. His ministry at Saint Mary's was marked by great growth. He made many costly improvements himself, especially to the Rectory. The church and Rectory were air-conditioned; the grounds were landscaped; the old house on the corner of King and Masonic was purchased and was used for additional church school classes and an office for the priest. By 1955, when Mr. Woods departed, Saint Mary's was debt free.

July 1, 1956, the Rev. Warren E. Haynes became Rector of Saint Mary's. A bachelor, without furniture, he won the hearts of the parishioners, who quickly furnished the Rectory, scrimpily but adequately. The church people were thrilled when they learned Mr. Haynes was taking a wife—and took the bride to their hearts.

In 1957, Saint Mary's became a full parish and the number of communicants passed the 100 mark. Also in 1957 a new organ was purchased.

In December of 1959 a gift of a beautiful silk damask Pall was given to Saint Mary's by Louis G. Norvell, Jr.

In 1960, the Rev. Sam A. Boney was called by Saint Mary's from Brownsville, Tennessee. He was young, eager and had his wife and three baby girls with him. The Rectory reverberated with a different sound. Mr. Boney remained at Saint Mary's for twenty years, resigning December 14, 1980.

During Mr. Boney's cure at Saint Mary's, there were many improvements made, both spiritual and temporal.

In 1964 a new parish house was built where the old house had stood on the corner of King and Masonic streets. After the new parish house was built, T. B. Rosser, Jr. had the old kitchen in Calcutt Hall converted into an office for the Rector, putting in shelves and other appurtenances to make for comfort.

The beauty of Saint Mary's church had been enhanced by many memorials and gifts over the years. In 1960 a hanging cross over the altar was given by Mrs. Louis G. Norvell, Jr. in memory of Louis G. Norvell, Jr. Twelve stained glass windows for the nave of the church were given as memorials by the following: Mrs. Henry K. Rice; Mr. and Mrs. Danal Hotaling; Members of Saint Mary's; Mr. and Mrs. Edward M. King, Jr.; Mr. and Mrs. E. H. Lannom, Jr.; Mrs. A. M. Bowen, Sr.; Mr. and Mrs. Drennan Albrecht; Mr. and Mrs. Carney Calcutt; and Mr. and Mrs. John Lamb.

Six brass plaques were placed on the walls in the nave of the church in memory of the following: Ross Crenshaw Moore; Robert Lee Bird; Thomas B. Rosser, Jr.; H. Scott Rosser; John H. Reed and Nell Blood Reed.

Also, a brass plaque and organ chimes were given in memory of Jeffery Vern Forcum by Mr. and Mrs. John Lamb.

Eucharistic candlesticks were given by Mrs. T. B. Rosser, Jr., in memory of H. Scott Rosser. A brass flower container was given by Helen S. Albrecht in memory of her mother, Mrs. Maud Slater.

A Book of Remembrance was given by Monica Scott King (Mrs. Edward). Needlepoint kneeling cushions were made and given by Dudley Davis in memory of her uncle, Walter Chandler. The cushions for the Bishop's and Priest's chairs were made and given by Monica Scott King.

An Advent wreath was given by the Paul Welborns in memory of Henry R. Rice. A Paschal candle was given in memory of Mrs. Mary Kennedy Wheeler by members of Saint Mary's.

The twin daughters of the Paul Hallocks, Brooke Noel and Eve Shirl, gave to Saint Mary's three beautifully bound books in memory of their grandfather, James Franklin Luke. They are The Altar Book, The Jerusalem Bible and The Book of Gospels.

All monetary memorials are put into Saint Mary's Endowment Trust Fund handled by the First-Citizens National Bank.

During the years there have been many other gifts. A Nativity Scene was given by Mr. and Mrs. John Lamb. Office candlesticks were given by Mrs. Dan (Maxine Fowler) Gary. A large silver chalice and paten were given by Henry K. Rice, Sr., also a pair of large brass vases.

A most generous benefactor has been Mr. Richard H. Wheeler. Due to his generosity, Saint Mary's church has been endowed with an annual income. The new reception room added to Calcutt Hall has been completed and will be dedicated to Richard H. Wheeler.

At the present time Saint Mary's has 140 communicants.

The Rev. James J. Diffee, Jr., non stipendary priest assistant at St. Luke's, Jackson and Vice-President of McCowat-Mercer Printing Company, was sent to Saint Mary's on a temporary basis. He provided a positive healing influence at a time of confusion and misunderstanding within little Saint Mary's Church family. Father Diffee pulled all sides together and the church proceeded through Christmas and into 1981 under his most inspiring leadership. He smoothed the hurt of the various factions and steadied Saint Mary's on her course.

The Committee to Select a new minister was appointed and in due time, the Rev. John Sterling, priest at St. Joseph of Arimathia in Hendersonville, Tennessee was extended a call. In July, Father Sterling accepted the call. He and his charming wife, Shirley, moved into the Rectory. His first sermon and Holy Eucharist at Saint Mary's Church was on the first Sunday in September, 1981.

The Sterlings transformed the modest Rectory into a charming, warm home.

Saint Mary's Church, Dyersburg, Tennessee is growing and moving again.

June Fearnside Lannom

St. George's, Germantown

St. George's Church, Germantown

St. George's Episcopal Church, Germantown, began as a mission in 1934 by seventeen residents of Germantown some of whom later petitioned the Bishop and Council to establish a mission. A meeting was held in the home of one of the petitioners, Joseph A. Martin, in early June, 1934 at which Archdeacon Charles K. Weller outlined the requirements of establishing a mission. It was established by the petitioners and supported by them and additional communicants with only the aid of the Diocese which supplied clergy once a month for Holy Communion.

Those who signed the petition dated August 1, 1934 were as their names appeared: John Bell Hebron; Mary Hebron; Carl R. Graves; John B. Scruggs; Mamie Cloyes; Charles E. Speer; Mrs. H. T. Adair; Edwin S. Williamson; Elizabeth D. Speer; J. A. Martin; Francis Martin; and Geraldine Apperson Martin.

The first Senior Warden of St. George's was John B. Hebron (1934-1942) and the first Junior Warden was Carl Graves (1935-1942).

The first service was held on June 13, 1934 in the Germantown Masonic Lodge which had been secured for that purpose by John B. Scruggs,[10] who was a Lay Reader and a Mason. A building fund was begun for the construction of a chapel across the street from the Lodge on land acquired in a trade by the Diocese in 1924. In March 1937 the chapel was consecrated by Bishop Maxon.

The Mission grew slowly at first, but by 1940 had its first resident priest, the Rev. Guy S. Usher (January 1, 1940-1941). He had the responsibility of St. George's with 25 commuicants, St. Andrew's and St. Ann's. The Rev. Usher was succeeded by the Rev. Charles L. Widney, and he became the first Rector when parish status was achieved in 1944.

After World War II, a major addition to the chapel was made for Sunday School rooms and restrooms. Later about 1948-49 stained glass windows replaced the original chapel windows. The congregation continued to grow and by the early 1950's it was obvious the church facilities were woefully inadequate. Mr. Widney served from March 1, 1941-April 22, 1952.

In 1952 the Rev. Mr. Widney resigned and the Vestry asked Bishop Barth for the services of Thomas A. Roberts, then a deacon-in-training. The request was granted and the Rev. Mr. Roberts was called as Rector upon his ordination. However, while still a deacon, the opportunity came to the Rev. Roberts and the Vestry to provide more adequate facilities for the congregation. In 1953, a member of the congregation offered to sell the church a nineteen and a half acre tract on Highway 72 (Poplar) on which there was a home and a workshop housed in a barn-like structure situated on a hill. It was through the leadership provided by the Rev. Mr. Roberts, his Senior Warden, Charles Kortecht and the Vestry, that the church was able to make a property plus cash trade and obtain the property. After renovation into a sanctuary and rectory, the property became St. George's Church in 1954. Mr. Roberts was rector August 31, 1952-October 1, 1956.

After the congregation moved to "the hill," east of Germantown, the church experienced increased growth which continued through the late 1950's. The Rev. Mr. Roberts, a most popular and dynamic Rector, resigned in 1956 to accept a call from Christ Church in Greenville, South Carolina. The Vestry issued a call to a young, scholarly priest who had recently became Rector of St. Andrew's in Harriman, Tennessee. The Rev. Frank McClain had been appointed priest-in-charge at St. Andrew's in 1953 and in 1954 became the first Rector of that parish which had been a mission for seventy years. Mr. McClain was rector June 1, 1957-August 15, 1962.

As the parish grew, its ministry was directed in a different direction—toward elementary education. It was the idea and support of Eric and Margaret Catmur, Dr. Steve Bledsoe and others who moved the Rev. Mr. McClain to spearhead the creation of a school on the church grounds. St. George's Day School thus began in the Fall of 1959. As the needs of the school increased, work began in 1961 on a six classroom building. This was followed by the construction of a rectory in 1964. Meanwhile, Mr. McClain resigned in April 1962 to accept a position at Sweetbriar College in Virginia.

In July 1962 the Vestry called the Rev. David E. Babin, an assistant at St. John's in Knoxville. With this choice the Vestry embarked on a four year period in which the Rector did not meld with the congregation. (September 1, 1962-August 31, 1965).

The rectorate of Mr. Babin and his successor, the Rev. Robert Cherry, were relatively low points in the fifty years of St. George's existence. Mr. Babin's personality apparently did not blend with that of many of the congregation, while Mr. Cherry was personable—even likeable, his domestic difficulties and his private life were not what many in the congregation thought befitted a clergyman. Both subsequently left the ministry after their resignations as Rectors at St. George's. Despite these somewhat unhappy rectorates, the Church continued a steady growth of 279 communicants at the end of 1965, the year Mr. Babin resigned. Total communicants numbered 341 when Mr. Cherry left. He was Rector, September 1, 1965-January 1, 1967.

In the early months of 1966 the congregation began to voice opposition to the social and political actions of the National Church. This opposition was not unusual in the South and became very serious and divisive in those more conservative congregations like St. George's. The controversy continued to exacerbate into the next rectorate of Sidney Ellis. (April 1, 1967-August 1, 1971).

With the sad and rather sudden resignation of Mr. Cherry in December 1966, the Vestry turned to the work of finding a new Rector. In February 1967, the Vestry called the Rev. Sidney Ellis, Associate of St. George's in Nashville. The Rev. Mr. Ellis, an Englishman, with a quiet and respectful manner had the misfortune of becoming Rector of a conservative congregation at a time when the policies of the National Church had become controversial. He, being a priest, was therefore duty bound to support the National Church, a position objectionable to a substantial number of those of more conservative persuasion within the congregation. In addition, the Rev. Mr. Ellis was a relative sedentary individual at a time when a great many in the congregation believed a vigorous and aggresive Rector was needed. Despite the problems both the church and school continued a steady growth. By the end of 1971, communicants of the church had grown to 478 and the Day School enrollment 140 with a new six-classroom building under construction which would almost double the enrollment capacity.

With the resignation of Mr. Ellis in July, 1971 to make room for "a younger man", the Vestry again turned to the task of finding a new Rector. In August, C. Allen Cooke, a native Memphian, was called, becoming the seventh Rector of St. George's Church. Mr. Cooke was a graduate of old Central High School and Southwestern at Memphis. Prior to his call, he was Rector of St. Andrew's in Maryville, Tennessee.

The Rev. Mr. Cooke began almost immediately efforts designed to establish a closer relationship between the congregation and his rectorship. After only two months, he announced the formation of a couple's club for Christian Fellowship meeting one Sunday evening a month with a potluck supper and a cocktail period. At the same time the 9:30 a.m. service was eliminated leaving only the 7:30 communion service and the 10:30 a.m. Worship service.

This was an effort to unify the congregation which still relatively small for three Sunday services. Next, Mr. Cooke undertook to rebuild the Christian Education Program. When he arrived in August 1971, the Sunday School was in a state of decline and there was only one adult class. Within the next few years Sunday School enrollment had increased and several adult classes were being offered. Then in 1978, the Rev. George C. Gibson became the Director of Christian Education. It has been through his leadership that adult Christian Education has grown in variety and quality during the past five years.

Several years after the Rev. Mr. Cooke became Rector, Germantown experienced a population explosion which resulted in a rapid communicant growth. It was clear that by the middle 1970's the need for a larger sanctuary had become obvious, therefore, the Vestry undertook a building program which culminated in the third church building for the congregation. Vestry action began in 1976 and the first service in the sanctuary was held on February 18, 1979. The new building which seats 450 was consecrated by Bishop William E. Sanders on March 4, 1979. By the end of 1980 the communicants numbered 707 and the total baptised persons 961. The budget in that year had grown to over $265,000.00.

With the number of communicants and the size of the church operations, the need for additional clergy was apparent. In December 1980, the Vestry authorized the employment of an Assistant Rector and adopted a budget for the year 1981 to meet that need. The Rev. James W. Cubine came to St. George's July 1, 1981, and was ordained on May 17, 1982 at which time, he became St. George's first Assistant Rector. Under the Rev. Cubine's leadership the E.Y.C. has been revitalized and the organization and number of its activities has grown into one of the parish's most important organizations.

In the meantime, the Rev. Mr. Cooke approached his tenth anniversary as Rector in 1981. At the initial suggestion of the Rev. George Gibson, the congregation gave Mr. Cooke and his wife a Festal Evensong Service in thanksgiving for his ministry. After the service, they were presented with an expense paid trip to Canterbury, England.

Another high point in the rectorate of Mr. Cooke was the removal and restoration of St. George's first church building. During the period from 1954 to the end of 1980, the building located immediately west of the Germantown Presbyterian Church had been used as the Germantown Library and Community Theater. In

November 1982, the building was offered to St. George's for removal by the Germantown Presbyterian Church, the owner. After a rather brief fund raising program, the building was moved on April 10, 1981 to its new site, west of the parish hall (second church building) on the same axis with the Church sanctuary completed in 1979. Renovation and restoration of the chapel building continued through April 1983. On April 23, 1982, St. George's Day, the cornerstone was laid with the same copper box sealed therein again with a history of the building, members of the congregation, clergy and a copy of the New Testament. The chapel was consecrated on June 15, 1983 by Bishop Alex D. Dickson, being the first consecration in the Diocese of West Tennessee.

The Women of the Parish were always active in their Guilds and in the Episcopal Church Women began an activity in 1971 with the sale of antiques donated to the Church by Mr. and Mrs. Eric Catmur. Through efforts of the E.C.W., this event has been scheduled each year in October and has blossomed each year into St. George's Antiques Arcade.

Within the past ten years St. George's choir and music program has gained recognition. St. George's was honored in June 1982, to host the Association of Anglican Musicians. On the night of June 24, 1982 the choirs of St. George's and Calvary Church performed a concert for the occasion. Then, in November 1982 and March 1983, the choir performed Festal Evensong concerts which were well attended by the parish and the community.

On the eve of its fiftieth anniversary in June 1983, St. George's parish has fulfilled the expectations of its founders through its ministry in the community and given those of the Anglican persuasion a story and caring church home.

Leonard V. Hughes, Jr.

St. Thomas the Apostle, Humboldt

St. Thomas The Apostle Church, Humboldt

St. Thomas the Apostle was founded August 30, 1959 by five families in Humboldt. There were five organizing members: Fred Zahrndt, Jessie Hill Ford, Clinton Bell, Tom Miller and Hal Hodgson.

In early 1959, the Rt. Rev. John Vander Horst, Suffragan Bishop of the Diocese, was contacted about the establishment of an Episcopal Church in Humboldt. St. Thomas the Apostle was accepted by the 1960 Convention as an Organized Mission. The Rev. Tom Hutson was the first Vicar.

Two and one half acres of land on the Jackson Highway were purchased from Frank Warmath as the site for the church.

Ground for the building was broken in early 1960, the building was completed and the first services were held later that year. Prior to that time, services were held in the War Memorial Building and at the J. Hungerford Smith plant.

On July 4, 1976, the Rev. Joseph Pinner, Jr. became Priest-in-Charge of St. Thomas. Since that time, the congregation has once again begun to grow and to become an active and vital part of the Humboldt community. On the Fourth Sunday of Easter 1978, St. Thomas' Church and Holy Innocents' Church, Trenton, a congregation whose history dates back to February 12, 1878 when it became a mission (See 1887 Tenn. Diocese Jl.), were joined to make one congregation located in Humboldt. Thus the Episcopal Church in Gibson County was unified. This was a significant step. It served to strengthen St. Thomas, and brought to a focus the Episcopal Church's ministry to all of Gibson County.

In the Fall of 1979, work was begun on an addition to the church. Additional space for the life and ministry of the congregation had long been needed and this hope was finally fulfilled. The new Parish Hall was completed in 1980.

The Rev. Thomas Hutson served as Vicar of St. Thomas the Apostle from 1959-1960. Other ministries who followed were: Armond Eyeler, 1960-1965; Gene Hawes, 1965-1968; David Hackett, 1968-1971; Bill McGill, 1971-1973; Ross Moore, 1973-1975; Joseph Pinner, 1976-1980; Paul C. Dickenson, (Interim-Priest) 1981-1982. The present Rector is the Rev. M. Scott Davis. Tom Miller served as the first Senior Warden. Mrs. Fred (Alice) Zahrndt served as the first president of the Church Women of St. Thomas. The present organist is Anthony Edwards.

Compiled by Mrs. Fred Zahrndt (and the Author)

St. Luke's, Jackson

St. Luke's Episcopal Church, Jackson

From July 25, 1982-May 29, 1983 St. Luke's Church, Jackson held a notable Sesquicentennial Celebration. A very attractive brochure was published for this important period in the life of the church. Topics which received attention were: General Parish Information; Our Parish Life and Fellowship; Christian Education; Worship, Music; Outreach, Caring About Others; and Youth, Our Most Important Blessing.

A very significant part of the brochure was the History, Determination and Strength 1832—Today, much of which is quoted in this account. The final and crowning event of the 150th anniversary celebration of St. Luke's, Jackson, was a visit by the Presiding Bishop, the Right Rev. John M. Allin. Bishop Allin, and Alex D. Dickson, Jr., Bishop of the Diocese of West Tennessee, celebrated the Eucharist at St. Luke's Sunday, May 29, 1983. They were assisted by the Rev. Alexander Comfort, new rector of St. Luke's, the Rev. John Bull, the Rev. James Diffee and the Rev. Frank Butler.

Historical Sketch

On July 23, 1832 (a decade after Madison County was organized) a small group of persons "friendly" to the Episcopal faith met at the Masonic Hall to establish the Episcopal church in Jackson. The Rev. Mr. Thomas Wright of North Carolina presided over the meeting which established St. Luke's Parish. Eighteen persons signed the Articles of Association.

Until 1834, the Rev. Mr. John Chilton, the first rector, served both St. Luke's and the church in Brownsville, which had been established only a month after the one in Jackson.

In 1839, the parish was honored with a visit from Tennessee Bishop, the Right Rev. James H. Otey, who held services in the Madison County Courthouse. St. Luke's labored under many difficulties in these early years because of the lack of money and of members. There were only six communicants in 1837 and no rector until Mr. Chilton returned in 1840. Services were held where space was available. It is obvious from historical data of the period that the parish's very survival can be attributed in a large part, to the devotion and work of its women members, notably Mrs. Eliza Vaulz.

The Rev. Mr. Thomas West became rector of St. Luke's in 1842. He also served Haywood, Fayette and Tipton counties and reported at the time "this has been a year of considerable debility and hard labor to the missionary . . . my rides are (from) 20 to 50 miles from place to place. My services have been two or three times a week in dwellings, school houses or some place of worship . . . The Lord gave me favor in the sight of the people, so that my poor labors have not been in vain in the Lord. . ."

In 1845, a church building was finally erected at the present location, Church and Baltimore Streets (the lot was purchased for $450.00 in 1844.) Although only partially completed by the fall of that year, St. Luke's hosted the Tennessee Diocesan Convention in July, 1846. The original, hand-pumped pipe organ was installed in 1853, as was the church bell which today still calls the congregation to worship and tolls the death of a parishioner at funerals. Pews and the chancel completed the building and St. Luke's was consecrated by the Right Rev. Otey on May 14, 1853.

In 1855, a five-acre lot in the suburbs was given to the parish by James L. Talbot, on which a rectory was built. Jackson Central-Merry High School is now located on the site on Allen Avenue. The Rev. Mr. John A. Harrison was rector of St. Luke's at that time and walked to many of the services of his downtown church during the 25 years he served the parish. This property was sold in 1874 and a lot east of the church was purchased for a new rectory.

The unique brass altar cross and the brass alms bason in use today were presented to the church in 1867 by Tennessee Bishop, the Right Rev. Charles T. Quintard. (The cross is a copy of one in a Westminster Abbey chapel.) They were gifts of the British Duchess of Teck, who met the bishop while he was in England raising funds for the University of the South at Sewanee, Tennessee. She suggested he give them to "one of his parishes." He chose St. Luke's.

Jefferson Davis, President of the Confederate States of America, was imprisoned by the U. S. Government after the defeat of the South in the Civil War. In 1870, having been released from prison, he was scheduled to make his first address as a free man to members of St. Luke's congregation and their friends. It was soon obvious that the crowd would overflow the small church building so the meeting was moved to a grove of trees in front of the home of a parishioner, Confederate General Samuel Jackson Hays.

The original church building was enlarged and remodeled in 1883. The nave was extended, a vestibule and the towers added, a new floor was laid and the church furnished in black walnut. Modern additions have been made from time to time.

The first communion service was made in the 1880's from "love gifts" of silver and other valuables from members of the congregation. Such personal treasures as baby cups, tablespoons, cuff links, jewels and other heirlooms were donated. These communion vessels are still in use today.

The present reredos was acquired in 1885. Of quartered oak, the expertly carved wall screen encloses a trilogy of paintings representing the resurrection of Christ. The Rev. Dr. Johannes A. Oertel, a professor of art at Vanderbilt University, Nashville, Tennessee, and an artist of repute, created the paintings.

The rare triple mosaic windows over the chancel arch were made in Switzerland and installed by an expert Swiss glass worker. The center window of the three stained glass panels in the rear of the church is by Tiffany. These windows were moved from behind the altar when the church was remodeled.

The Convention of the Diocese was again held at St. Luke's in May, 1884. The rector at that time, the Rev. Mr. George Hinkle, reported to the Convention that the church had 240 communicants.

Under the guidance of the Rev. Dr. Joseph E. Martin, (St. Luke's rector 1892-1900), St. Thomas Episcopal Church was organized and built, at the corner of Hale and Cumberland Streets, for the black Episcopalians in Jackson. It became a diocesan mission and was used for many years. In 1962, St. Luke's began welcoming minorities to its services under the spiritual leadership of the Rev. Dr. Frank N. Butler. The St. Thomas building was deconsecrated in December, 1969.

The Rev. Mr. Robert Jackson, who became rector of St. Luke's in 1930, stayed less than a year but in that time met and married a young woman parishioner, Miss Mary Anne Cocke. Also in the year 1930, the Rev. Dr. William J. Loaring-Clark became rector of St. Luke's at the request of the bishop, the Right Rev. Thomas F. Gailor. Under the expert guidance of Dr. Loaring-Clark, a financially faltering parish made great strides, both materially and spiritually. Extensive improvements were made in church property including building a new parish house. Church membership was increased and finances were put on a sound basis.

Dr. Loaring-Clark's wife, Ada, was prominent in national church affairs as well as those of St. Luke's and the community. She was the first woman to serve on the National Council of the

Episcopal Church and organized the United Church Women in Jackson, which is still active today. She also formed St. Luke's Chapter of the Daughters of the King in 1932 and was national president of that order at the time of her death in 1936. The Loaring-Clarks lived at the New Southern Hotel, just a block from the church, for the larger part of his ministry at St. Luke's.

The Great Depression and World War II occurred while Dr. Loaring-Clark served the parish and he guided his congregation through these and all such tribulations with strength, humor and spiritual sustenance. He retired in 1954 and was rector-emeritus of St. Luke's until his death in 1959.

The Rev. Dr. Frank N. Butler was called from the Arkansas diocese to fill the pulpit at St. Luke's in 1954. He and his family occupied a new rectory on Mimosa Drive which had been purchased for their use. Dr. Butler contributed much to the spiritual growth of the parish. His work with the young people was outstanding. The church had active junior and senior Episcopal Young Churchmen organizations and participated in district and diocesan camps. He was a splendid Bible teacher and held mid-week classes in the parish house.

The Rev. Mr. Frank S. Cerveny came to St. Luke's in October, 1963 from the staff of Trinity Episcopal Church in New York City. He remained at St. Luke's until 1969. During his tenure, he provided the parish with spiritual enrichment and motivation for new programs such as planning for the establishment of the Episcopal Day School in the city. Father Cerveny is now bishop of the Diocese of Florida, a position to which he was elected in 1975.

The Rev. Mr. Paul Shields Walker assumed the rectorship of the parish in March, 1969, coming from Holy Trinity Church, Memphis. Under his leadership and that of St. Luke's vestry, the Episcopal Day School was chartered in January, 1970. With 24 students enrolled, the first EDS classes in grades one through five met in the Sunday School classrooms of St. Luke's parish house from September, 1970 until January, 1971. Father Walker served as school chaplain, conducting daily morning services. At present, EDS offers instruction in grades K through nine and is planning to add grades ten, eleven and twelve in the future.

In November, 1969, after much planning, the church dedicated its present organ, an instrument custom built by the Wicks Organ Company in Highland, Ill. It possesses a 12-rank distribution of 775 pipes, all of which speak, and is one of the finest small pipe organs made in this country.

A memorial church garden was begun in the north churchyard and a brick wall to surround it erected in 1966. Under Father Walker's direction, a patio entrance to the garden was built through remodeling of the parish hall in 1972. Today, with a parquet floor, paneling and crystal chandeliers, the hall is ideally suited for wedding receptions and other church functions.

The carved oak reredos with paintings of the Resurrection; black walnut pews, rare triple mosaic windows over the chancel; the many beautiful stained glass windows and other memorials. . . all are symbols placed in this church by faithful parishioners for more than a century. They make this Gothic ediface not only the oldest continuously used church building (since 1845), but one of the most beautiful historic buildings in Madison County.

Mary Jo Tate (Mrs. Joseph G.) Mulherin

Immanuel, LaGrange

Immanuel Church, La Grange

Serene, confident and majestic stands Immanuel Church, LaGrange, Fayette County, Tennessee. Truly it is of God!

More than architectural beauty and ecclesiastical dignity infuse this heritage house of worship. Precision laid bricks of age are secured by stout stone pilasters. Undergirdings of giant hand-hewn timbers provide obvious strength to cause of the construction a creation.

In the midst of tradition every feature of the setting expresses a continuity in love, in faith, in fortitude. All these are enduring evidences of lofty courage, self-sacrifice, and determination consecrated by Christian association.

No account of the Episcopal Church, its founding and growth in Tennessee can be accurately recorded without consideration of the place of its beginning. A peculiar and lasting influence on the Church in Tennessee, and particularly in the Western District was wielded by Emmanuel Church, Warrenton, North Carolina, consecrated in 1824. Dedicated men and women of distinguished religious zeal comprised the congregation. Among these were the families of Gloster, Anderson and Alston. On Emmanuel's vestry in 1824, were George and John Anderson, James Hervey Otey and Kemp Plummer.

"We removed to Fayette County from North Carolina in the Fall of 1827" wrote Elizabeth Willis Gloster (Mrs. John) Anderson. Those who came from Warrenton to LaGrange were Mary Hayes Willis (Mrs. Thomas Benn) Gloster, widow of Dr. Gloster; her son, Arthur Brehon Gloster; her daughter, Elizabeth Willis Gloster, and husband, John Anderson, and their five children, and George Anderson, John Anderson's brother.

Between 1825 and 1827 members of the Alston family came from Warrenton and founded Ravenscroft Plantation near Ramdolph, Tipton County, Tennessee. In 1831, Elizabeth Whitmel W. Johnston Alston, widow of Philip Alston, came from her home on Fishing Creek, Warren County, North Carolina with her sons and daughters to Ravenscroft Plantation. Philip Williams Whitmel Alston, her youngest son, became an outstanding Episcopal minister and rector of Calvary Church, Memphis.

At the time of Mrs. Gloster's arrival, LaGrange was a community of approximately two hundred fifty persons of wealth, education and culture. No church had been established within its borders. The town was incorporated October 17, 1831.

James Hervey Otey came to Franklin, Tennessee, in 1821 and founded Harpeth Academy, a school for boys. In 1823, he became principal of the Warrenton Male Academy, Warrenton, North Carolina. In 1825, he returned to Harpeth Academy to continue his role as teacher and to begin the extensive missionary effort in Middle Tennessee which resulted in the organization in 1827, of St. Paul's, Franklin, the first Episcopal Church in Tennessee. At the Fourth Diocesan Convention, 1833, James H. Otey was elected the first Bishop of the Protestant Episcopal Church in Tennessee.

In 1832, Mrs. Gloster, determined to do all within her power to establish the Episcopal faith in the town of LaGrange and in the communities of West Tennessee, made an eventful and rewarding horse-ride. Mounted on her gentle steed, capable of long travel, she set forth from her home in LaGrange to ride to Franklin to confer with her godson, Mr. Otey.

Two historic markings in LaGrange commemorate Mrs. Gloster's gallant achievement in behalf of her Church. They are a roadside marker and a bronze plaque in Immanuel.

Mrs. Gloster's appeal to influential, able Mr. Otey was that he come to West Tennessee and establish the Church, or that he request missionaries be sent by the Domestic and Foreign Missionary Society of New York to supply this great need.

The religious fruitfulness of Mrs. Gloster's journey was evidenced by the coming of the Reverend Thomas Wright, John Chilton and Samuel George Litton which resulted in the organization in 1832 of St. Luke, Jackson, July 23rd; Calvary, Memphis, August 6th; Zion (Christ), Brownsville, August 25th; St. Paul, Randolph, September 16th; Immanuel Church, LaGrange, October, and St. Matthew (Grace), Paris. The founding of these churches is in reality the record of the journey of the pioneer missionary-organizer who came from North Carolina and arrived in Tennessee on June 12, 1832, the Rev. Thomas Wright.

A very complete and fascinating travelogue of his entire journey was kept by Mr. Wright. Evidently he wrote much of his diary as he rode his horse on this historic trek to the Western District.

Mr. Wright made three trips to LaGrange in 1832 as recorded by him:

> "July 28, reached LaGrange and soon met with our good friends, the Andersons and others (Mrs. Gloster). 29th—the Male Academy being the only place we could worship and the Baptist having it occupied in the morning, I could not preach until 3 o'clock in the afternoon. The people

never having heard an Episcopalian before filled the house and some could not get in, and were attentive. Our Warrenton friends are the only Episcopalians, but we can make some if our services are regularly celebrated once or twice a month. 30th and 31st—Remained in LaGrange and preached at 4 o'clock on the first of August. August 2nd—I left Mr. Anderson. . . ."

Mr. Wright's second trip to LaGrange:

"Tuesday, August 17th—arrived at LaGrange, preached Saturday and Sunday, twice on the latter day. 23rd—left LaGrange. . . ."

And his third trip:

"September 1st, twice on Sunday, 6th; left LaGrange and arrived on the 7th at Memphis, and from LaGrange to Memphis is 50 miles."

Dr. George Weller introduced this resolution to the 1833 Diocesan Convention:

"Resolved, that the articles of association of Immanuel Church, LaGrange, Fayette County, be approved and the said Church admitted into union with this Convention."

Unanimous agreement followed (June 27th). A certificate of the election of John Anderson as a Lay Delegate from Immanuel was read and approved. Mr. Anderson took his seat.

In 1833, In Mr. Wright's first report to a Tennessee Diocesan Convention, he stated:

"I take the liberty of mentioning here the organization of Immanuel Church, LaGrange, in October (1832) and am happy to state that a gentleman of the congregation has offered a pleasant and convenient lot adjoining the town, for the erection of a church. There are four communicants at LaGrange and two at Randolph."

The Rev. Samuel George Litton, Deacon in charge of Immanuel reported:

"I feel thankful there is a spirit of anxiety and deep concern manifested by many of the congregation, to inquire after the things that belong to their eternal welfare. May God shed his divine influence on my efforts. . . ."

Recorded by Bishop Otey, 1834:

"April 10th. We came to Mr. Anderson's, LaGrange, and were pleased to find this old and tried friend of our Zion, 'with the Church in his house', as we may properly term it, enjoying health and every worldly comfort; rejoicing that they were once more blessed with the privilege of—'treading the sacred paths, that to God's dwelling lead!' April 12th. Preached in the Methodist meeting house; Mr. Wright and Mr. Litton, prayers."

The Diocesan Convention met in Immanuel Church, May 6-9, 1840. Bishop Otey recorded:

> "In the afternoon (May 9th) the cornerstone of Immanuel Church was laid by me accompanied by suitable religious exercises, and address by the Rev. Philip Alston . . . . At night . . . . Bishop Leonidas Polk (Louisiana) addressed the Church assembled. Sunday, May 10th . . . I admitted to the order of Priesthood . . . the Rev. Philip W. Alston . . . It is hoped and believed that the exercises of the Convention week at LaGrange, made a happy impression upon many minds in behalf of virtue and religion."

The Rev. Philip Alston concluded his address at the laying of the cornerstone of Immanuel:

> "We rejoice to behold the promise of a permanent beacon of the gospel, to guide souls aright which are tossed on the waves of this troublesome world; a beacon—which is built on the foundation of the Apostles and Prophets, Jesus Christ himself being the chief cornerstone—. Here the wayfaring brother of our communion shall turn aside, and be refreshed in his travel, as by the shadow of a great rock in a weary land. Here the poor shall find that godliness which is great riches; here the afflicted shall be led forth by waters of comfort; here the ignorant shall be made wise unto salvation; here the fallen shall be raised up and the feeble supported—. Here He who walketh in the midst of golden candlesticks, the churches of His love, will vouchsafe His peculiar presence—."

Immanuel Church was consecrated by Bishop Otey on Sunday, October 1, 1843. As he recorded:

> "With the rites and solemnities prescribed, I, this day, set apart and consecrated to the worship of Almighty God, Immanuel Church, LaGrange, according to the order of the Church. Rev. Mr. Alston read the Morning Prayer, and the Rev. Mr. Litton the lesson. The letter of request from the vestry was read by Mr. John Anderson, senior warden—the instrument of consecration by Mr. Alston. The Church is a neat substantial, and commodious edifice, built of brick, having a cupola, surmounted with a cross, an organ loft, and seats on the lower floor for the colored population—."

In 1848, the list of subscribers from LaGrange to the Diocesan Missionary Society gave the names of Mrs. John Anderson, Mrs. Mary H. Gloster, Mrs. Thomas (Mary Hostler Green) Wright, J. W. Burton, Mrs. M. Potts, Mrs. Beauchelle, Mrs. Leonidas (Sarah Eliza Wright) Cotten, T.R. Polk, George G. Cossitt, J. J. Potts, and T. G. Anderson. The Rev. William Fagg was rector of Immanuel.

Bishop Otey died during the Civil War. Dr. Charles Todd Quintard succeeded to the episcopate. The Rev. George James reported to Bishop Quintard:

"January 26-28th, 1866. At LaGrange, Fayette County. A church of brick, which was used for hospital purposes and for ordnance storage, during the war; the windows and window blinds, broken; chancel surroundings destroyed; the seats gone, (having been used for coffins); stoves gone; vestry-room destroyed, (having been used as a privy); walls, written over with charcoal and pencil, (sad to look on). Communicants, in and around LaGrange, about twenty, (nearly all females). Sunday, January 28th, I held services and preached twice in the Presbyterian meeting house—. One of the lady communicants, Miss Cossitt, was making money to repair the windows and fix up a stove, so as to have a Sunday School in operation. April 20-24th—Accompanied the Bishop on a visit to LaGrange; took with us a lectern, litany, stool, lamps and oil. —Miss Cossitt had got the windows mended—regularly instructing in the Sunday School. I assisted the Bishop in tacking some pieces of carpet on the chancel floor—people borrowed some benches—I held the first service that had been in the church since the war."

On September 17, 1867, Robert H. Parham, J. J. Pulliam, Henry Biggs, W. A. Houston, vestrymen, and the Rev. J. M. Schwrar, rector, petitioned the United States government for payment of damages done to Immanuel Church by Union soldiers during the war. The claim set forth that about November 2, 1862, General Grant, with the Army of the United States under his command, being stationed at and in the neighborhood of the town of LaGrange, Tennessee, took possession of the church building called Immanuel, (the same being a building erected and used for the exclusive purpose of worshipping therein Almighty God according to the discipline and rites of the Protestant Episcopal Church in the United States.) A full account of the damage was set forth in the petition. The reply was that an army in the territory against which it is warring has a right to compel the supply of its wants from its opponents, hence the absolute necessity of showing the positive loyalty of the claimants. No claim from a seceding community will be entertained by the government! Mr. Schwrar wrote in part:

"The church is not the property of any man, or body of man; it is a building consecrated to the service of Almighty God, and such claims as we have presented, being just and equitable, should, it seems to me, be allowed without reference to the political opinions of those who might, for the time being, be guardians of the property."

In further correspondence it was disclosed that an Episcopal Church of which the Secretary of War was a member did receive a small sum to pay for repairing benches! Finally, Mr. Schwrar wrote on the back of the letter received: "The experience of the churches in Washington and the tenor of this letter do not encourage a further prosecution of our claim at the present time!"

An eternity of hours of church occupation and the desolation were factual. Guided and inspired by the dedicated members of Immanuel, the gracious townspeople of all faiths in LaGrange made possible the necessary restoration of the building and did not permit dilapidation.

The many dedicated ministers who served Immanuel pass in dramatic panoply. Among them—Samuel George Litton, J. J. Vaulx, William Fagg, William Crane Gray (who became, 1892, the first Bishop of Southern Florida), J. M. Schwrar, Irenaeus Trout, Dr. Arthur Howard Noll, J. F. Plummer, Charles Woodward.

All Saints' Church, the Rev. Robertson Eppes, Jr., rector, Memphis, provided pastoral and liturgical ministry to Immanuel for more than fourteen years. The Rev. Paul Dickenson followed Mr. Eppes and the Rev. Dr. James P. McKnight is presently in charge.

Of great interest is the diary of the late Bishop William Crane Gray once minister of St. James, Bolivar and Immanuel:

"Saturday, October 29, 1859—took a delightful walk—the beautiful hills that rise around LaGrange covered with green pines give a varied aspect to the country which few places in the Western District enjoy. —May 16, 1860—I walked home with Miss Maggie Trent.—November 7, 1860—At Mrs. (Thomas) Wright's. LaGrange. Rose early. Conducted family prayers. —Wednesday, May 20, 1863—"A day ever to be remembered by me. The day of my entrance upon wedded life. A delightful era in my existence! This day at 12 o'clock in Immanuel Church, La Grange, by the Rector, Rev. J. J. Vaulx was united in marriage to Miss Maggie Locke Trent. We drove in carriages from the residence of her brother-in-law, Captain Anderson, and when we arrived at the gate of the churchyard the Sunday Scholars of the Parish all dressed in white and covered with pure white flowers were arranged on either side of the walk leading up to the Church and we walked between them. A goodly number of friends were present at the Church and after the ceremony was over we were greeted with warm and numerous congratulations."

A rich and rewarding experience awaits all who journey to LaGrange annually on Sunday morning to attend the Harvest Eucharist, a service of communion and thanksgiving. The great double walnut doors of Immanuel will open wide to welcome all who come. And every person who enters will be drawn more closely one with another in Christian fellowship by the ageless message inscribed in letters of gold above the altar: "Thou God Seest Me."

A number of original appointments which have withstood the exigencies of the years are brought from vault-storage (in a nearby town) and used in the service. Two silver chalices, a silver tankard, a square glass wine cruet, a small silver baptismal font, fair linens, a lace-edged chalice veil and altar coverings, with original gold fringe and insignia, are among Immanuel's cherished possessions.

A harbinger of hope she stands, a monument to the devotion of her founders, a blessing to be appreciated and a venerable edifice to challenge gratifying religious experiences for generations yet unborn.

Well art thou named "Immanuel" —God with us—thou stately Church of Grace!

> "And quiet, so quiet, the Autumn sky,
> Smiling on all below,
> Promises splendor that shall not die
> For such as listen, and live thereby,
> And the cross of the Faithful is rising high,
> A shout in the morning-glow."
> (by Dean M. Stewart)

Ellen Davies-Rodgers

"Religion is the first thing and the last thing; and until a man has found God, he begins at no beginning and works to no end."

—unknown.

St. John's, Martin

St. John's Church, Martin

Sometimes I feel the Diocese of Tennessee was primed and waiting for ten Episcopal adults to request a Student Center (Canterbury Center as it was referred to in the 1950's) in Martin, Tennessee.

There were three families that trailed to Fulton, Kentucky each Sunday to celebrate the Lord's Day in the nearest Episcopal Church. A young concerned priest, the Rev. George Laib, encouraged such a move and met with us and the Rev. Sidney Sanders of Union City, St. James Church (Sid is now Bishop of East North Carolina) in the James Wilson home to organize such a Mission. This meeting was held in the Spring of 1956 with the following people present: Dr. and Mrs. James Wilson, Pamela and Paul Wilson, Allan Strawbridge, Sr., Mr. and Mrs. Robert Swaim, Debbie Swaim, Mrs. Ned Ray McWherter, Mrs. Margarite Walker, Mike Walker and two other Walkers, Mr. and Mrs. Pete Smith, and Mrs. Milton Miller, Mike, Penny and Jan Miller.

A letter was sent to the Rt. Rev. Theodore Barth, Bishop of Tennessee requesting help in organizing in Martin. Following the same pattern of being University oriented it was not until September 23, 1956 that the first service of St. John's Episcopal Church and Canterbury Center was held with the Rev. George Liab and the Rev. Sidney Sanders officiating. These first services were held in the Vanguard Theater then located in an old army barracks, vintage WWII, on the site of the present Clement Hall. The time of our service was 5 p.m. When plans were made for Clement Hall we met in any available University building from English classrooms in the old Administration Building to Music Department to Food Lab in Home Ec finally to the Nursery School. All this time using an improvised altar and hand-me-down appointments. On December 2, 1956, we were recognized as an Organized Mission. It was not until we moved into the nursery school in January, 1957 that we had a place to store kneelers and an altar on the site of the service. The Altar we used is the one you see on the Epistle side of our present building. It is hollow and after each service we stacked our kneeling cushions in it along with our candlesticks and communion vessels and two strong men lifted it atop a row of lockers to await the following Sunday. So you see in those days our very survival and a roof over our heads depended on the University.

Our present property was purchased in Spring of 1958. On April 13, 1958, following Holy Communion in the nursing building, the congregation marched across campus and observed the old English custom of "the Beating of the Bounds". That is to say a procession led by the Cross and Priest, with congregation following, march around the edges of the property singing "Onward Christian Soldiers" followed by the traditional ground breaking.

In July 1958, M. Clark Baker, a young deacon took the reins of St. James, Union City and with it the responsibility of Martin. On March 4, 1959, Bishop Theodore Barth, with Mitre and Crozier, dedicated St. John's.

There followed a succession of vicars. Clark Baker was ordained at St. James in 1959 and was a strong influence on the life of St. John's and the college students.

The Rev. Richard Clark inherited us. Then the Rev. Lee McClain, who was in charge of Grace Church, Paris, was with us from August 1967 until October 1970. Lee was very good with the students also. During these years the ECW flourished as well.

In June 1971 the Rev. William T. Patten took over in Paris and again St. John's had a new priest. Bill Patten was priest when we agreed to share worship area with the First Christians. This was at first an effort to work more closely with the students of both denominations jointly. A set of bylaws was drafted, a governing board set and officers from both churches selected to administer this . . . All this time our services had been at 9 a.m. so our priest could hold his "Holy Hour" service in his own church. The Diocese only loaned him to us for Holy Communion and student work. The First Christian held their worship service at 11 a.m. It was good to have our building used more than one hour a week.

In September 1972 at long last, the Diocese sent us our first Resident Priest, Cameron Hess. We had to find him a place to live with six children and a wife! A house was rented on Peach Street for temporary housing. The present Vicarage was bought in 1973.

The University students found a true friend in Cameron and an open heart to share their griefs, problems and joys. But it was obvious we needed more space to share with these students who are truly the reason St. John's exists. The Parish Hall was planned and one half of it built in 1974-1975. The back wall was knocked out to make room for the double doors, the vestibule and the three classrooms built. To get food and drink to the Parish Hall the kitchen window was remodeled into a "pass thru". Now we had space to gather together as a family; college students and the families of St.

John's. Later the plan was to build three more rooms opening off the existing hall. Under Cameron's guidance St. John's made firm steps outward and upward. And as we knew he would, Cameron accepted a call to a larger parish!

Tom Hughes was our second resident priest beginning in July 1976. The Bishop was wise again. Tom related to the students, organizing Agape Suppers for them, holding outdoor services, picnics, fishing contests and joining with our Jewish friends in Celebration of Seder.

In September 1980 our present and eighth vicar arrived on the scene. The Rev. Laurence K. Packard brought new energy and insight to St. John's. He instigated the idea of a three year Master Plan formed by the entire congregation involving 1) Capital improvements 2) Finances and 3) Community life and Outreach. Within one year most of the major goals had been met. Pulpit constructed, pews refinished, fresh paint, carpeting, Sacristy remodeled, new siding and inside-outside trim painted, landscaping, Day Care Center started, air conditioner installed in Parish Hall, door cut through kitchen, opening in Nave of church to kitchen closed off, and new vinyl in kitchen to name a few.

Dial-a-Burger and carepackages were started as added outreach to students, but actually resulted in all families becoming involved and a major project for St. John's. "Ministers of the Month" has been instigated and allows all families the privilege of Altar Guild work and hospitality hostesses.

Sunday School taught by the vicar is offered. An interdenominational youth group between St. John's, St. Jude's (Catholic) and Trinity Presbyterian is active.

When our pledges reach the level where we are self-supporting we can become a parish, until that time we are a Mission organized to look to the needs of the University of Tennessee, Martin Branch, students and the community of Martin.

In August 1982 a Before and After School Place was instituted for "latchkey" children. A Venture In Mission "seed money" grant made this possible and the project is now self-supporting. The Center will be in operation again this year.

Presently there are 86 communicants.

Allen Hammond serves as Senior Warden of St. John's, 1983.

Mrs. Milton (Elizabeth Sudlow) Miller
Organizing Member, St. John's

St. Paul's, Mason

St. Paul, Mason

The congregation of St. Paul's, Mason, began with the baptism of four infants of slaves from Colonel George Tarry Taylor's plantation August, 1847, by Reverend James W. Rogers. On November 5, 1850, two slaves were confirmed. This congregation worshipped in Trinity In-The-Fields in the afternoon. By 1866, there were 40 to 100 members.

The church was admitted to the Diocese in 1873. The cornerstone of the first church-house was laid February 8, 1873. The Reverend Henderson Maclin was the first Deacon-in-charge.

In 1880 a day school was organized with 138 pupils by Deacon Isaac Black, a former instructor at Meharry Medical College. The school continued, periodically, until 1915.

Dr. George W. Honesty, Rector of Emmanual Church, Memphis, contributed greatly to the work of the mission, 1894-1901.

Old St. Paul's, located on the Memphis-Brownsville Road, served this congregation until 1941. In 1954, the congregation of St. Paul's was merged with St. Mary's on the campus of Gailor Industrial School. There were forty communicants.

A vast program of renovation has been recently in progress at St. Paul. The church has been completely repaired and painted during 1983.

The Rev. W. Joe Moore has held services twice a month at St. Paul since October 1974. A Lay Reader from Emmanuel, Memphis is in charge of services for the other two Sundays each month. John Cochran has served as Warden for many years; Alice Grant is the church treasurer. Priscilla Brown Cochran continues as organist.

There are twenty-seven communicants at present.

Priscilla Brown Cochran

Trinity, Mason

Trinity Episcopal Church, Mason

"In the month of March 1834, the Rev. John Chilton, then in charge of the congregations at Brownsville and Jackson, visited the neighborhood where the county lines of Haywod, Fayette and Tipton Counties corner, and preached at the residence of Mrs. Hunt, relict of Captain Christopher Hunt, after reading the morning service of the Church with a few respondents. At that time there was but one communicant of the Church in the neighborhood. There were three or four families friendly to the Church, and several persons attended from motives of curiosity, her forms and ritual being entirely new to them. From the interest manifested, Mr. Chilton was induced to conduct the services and preach several times during that and the years 1835 and 1836 alternately at the dwelling houses of Mrs. Hunt and Mr. George T. Taylor."

So begins the history of Trinity Church, Mason, as recorded by the Rev. William M. Steel in the old parish register.

The neighborhood was also visited by the Rev. Samuel Litton who had charge of Immanuel, LaGrange.

In the spring of 1837 the Rev. John Drummond came to the neighborhood as a missionary. He organized a congregation and directed them in electing a vestry and purchasing a "storehouse" from Mr. Robert Hightower, which was fitted up as a house of worship. "It was called St. Andrew's and admitted into union with the Convention by that name." At the Bishop's visitation eight persons were confirmed.

Mr. Drummonds resigned that year and the vestry elected the Rev. William Steel to take his place. Mr. Steel stayed two years and was followed by the Rev. Mr. West. After Mr. West left the people were left without services for some time.

In 1844, services were held once a month by the Rev. Samuel Litton. He was followed in 1845 by the Rev. James W. Rogers.

In 1847 Major William Taylor, brother of George T. Taylor, gave the church "one acre of land near his residence and the friends of the Church erected a small house on it for the worship of God naming it after the Holy Trinity." This is the present Old-Trinity-in-the-Field. Mr. Rogers was succeeded in 1848 by the Rev. William M. Steel who received a salary of two hundred dollars and "board for himself and horse."

The Rev. J. A. Wheelock took charge of the parish on July 14, 1854. He held services on alternate Sundays for the white and colored congregations. On the 18th of July 1859, the Rev. Charles F.

Collins "was called to the rectorship of the parish and entered upon the duties of the same." The number of communicants was—White 41: Colored 21. The rector's salary was $800.00 and the use of the parsonage. Bishop Otey visited the Church and preached and confirmed for the last time November 17, 1861. In the words of Mr. Collins, "During the War our Church services were at no time interrupted and we found our chief comfort in our troubles and adversities in seeking God's help in His holy Sanctuary." On December 31, 1865, Bishop Quintard paid his first Episcopal visitation to the parish and confirmed 13 whites and 13 colored.

Meanwhile the railroad came through and the town of Mason was established. People moved to town and wanted their church close at hand. On December 8, 1869, Bishop Quintard laid the foundation stone. The following summer the building was begun on land given to the church by George Tarry Taylor. The church was completed in October, 1870. On the 30th of March, 1871, in the presence of a large congregation the Church was consecrated by Bishop Quintard. Mr. Collins was instituted as rector, and twenty-seven people were confirmed.

On May 7, 1871, the following item appeared in the Commercial Appeal: "The new Episcopal Church at Mason's Depot, consecrated recently by Bishop Quintard is the neatest bit of architecture between Memphis and Nashville. Designed by John B. Cook of Memphis it is a veritable gem of pure Gothic style. The magnificent stained glass windows would do credit to a European cathedral. They were made by Hughes the famous Memphis stained glass artist who recently completed windows for St. Mary's on Poplar. The new church was built by members of the Rev. Charles Collins' flock at the cost of $10,000." The windows were designed by Mr. Hughes but the stained glass in them was imported from Venice, and according to the noted Church historian, Dr. Arthur H. Noll, is irreplaceable, since it was made by a process that is no longer known.

In his history of the Church Mr. Collins wrote: "The Parish is under especial obligation to Col. John F. Jelt, a faithful vestryman of the parish, who superintended the erection of the Church and most liberally contributed to the same." The Church building was all that was new for the congregation was the same and they gave the name Trinity to the Church after its parent church which now became known as Old Trinity. (Trinity-in-the-Field).

On December 31st Mr. Collins resigned the rectorship of Trinity Parish, which he had held for fifteen years and moved to

Covington to take charge of St. Matthews. The number of communicants at this time was 82. The Rev. Flavel Mines followed Mr. Collins as rector and continued in charge until 1877. In 1878 the Rev. Charles F. Collins was again called to the rectorship and remained in charge until his resignation on May 1st, 1882. There were 96 communicants. The foregoing history is for the most part taken from the old church register compiled by the Rev. William M. Steel, the Rev. J. A. Wheelock and the Rev. C. F. Collins.

Mr. Collins was succeeded in 1883 by Edward de Seebach Juny, the son of an Episcopal priest, Frederick Augustus Juny, a Frenchman and a former Roman Catholic. Another son, Frederick Augustus Juny, Jr., was also a priest and we shall hear of him later in the history of Trinity Church. During the years 1885 and 1886, the Rev. Matthew Henry was missionary in charge of Trinity and held at least monthly services.

In 1887, Trinity Church was singularly blessed by having as their rector the Rev. Charles Thomas Wright. He was ordained to the priesthood that same year, and Trinity was his first charge. Mr. Wright was born in England, and left an orphan at an early age and became the ward of Bishop Quintard. When he was ready for college he was enrolled by the Bishop in the University of the South at Sewanee where he also received his degree in theology.

In her book, *"The Holy Innocents,"* Ellen Davies-Rodgers wrote: "Early in 1887 the Rev. Mr. Wright went to Trinity Church, Mason. There his abiding interest in music became even more vital. The Church organist was the attractive and talented Miss Annie Rivers Seay. Soon after their acquaintance, it was quite evident that heart strings, as well as an organ, were being played upon."

Mr. Wright married Miss Seay, the daughter of Mr. and Mrs. Charles Irenaeus Seay, on November 30, 1887 in Trinity Church. The ceremony was performed by the Rev. Mr. Patterson of Grace Church, Memphis, and Bishop Charles Todd Quintard. The local paper referred to the wedding as one of the largest and most fashionable in Trinity Parish. Mr. Wright was rector of Trinity from 1887-1889 when he accepted a call to Pulaski, Tennessee. He was followed by the Rev. Howard Murray Dumbell.

Mr. Dumbell, like Mr. Wright, was born in England, educated at the University of the South and the School of Theology at Sewanee. He was also like Mr. Wright in marrying a local girl, Anna Pattison Sherrod of Covington the daughter of Dr. John Irvin and Lucinda Smith Sherrod. They were married in St. Matthew's, Covington on April 8, 1889. Mr. Dumbell served Trinity until 1893 when he resigned to become rector of the Church of the Good Shepherd, Memphis. He was followed at Trinity by his friend and classmate, Daniel Troy Beatty. When he came to Trinity in 1893 Mr. Beatty had been married for only a few months to Miss Fredericka Mayhew. Although he remained for little more than a year, the handsome young clergyman won a warm place in the hearts of the parishoners.

On April 22, 1894, the Rev. Irenaeus Trout was placed in charge of Trinity. Mr. Trout, though only 18 at the time of the epidemic, was one of the heroes of the yellow fever disaster in Memphis. In her book *"The Holy Innocents,"* Ellen Davies-Rodgers quotes a fascinating story of the romance and marriage of Mr. Trout and a young lady he had rescued during the epidemic when she was only a baby. From his mother, an accomplished musician, Mr. Trout inherited a love and talent for music. While he was at Trinity he trained an excellent choir, often playing the organ as well as preaching. During this time his soloist was Mrs. William Rivers Seay who had a beautiful and highly trained voice. She was a young bride who had just been presented for confirmation by Mr. Trout after her marriage to Mr. Seay in 1895.

Late in 1896 Mr. Trout was sent to St. Thomas, Somerville and Immanuel, LaGrange. He was replaced by the Rev. Frederick Augustus Juny, Jr., brother of Edward deSeebach Juny who was rector of Trinity from 1880-1883. When Mr. Juny resigned in 1898 to go to Dalton, Georgia, he was succeeded by the Rev. Matthew Nevill Joyner in April, 1898. Few rectors have been as close to their parishoners or been as dearly beloved as Mr. Joyner, and he returned their love keeping in close contact through the years with visits and letters. Evidence of his love was the fact that he wished the memorial to his father and mother to be placed in Trinity Church. Before his death he left a sum of money for this purpose with his son, Quintard Joyner. The beautiful walnut pulpit which now stands in Trinity is the memorial gift. The old church register contains this entry: "My first rectorship. I become rector of Trinity Parish April 1898 and resigned September 1902. It was a happy relationship, Nevill Joyner." Mr. Joyner accepted a call to become the rector of St. James, Bolivar and chaplain of St. Katharine's School.

In 1904, Bishop Gailor sent the Rev. Francis Moore to Trinity. He and his wife became a vital force in the community. With Mrs. Moore as hostess, the rectory became a gathering place for the young people of the community. She had a number of "young fry" of her own and their friends were always welcome in the rectory.

Mrs. Moore would play the organ for them to dance which seemed strange but none the less enjoyable to the boys and girls of all denominations who gathered there. She fed them her famous gingersnaps as refreshments. Mr. Moore was by nature a teacher and in his sermons taught his congregation much about Church history and the early Church fathers. He was also athletic and an outdoors man. He was a skilled ice skater and thought nothing of walking the thirteen miles from Mason to Arlington to hold a service.

After Mr. Moore resigned to go to St. Thomas, Somerville, there followed in rapid succession, J. Coleman Horton, 1911; Thomas Dyke, 1912; John James Patrick Perry, 1915; Harry F. Keller, 1917, — A charming young man just out of seminary who, although his tenure was brief, made a deep imprint on the church and formed friendships that lasted all his life long; Paul F. Williams, 1918 and Howard Cady, 1921. During this time there were long stretches when Church services were irregular or entirely lacking.

On January 5, 1924, Bishop Maxon placed Archdeacon Benjamin F. Root in charge of the missions—Christ Church, Brownsville, Trinity, Mason and Holy Innocents, Arlington. He was assisted by Trinity and Holy Innocents by Stanley Young, a business man and perpetual deacon, who gave unstintingly of his services wherever he was needed. On January 1, 1922, Mr. Young recorded a revised list of communicants in the parish register. The number of communicants was thirty-six. In 1928 Bishop Maxon sent Archdeacon Charles K. Weller to replace Archdeacon Root.

Archdeacon Weller was an indefatigable worker and traveled miles over West Tennessee with the ever faithful Mrs. Weller in his trying to minister to the many churches in West Tennessee who had no priest. Mr. Weller had a missionary spirit and brought several families into the church at Mason who had no former ties with the Church. Among these were Mr. and Mrs. B. F. Thomas of Arlington. Mrs. Thomas played the organ at Trinity for more than 25 years.

When Archdeacon Weller retired he was replaced by the Rev. Paul Earl Sloan, February 2, 1937. Mr. Sloan with his lovely young wife and baby son, Paul Earl, Jr., lived in the rectory in Covington. He had charge of St. Matthew's, Covington; Trinity, Mason; Immanuel, Ripley and Ravenscroft, Brighton. The churches prospered under Mr. Sloan and he united them in a County parish, something unique in the Diocese of Tennessee. Mr. Sloan made extensive repairs on the church properties doing much of the work himself. During this time the walls of Trinity were replastered. Mr. Sloan was greatly beloved not only by his church people but by those outside as well since he ministered to them in their troubles and sorrows just as he did his own people. On July 7, 1937, a second son, Theodore Bradford Sloan, was born to the Sloans. This young man has remained in Covington and occupies a position of great respect in the church and community. In 1949 Mr. Sloan was stricken by a fatal illness. His untimely death brought an end to a happy time in the life of the parish. The church was stunned with grief.

During Mr. Sloan's illness the church was served by the Rev. Max Damron, a young man beautiful in body and soul. After he returned to his studies at the University of the South School of Theology he was followed in rapid succession by the Rev. Ellis Bearden, the Rev. Robert G. Tatum, the Rev. Sterling Tracy, and the Rev. Alfred Snively, fine, intelligent men who ministered as well as they could in view of the short time allotted them to the needs of the church.

In 1952 the parish called the Rev. John H. Sivley as rector. In July he and his wife, Martha, came to live in the rectory in Covington and once more the four churches functioned as a parish. Under Mr. Sivley's leadership an extensive restoration program was carried out at Trinity. The floor was repaired, the beautiful old handmade brick were pointed up, and a new roof was put on the church. During their stay in Tipton County the Sivleys became the parents of twin boys, John and James.

On Palm Sunday, April 3, 1955, Nevill Rivers Seay, Senior Warden and principal of the Mason School was licensed as a lay reader and held his first service. Since this time services have been held every Sunday in Trinity Church, Mr. Seay holding services when no priest was present.

On November 3, 1955, Mr. Sivley held his last service at Trinity. The search now began for a new rector.

On January 1, 1956, Trinity was extremely fortunate to have as guest preacher and celebrant, the Rev. H. Sheldon Davis, a Canon at St. Mary's Cathedral. The congregation realized this was the man for them. Shortly thereafter a call was issued to Mr. Davis and happily for the parish he accepted. On April 29, 1956, he held his first service as rector at Trinity. These were joyous days in the parish.

Under the leadership of Mr. Davis, St. Matthew's grew to such an extent that it wished to become a parish with Mr. Davis as their rector. This was accomplished and Trinity once more became a mission. Mr. Davis' last service was Quinquagesima Sunday, February 8, 1959. In their grief over the loss of Mr. Davis the people were comforted by the Rev. Warwick Aiken. No priest has ever been more beloved by the people of Trinity than Mr. Aiken.

In 1960 Bishop Barth placed the Rev. Ben H. Shawhan in charge of Trinity. Mr. Shawhan, his wife, Diana, and little son came to live in Mason. A house left to the church by Mrs. Elizabeth Elcan was made suitable for occupancy. For the first time since Mr. Perry in 1917, Trinity Church had a resident priest. On January 24, 1961, Mr. Shawhan was ordained to the priesthood by Bishop Vander Horst in Trinity Church. A reception given by the people of Trinity followed at the home of Mr. and Mrs. J. N. M. Taylor in Mason. Mr. Shawhan held his last service at Trinity on August 29, 1962.

The Bishop next appointed the Rev. M. C. Nichols priest-in-charge. He held his first service on September 2, 1962. Every Sunday Mr. Nichols drove from Memphis and brought with him Eric Greenwood, Jr., to serve as organist, an office he performed most proficiently.

With his great ability as leader and organizer Mr. Nichols soon persuaded the congregation to proceed with their plans for a parish house. Some feared that a parish house would detract from the classic beauty of the old church but the building designed by Wells Awsumb, Memphis Architect, so successfully blended the new with the old that their fears were allayed.

William B. Cuningham was treasurer of the church at this time and secured donations and pledges that made the financial future of the venture secure. Mrs. James N. M. Taylor led the women of the Church in making money for the project. She organized a thrift shop and opened her home for spaghetti suppers given by the Woman's Auxiliary, for which she made her justly famous spaghetti sauce, doing all the cooking herself.

On All Saints Day, 1964, the new parish house was used for the first time and dedicated by Bishop Vander Horst. The joy of the occasion was turned to sadness when the Bishop announced he was sending Mr. Nichols somewhere else. In spite of the small number of the congregation the building was paid for in full in 1976.

On December 20, 1964, the Rev. Carter Gregory, assistant at St. John's, Memphis, held services at Trinity. He was a fine, intelligent, attractive young man and it was with great regret that the church parted with him on April 25, 1965. On May 2, 1965, the

Rev. William P. Nevils was placed in charge of the church. He was young and dedicated and served faithfully and well but remained at Trinity little more than a year. His last service was July 10, 1966.

From August 7, 1966 to May 28, 1967, the Rev. E. S. Ballentine was priest-in-charge. At this time he retired for reasons of health. During the next four months services were held by Nevill R. Seay, lay reader.

On October 1, 1967, the church joyfully welcomed back the Rev. Warwick Aiken. Mr. Aiken served until June 30, 1968 when Bishop Vander Horst placed the Rev. M. Clark Baker in charge. Mr. Baker, his wife, Lila, and their three little girls became a much loved part of the church family.

On October 4, 1970, Trinity Church celebrated the one hundredth anniversary. Bishop Sanders was the Celebrant. Officers of the Church at this time were: Nevill R. Seay, Warden, W. E. Harper, Jr., Treasurer, Members of the Council: Nevill R. Seay, J. N. M. Taylor, William B. Cuningham, Mrs. J. N. M. Taylor, Mrs. William B. Cuningham, A. E. Waddell; Priest-in-charge, M. Clark Baker.

On February 28, 1971, Mr. Baker resigned. He was replaced by the Rev. E. Dargan Butt, who was enjoying a well earned retirement in Collierville, Tennessee. Mr. Butt was a scholar of note and an authority on rural work. He served the church from March 21, 1971 to April 27, 1973, when ill health forced him to retire. He was dearly loved and it was with deep regret that the Church gave him up. On April 6, 1973, the Rev. Montague Hope replaced Mr. Butt. He was a loving and lovable Englishman who served the church from April 6, 1973 until September 22, 1974, when he returned to his native England.

At the present time the church is under the charge of the Rev. W. Joe Moore who succeeded Mr. Hope on October 7, 1974.

Mr. Moore had retired with his wife, the former Jane Allen, to his farm near Cordova, but he responded to the pleas of the Bishop and once again put his hand to the plow. Since that time he has faithfully and ably served the church, giving generously of his time, effort and means. Although the membership of the church at the present time is only fourteen active communicants, they participate fully in the program of the church. The church property is kept in excellent condition and there is an active branch of the Episcopal Church Women, composed of six members.

The members of Trinity know that this is the Lord's work and "in due time we shall reap if we faint not."

Frances Seay (Mrs. William B.) Cuningham

"The Bible contains 3,566,480 letters, 733,746 words, 31,163 verses, 1,189 chapters and 66 books. The longest chapter is the 119th Psalm; shortest, the middle chapter, the 117th Psalm. The middle verse is the 8th of the 118th Psalm. The longest name is in the 8th chapter of Isaiah. The word "and" occurs 46,227 times; the word Jehovah 6,855 times. The thirty-seventh chapter of Isaiah and the 19th chapters of the 2nd book of Kings are alike. The longest verse is the 9th of the 8th chapter of Ester; the shortest verse is the 35th of the 11th chapter of John. In the 21st verse of the 7th chapter of Ezra is the alphabet. The finest piece of reading is the 26th chapter of Acts. The name of God is not mentioned in the book of Esther. The Bible contains two testaments. The Old is Law, the New is Love. The Old is the Bud, The New is the Bloom. In the Old, man is reaching up for God. In the New, God is reaching down for man. In the Old, man is in the valley but can see the sun shining on the mountain tops. In the New he is on the mountain top basking in the sunlight of God's infinite love."

—Leaves of Gold—p. 44

All Saints', Memphis

All Saints' Church, Memphis

All Saints' Mission held its first Service on August 12, 1956, in the home of Miss Ruth Neil Murry and Miss Caroline Jenkins and moved shortly thereafter to Colonial Kindergarten. From there, the Services were moved to Memphis University School, where they were held until the church building could be used. On September 4, 1956, a Mission Organization meeting was held by Bishop Barth.

Mr. Edmund Orgill purchased 3.9 acres in behalf of Bishop Barth in 1955-1956. The congregation was begun by Bishop Barth as a "Diocesan Mission" with ten volunteer families. The congregation later reimbursed Mr. Orgill after loans were arranged.

In January 1957, the congregation began the work of clearing the lot which is the present church site at White Station and Quince. There "work parties" were to become a regular event of the congregation until after the completion of the original church structure.

Ground-breaking ceremonies for the church building were held January 13, 1957; the first Service in the building was held on Maundy Thursday (April 18); and the cornerstone was laid in the original structure on June 23, 1957, by Bishop Barth. The final completion of the building was accomplished by late summer of 1958, with the floor tile being laid and the site being fully graded.

On January 20, 1960, All Saints' Mission was accepted by the Convention of the Diocese of Tennessee and admitted as a Parish. The Reverend Robertson Eppes, Jr., Priest-in-charge of All Saints' Mission, was called to become the first Rector of the Parish.

Ground-breaking ceremonies for the Church School addition were held on March 18, 1962, and for the new church proper on December 7, 1967. Services began in the new church in August 1968. Alterations to the old church provided seven classrooms in the Nave, with the Chancel being walled off to provide a regular Chapel.

In 1980-81 all loans were paid off several years early—"Thanks be to God". The "main church" or "new church" was later connected to the buildings to its North by an attractive "covered walkway."

The congregation currently has around 279 communicants, (2/9/1983).

Mrs. Roberts (Audrey) Espenshade serves as Senior Warden.

Robertson Eppes, Jr., Rector

Bishop Otey Memorial, Memphis

Bishop Otey Memorial Mission

The organizational meeting for the current Church building was held in the Oakhaven Methodist Church in the Spring of 1961. The Rev. Joe Nichols, assistant to the Bishop, was responsible for getting the plans off the ground. The Chapel was to be located on a 10 acre wooded plot given by the Stidham family, Emrile Davis Stidham and Mary Edmundson Williams Stidham. Five acres were set aside for the relocation of The Church Home and 5 were given to the Chapel, with the stipulation that the Chapel maintain the family cemetery on the property. The 10 acres were located at the corner of Tchulahoma Road and Raines Road, East. From its organization in the Spring of 1961, the Rev. Gordon Bernard, assistant at St. John's Parish was the priest-in-charge. The Mission celebrated the first service in the new building on the Stidham property on Christmas Day, 1961. The pews were taken from St. John's Church, Memphis and were shortened to fit the new Chapel. The altar, reredos, rail, choir stalls, font and communion vessels came from the Nun's Chapel of The Church Home (formerly located on Lamar Avenue). The windows came from the Nun's Chapel at The Church Home; Chapel of the Holy Ghost and the two Tiffany windows from a tiny Chapel, St. Mary's-of-the-Woods, built under the guidance of Sister Anne, as a part of the summer camp for girls of The Church Home in Hardy, Arkansas. Over the years, the statuary that belonged in the reredos came to be restored and placed in the Otey Chapel.

Vicars of the Chapel since its founding: Gordon Bernard, John Paschall Davis, Jr., Richard Maddock, Jack Wilhite, Samuel Cross, Noble Walker.

The cornerstone from the Nun's Chapel at The Church Home when it was on Lamar is incorporated into the southwest corner of the current Chapel and is dated, June 24, 1910.

Wells Awsumb was the architect.

The initial congregation came from St. John's and people in the immediate neighborhood of the Church.

Noble R. Walker, Vicar

Calvary Church, Memphis

Calvary Church, Memphis

The first church of which the Rev. Thomas Wright served as rector was Calvary Church, Wadesboro, North Carolina, from 1821-1826. From 1826 to February 1832, he held services there five Sundays each year. The years spent by Mr. Wright at Calvary Church, Wadesboro, which he established, named and served as the first rector were evidently among the happiest of his early ministry in North Carolina. *Calvary* was the name he chose for the first church of his ministry. Ironically, he saved the name for the last church of his ministry,—Calvary, Memphis!

After having written *The Great Book, Calvary Protestant Episcopal Church, Memphis, Tennessee, 1832-1972*, covering nine hundred ninety-four pages of history, the Author finds it difficult, indeed to condense in this sketch the important facts pertinent to the Church's founding and achievement of one hundred forty years. Then to this period must be added the accomplishments of the congregation for the past ten years! It is a sincere wish that the volume—*The Great Book*—may be read and re-read, for its historical accuracy, most carefully researched—that the full history of Calvary, Memphis may be appreciated.

The *Travelogue* kept by Mr. Wright as he rode his horse from North Carolina to Memphis is not only an authentic record but it is a simple factful account of his magnificent missionary journey to and through West Tennessee. The entire diary is carried in *The Great Book*.

A small Bible, a Prayer Book and Hymnal and a minimum of garments for his personal attire comprised the contents of his saddle bags, flung across his horse. Mr. Wright's Prayer Book is one of the prized relics of Calvary Church, having been presented to the Church in 1968.

On August 3, 1832 Mr. Wright arrived in Memphis as stated in his *Travelogue:*

> "3rd at 12 o'clock in Memphis—4th August. Preached at 5 o'clock in the Accy (Academy) to a small company and twice on Sunday and again at 8 o'clock on Monday, . . ." "This morning the 6th, I was taken sick and was greatly exhausted after sermon. 3 o'clock I met the Gentlemen when a *Church was organized by the name of Calvary Church."*

It is noted that Mr. Wright gave additional information about the founding of Calvary in his report in the *Missionary Record:*

> ". . .on the 6th. After service though feverish and otherwise indisposed, I was enabled to meet a number of the friends and members of the Church, who kindly attended at Major B's where a congregation was organized under the name of the Wardens, Vestry etc., of Calvary Church.
>
> Memphis has about 1200 inhabitants, and it is thought by some persons, that it will be in a few years number many thousands."

Calvary's records have carried since 1839 a list of ten persons designated as the first ten original members of Calvary. However, the only reference found of that period 1832-1835, was the parochial report made in June 1825 by the Secretary of the Vestry of Calvary:

> "Communicants-added 2, died 1, present number 10."

It is believed there were more than ten organizing members. This statement by Dr. Arthur H. Noll gives some authority to this opinion:

> "...the parish of Calvary Church was organized that year (1832) though only ten communicants of the Church remained in Memphis in 1835."

Listed in readable manuscript, evidently the handwriting of the Rev. Philip W. Alston, February 10, 1839, are the names of ten original members of the Church:

> "Thomas B. Beatty, Va.; John Boothe, Tenn.; Eliza Brothers (Mrs. Edmund D.) Bray, N.C.; Anna H. (Mrs. James) Hart, S.C.; Elizabeth Taliaferro (Mrs. James) Rose, N.C.; Dr. Lewis Shanks, Va.; Virginia Cary (Mrs. Gray) Skipwith, Va.; Hannah (Mrs. James) Truelove, England; Sidney Gatlin (Mrs. Isaac Newton) Lamb, Va.; Samuel Rembert, S.C."

The Rev. Thomas Wright made a second visit to Memphis on September 7, and by his effort to strengthen the month old Church, Calvary. He remained in Memphis through September 13:

> "I am now in Memphis and am happy to state that there seems to be an increasing desire among our friends here to have a resident minister.
> ....The Church ... in the language of others is 'popular.' Her ministry and ordinances are highly esteemed and respected. She is no longer a stranger in the Western District..."

On December 17, 1832 Mr. Wright wrote in his *Report* to the Society:

> "I have been invited to take charge of the little flocks on the Mississippi." (Calvary, Memphis and St. Paul, Randolph). "...and to give such occasional service to LaGrange, as other duties will permit."

Mr. Wright gave the first parochial report for Calvary Church to the Convention on June 28, 1833. The Rev. George Weller reported on admissions on June 30, 1833. Calvary Church was admitted as a parish by the Diocesan Convention. In a *Report* to the Society late in 1833 Mr. Wright stated:

> "At Memphis, the prospect of my being usefully employed is as encouraging as I had reason to anticipate. The Vestry talk of building a church ...the Senior Warden has already engaged to give half of the necessary lumber."

The Sixth Convention of the Church in Tennessee was held in Columbia, April 1834. From Calvary the Lay Delegates were Edmund P. Gaines, Samuel Rembert and Augustine Smith. It is noted that Mr. Wright accompanied Bishop Otey on his visitation to the Western District in 1834. Therefore, Calvary's founder and first Rector went with the first Bishop of Tennessee on his first visitation to the Churches in the Western District!

The Rev. Thomas Wright died April 28, 1835, of cholera and lies buried in an unknown grave in Memphis. Far reaching and human had been the price,—yet Calvary Parish had been Founded!

The years from 1835-1838 in the life of Calvary was one of the most important periods in the long and distinguished history of the Church. To Bishop Otey must be accorded the praise and credit for his determined interest during those years in behalf of Calvary. The Bishop made great effort to fill the rectorship of the Church. The Rev. Mr. Waldo came and left; two Lay Readers were licensed by the Bishop—William H. Bowman and Thomas Beatty. Another effort by Bishop Otey was the preparation of Philip W. Alston for the ministry.

The history of Calvary in chronological sequence by the Rectors who served follows:

1838-1839, The Reverend George Weller, Second Rector
   A lot was bought and a two-story frame building erected.
1839-1847, The Reverend Philip W. Alston, Third Rector
   Land purchased and brick church built—consecrated by Bishop Otey, May 12, 1844. There were 115 communicants. Philip Alston died June 17, 1847.
1847-1854, The Reverend David Cook Page, Fourth Rector
   There were 74 families, 105 communicants at Calvary in 1850. A parochial school, later St. Mary's Episcopal School, was started, 1847. Grace Church, a mission organized. Dr. Page resigned December 7, 1854.
1855-1856, No Rector
1857-1858, The Reverend Charles Todd Quintard, Fifth Rector
1858-1860, The Right Reverend James H. Otey, D.D., Sixth Rector
1860-1883, The Reverend George White, D.D., Seventh Rector
   Rector Emeritus, April 1883-April 30, 1887
1884-1886, The Reverend Davis Sessums, Eighth Rector
1887-1891, The Reverend E. Spruille Burford, D.D., Ninth Rector
1891-1905, The Reverend Frederick P. Davenport, D.D., Tenth Rector
1906-1911, The Reverend James R. Winchester, D.D., Eleventh Rector
1911-1920, The Reverend Walter D. Buckner, LL.D., Twelfth Rector
1920-1939, The Reverend Charles F. Blaisdell, D.D., Thirteenth Rector
   Rector Emeritus, September 1, 1939-June 24, 1943.
1940-1948, The Reverend Theodore N. Barth, D.D., Fourteenth Rector
1/23/1949-2/13/1949, The Reverend Everett Carr, D.D., Fifteenth Rector
1949-1964, The Reverend Donald Henning, D.D., Sixteenth Rector
1964-1973, The Reverend Robert P. Atkinson, D.D., Seventeenth Rector

9/15/1973-9/25/1977, The Reverend Warren E. Haynes, Eighteenth Rector
9/1/1978   The Reverend Douglass Moxley Bailey III, Nineteenth Rector

Through the years the Women of Calvary have played a vital role in the Church's program. Mrs. Thomas (Mary Hostler Green) Wright, wife of the Founder, was the first to organize the effort of the women of Calvary—she named the group the "Working Society." A listing of the present chapters of the Women of Calvary follows: Altar Guild, Barth Chapter, Blaisdell, Mary and Martha, St. Elizabeth and St. Margaret. The Waffle Shop started by the ladies of Calvary Circle in 1928 as a Lenten feature continues as a most successful annual project. The Hester Shortridge Memorial Library with Mrs. George Bresslar and Miss Martha Turley Jack in charge serves a great need in the life of the parish. Mrs. Thomas Williams in the present president of the Women of Calvary.

Always there has been exceptional music at Calvary Church. Especial credit must be given to Dr. Adolph Steuterman who was organist-choirmaster from 1919-1975. The present organist is Dr. John Hooker who came January 1, 1976.

The many parish meals served at the Church have been highlights under the direction of able hostesses. Mrs. Mae Garner served as dietician for fifteen years and following her retirement, November 1982, Mrs. Martha Bernard Kimball took charge. Among the names of able assistants and sextons through the years are of interest: Silas Carter; Herman Fields; Roe Goodman has served for thirty-three years and Jerry Buckley since 1970.

Three giant scrapbooks are prized possessions of Calvary Church. These volumes contain the bulletins, clippings and miscellaneous important items which depict the history of the Church. In 1922, Dr. Charles F. Blaisdell motivated the keeping of the first volume which he entitled "The Great Book." In 1949 another book was started and presently another large book has been filled. The Parish Secretary who has spent hours in compiling the records has been Mrs. Joseph C. (Isabelle Ridley) Eggleston who has served the Church in this capacity since April 15, 1953; she resigned in September 1981.

The Men's Loyalty League was organized by Dr. Walter D. Buckner, Rector, on the second Tuesday in January 1920. John McCleary, Jr., served as the first president. Edward Tuggle is the present leader of Calvary's Loyalty League. The League has been since its organization a real institution and fixture in the life of the Church.

From Calvary have gone the following who became Bishops: Charles Todd Quintard, Davis Sessums, William Thomas Manning, James Ridout Winchester, Theodore Nott Barth, W. Fred Gates, Jr., and Robert P. Atkinson.

The present Senior Warden of Calvary is William Lawson.

The present communicants number 1,753.

Thus far in this account no mention has been made of the beauty of the windows in Calvary Church. *The Great Book* carries full-page illustrations of all the windows in the beautiful colors depicted in the exquisite stained glass. Also, there is a history of each window in terms of its significance, a number of which are memorials.

Significant indeed is the fact that Saint Mary's Episcopal School for Girls was founded as a Parochial School at Calvary Church by Mary Elizabeth Foote (Mrs. LeRoy) Pope in 1847, Dr. David Cooke Page was Rector of Calvary. Quite a complete history of the school's founding and progress through 1972 is carried in the volume.

Interestingly *The Great Book* also carries recipes for the many delicious foods prepared and served by the Women of Calvary annually during Lent in the Waffle Shop.

The 150th Anniversary of Calvary was celebrated at the Church on August 6 and 8, 1982. A chorale evensong and a barbecue banquet comprised the festivities on the 6th. The Rev. Douglass M. Bailey, Rector, delivered the meditation. The Presiding Bishop John M. Allin, Bishop William E. Sanders and Bishop W. Fred Gates, Jr., were present for the Festival Eucharist on Sunday, August 8.

Missions sponsored by Calvary have been: Grace Church 1850; St. Mary's 1858; St. Luke 1892; Holy Communion 1938; St. Paul 1959; St. Anne, Millington, before 1964. The Grand-daughters of Calvary are: St. Elisabeth, sponsored by St. Mary's Cathedral, 1960 and Holy Apostles, sponsored by the Church of the Holy Communion, 1967.

This sketch of history about the founding and life of Calvary Church is concluded with the inscription on the marker placed by the Memphis Sesquicentennial Commission to Calvary and dedicated on May 24, 1969:

> "*Calvary Protestant Episcopal Church*
> 'The oldest public building in Memphis and the first Episcopal Church in Shelby County.
> Organized August 6, 1832 by the Reverend Thomas Wright.
> The church-house started 1838, was consecrated May 12, 1844 by the Rt. Reverend James Hervey Otey, first Bishop of Tennessee, the Reverend Philip W. Alston, Rector.
> The Reverend Robert P. Atkinson, Rector, 1969'."

By the Author

Christ Church, Memphis

Christ Church, (Whitehaven) Memphis

In 1947, interested Episcopalians in Whitehaven, a suburb of Memphis, Tennessee, gathered at the Community Center of Whitehaven High School, to petition Bishop Edmund P. Dandridge and the Bishop and Council to establish a mission church. The date of this organizational meeting was May 25, 1947; the Bishop and Council authorized the establishment of the mission church on June 10, 1947. Services were held in the Community Center under the sponsorship of Grace-St. Luke's, Memphis until such time as the sanctuary could be built. Ground for the first sanctuary with basement for church school and various nonworship meetings to use was broken on November 11, 1948, and Grace-St Luke's was the sponsoring parish. The first service held in the newly built sanctuary fell on the first Sunday after Easter 1949 (April 23); Bishop Theodore N. Barth consecrated the sanctuary on the second Sunday after Easter 1949 (April 30). The Reverend Mr. George Bladgett Stuart Hale, rector of Grace-St. Luke's, along with his sons (both assistant priests at Grace-St. Luke's) George and Edmund, Thomas Maitland, Thomas Hopper, and Clifton Kelly, lay readers, served as celebrants at services until the arrival of the first assigned mission priest, the Reverend Mr. Richard Kirkhoffer (1951-56).

Largely through the efforts and generosity of Robert E. Palmer and his family who gave the lot at the corner of Palmer Road and Highway 51 South (now known as Elvis Presley Boulevard) in memory of Mrs. Hestyr Shortridge Palmer, mother of Robert, John, and Marvin, the first sanctuary with basement was built. In a relatively short time, space was needed for the ever growing mission; therefore with the generous gifts from the communicants and the assistance from the Diocese a Parish Hall was built on property at the rear and adjoining the original lot. With the arrival of the Reverend Mr. Kirkhoffer and his family, a rectory was needed; and one was acquired on Raines Road. In the midst of the growth of the mission, the Reverend Mr. Kirkhoffer received a call to serve a mission church in Hawaii; and early in 1956 he left Christ Church with its blessings.

Upon elevation to parish status in 1956 and because of the rapid growth in communicants and finances, the Reverend Mr. George David Jones was called as first parish priest (1956-60). The Reverend Mr. Jones was ordained priest at a special service on Christmas Eve 1956 by Bishop Barth so that he might celebrate the Christmas Mass as priest rather than deacon. A new rectory nearer the church was purchased on Craigwood for the rector and his young family. This rector's concern was how he might secure for the parish adequate housing so that congregation might not feel separated because of multiple services on Sundays. With this concern in mind, he appointed a Building Committee consisting of William C. Abbett, Chairman; William M. McGill; William E. Gay, Jr.; Mrs. Robert E. Palmer; Mrs. James E. Alexander; Thomas E. Mitchell, Jr.; Robert E. Andrews; and the Reverend Dr. Donald Henning, consultant on matters liturgical. In addition to the building project, the Reverend Mr. Jones was much involved in the youth programs in the parish and in the whole Diocese of Tennessee; this concern brought him a call to the Youth Department of the National Church in New York. He accepted the call and left Christ Church in the Spring of 1960.

The Vestry called the Reverend Mr. Francis W. Kephart to Christ Church as rector in May of 1960, and he remained until 1968. During the tenure of the Reverend Mr. Kephart, he saw the manifestation of a new sanctuary and greater increase of communicants as well as the beginnings of a decline in communicants. Christ Church became caught up in the turmoils of the sixties and lost the Reverend Mr. Kephart as its rector and spiritual director. With space still needed, the rector requested that the rectory be sold and that he be given a living allowance with which he could purchase a house. With the approval of the Bishop and the Vestry, the rectory was sold and the money derived from the sale of the rectory was used to build an annex to the Great Church to be used for church school classes and choir practice. During the tenure of the Reverend Mr. Kephart, Bishop Vander Horst assigned the Reverend Mr. M. Clark Baker as assistant priest to the parish.

With the departure of the Reverend Mr. Kephart, the Reverend Mr. Baker served as rector until the Vestry called the Reverend Mr. Richard L. Clark (1968-1972) as rector. The Reverend Mr. Clark received a call as rector of St. George's, Clarksdale, Mississippi and left Christ Church.

In 1972, the Vestry called the Reverend Mr. John C. Hight to be rector of Christ Church. During his tenure (1972-79), the indebtedness of the Great Church was paid off, and the burning of the note was duly celebrated. At the behest of the Reverend Mr. Hight, the parish purchased a spacious and newly built rectory for his occupancy. Upon being called by the Vestry of St. Barnabas, Tullahoma, Tennessee, the Reverend Mr. Hight left.

In November, 1979, at the call of the Vestry of Christ Church, the Reverend Mr. Curtis T. Allen came to serve as rector. With the preference of the rector in mind, the Vestry sold the rectory and granted him a living allowance which provided him the opportunity of purchasing his own housing. The profit realized from the sale of the rectory was put in a money account with very rigid and strict governance of such.

William C. Abbett

Bible Be's

"Be ye therefore perfect." Matthew 5:48.
"Be ye holy in all manner of conversation; . . .
    be ye holy; for I am holy." I Peter 1:15, 16.
"Be patient." James 5:7
"Be at peace." Job 22:21.
"Be of good cheer; it is I; be not afraid." Matthew 14:27.
"Be diligent that ye may be found of him in peace,
    without spot, and blameless." 2 Peter 3:14.
"Be subject one to another." I Peter 5:5.
"Be clothed with humility." I Peter 5:5.
"Be sober, be vigilant." I Peter 5:8.
"Be ye kind one to another, tenderhearted, forgiving
    one another." Ephesians 4:32.
"Be strong and of a good courage." Joshua 1:6

Emmanuel Church, Memphis

Emmanuel Church, Memphis

Emmanuel Episcopal Church is located at 604 St. Paul at Cynthia Place, Memphis. No firm date of organization is of record, however, the movement to create the church started in the 1860's to culminate in the progress of 1874.

On November 23, 1975 a great Centennial Celebration took place. The account of this historic occasion in the life of this venerable Church was well recorded in a program especially printed for the event. Much of the material has been shared in this account.

Emmanuel Episcopal Church 1875-1975, one hundred years ago a divine commission was accepted:

"It is historic that dreams are dreamed and visions seen. In that same sense, so did Emmanuel Episcopal Church have its source in the persistent and enthusiastic dreams of five Negro men who envisioned an Episcopal church in Memphis for Negroes. These five men, Vernon Chalmers, W. B. Miller, John Pollard, Thomas Williamson, and Isaiah Pickett, discussed their hopes with the Right Reverend Charles Todd Quintard, then Bishop of Tennessee. Bishop Quintard later told these men to form a committee whose purpose would be the organization of the church. As a result, meetings were held in the homes of the committee members.

'In 1874, the new church was on its way. With permission of the Bishop, the first service was held on Whitsunday at Zion Hall. Located on Beale Street, Zion Hall has been known as a community establishment frequently used by various religious groups. During this embryonic period, Bishop Quintard was untiring in his efforts to establish a strong well-grounded church. His faith in the fledgling mission could be seen in his recordings in the Journal of Proceedings. On several occasions following his visits there, he wrote, ". . .the mission is very promising." "The services were admirably rendered, the responses hearty, and the singing excellent."

'In 1875, the Reverend George J. Jackson, an ordained deacon, was given charge of the congregation which continued to hold services at Zion Hall. The first class was confirmed by Bishop Quintard in Calvary Episcopal Church that same year.

'It was the Rev. Jackson who accompanied the delegation to the 1875 Diocesan Convention at which time Emmanuel Church was admitted into union with the Convention. This union was truly the birth of Emmanuel as an Organized Mission of the Diocese.

'The Rev. Jackson served until 1876. He was succeeded by the Reverend James B. McConnell, an East Indian, who was appointed by the Bishop. Mr. McConnell, also a deacon, served one year, 1877, and again from 1879 to 1881. The Reverend Charles C. Parsons was in charge of the church during the interim year, 1878.

'The Reverend Isaac Edgar Black was the first priest appointed to serve Emmanuel. Because of the growing number of communicants, the need for a resident priest had become most pressing.

'It was difficult to maintain a parish program of activities at Zion Hall and many meetings were held in the homes of the parishioners. During the tenure of Father Black, the first efforts to secure a church building were made. By 1883, Emmanuel had a church building of its own. This building, located on the east side of North Third Street between Jefferson and Court Avenues, was formerly a Lutheran Church.

'Bishop Quintard negotiated the purchase with a large cash down payment. The Diocese, Calvary Episcopal Church (with a monthly contribution of five dollars), and other interested friends aided Emmanuel to quickly liquidate the debt.

'Although the church was quite some distance from where most of the communicants lived, attendance at services and the program of activities increased immeasurably. One of the activities of Emmanuel in those early years was the organization of a parochial school. Children of the communicants of the church attended, as did many other children of the community. A branch of the Women's Auxiliary and a chapter of the Brotherhood of St. Andrew were among organizations initiated.

'After Father Black left Emmanuel in 1884, the church was without a resident priest for several years. The Bishop, however, appointed some of the local clergy in charge, on, perhaps, a temporary basis. It is reported that at the close of the century Emmanuel had one hundred twenty-seven communicants. Progress was indeed steady.

'Only scant information is available on the priests who served Emmanuel from 1885 through 1906. These men were: The Reverends William Klein, A. B. Anderson (a deacon assistant to Mr. Klein), William H. Wilson, Henry B. Sargent, George H. Fenwick, George W. Honesty, Joseph L. Berne, T. E. Tucker, and Maximo F. Duty. It was noted that Mr. Klein, Dean of St. Mary's Cathedral, expended a great deal of time and effort trying to revitalize and keep the sometimes faltering Emmanuel alive. Bishop Quintard was quoted as having commented, "Dr. Honesty renewed interest in Emmanuel, beautified its services, had an impressive vested choir."

'Early in the new century, members of the congregation began talking of a different location for the church, preferably in a Negro residential area. Such a move would put the church in a setting more accessible to the communicants and provide a better climate for growth. Two factors gave impetus to the move: (1) the Italian populace residing near by caused some unrest, and (2) the building was delapidated and fast becoming uninhabitable.

'It was at this stage, in 1907, that the then Reverend E. Thomas Demby became priest-in-charge. A committee, appointed to seek a new site under the guidance of the Right Reverend Thomas Gailor, third Bishop of Tennessee, selected property on the corner of St. Paul Avenue and Cynthia Place. Bishop Gailor negotiated the sale of the Third Street property for twelve thousand dollars and aided the members of Emmanuel to purchase the vacant lot for five thousand dollars. Construction, which began on the new church in 1909, was completed, and the building was consecrated by Bishop Gailor on March 25, 1910.

'The new building, a beautiful cruciform, brick structure, and a temporary frame parish hall, built in 1913, provided Father Demby the necessary equipment to institute a varied long-range program. Emmanuel moved steadily forward under Father Demby's leadership. The number of baptisms and confirmations increased rapidly. Emmanuel had indeed reached an unbelievable peak. The church soon became one of the largest and most outstanding missions among Negroes in the Diocese.

'In 1914, Rev. Demby was made Archdeacon and given charge of the Colored Protestant Episcopal Churches in Tennessee. Later, he was elected Suffragan Bishop for Negro Churches in the Diocese of Arkansas and the Province of the Southwest. The election and consecration of Bishop Demby on September 15, 1918, at All Saints Church, St. Louis, Missouri, gave Emmanuel the unique distinction of being one of the few Negro churches in the United States giving one of its men to the American Episcopate.

'Between the years 1915 and 1928, several priests served Emmanuel. In succession they were: The Reverends Joseph Wilberforce Livingston, Frederick A. Garrett, James Aladubi Johnson and Bernard Godfrey Whitlock. Father Johnson, a native of West Africa, endeared himself to the citizens of Memphis and Emmanuel's immediate community. He was especially remembered for his work with the young people. Under the leadership of the

Rev. Whitlock, a new Reuter organ was purchased. During these years, Emmanuel had its ups and downs, but the communicant strength remained constant. Not many new members were added.

'With the appointment of the Reverend Elmer Morton M. Wright as priest-in-charge in 1929, Emmanuel again began to move forward. He had come to Memphis at the request of Bishop Gailor who knew of his outstanding ministry elsewhere. Under Father Wright's most capable leadership, the church grew numerically more rapidly than during any other similiar period. Father Wright gave six dedicated years of ministry of Emmanuel.

'Four priests, the Reverends Charles S. Sedgewick, Julian F. Dozier, George A. Stams and Vernon W. Lane (who was also priest of The Church of the Good Shepherd), served Emmanuel for relatively short terms between 1935 and 1939. More is known about the Rev. Stams. Each member of his family was a staunch communicant and he had even served as an alcolyte when he was a young lad.

'The Reverend Morris Bartlett Cochran, appointed priest-in-charge in 1939, had received Holy Orders at Emmanuel. Prior to his ordination, he had served as deacon-in-training under the Rev. Lane. Father Cochran, described as dedicated and active in the growth of the church, remained at Emmanuel until 1943, when he transferred to the Diocese of Florida.

'The Reverend St. Julian A. Simpkins assumed duties of priest-in-charge of Emmanuel shortly after his discharge from the United States Army on March 1, 1944. A campaign launched in 1944 to reclaim some of the thirty-odd members proved quite successful as twenty-two persons returned to the church.

'The church facilities needed improvement and, thus a church-wide rally was proposed to raise one thousand dollars to repair and redecorate the church and the parish hall. A group of men at Calvary Parish, headed by Mr. Edmund Orgill, heard of the church's efforts and matched, dollar for dollar, the thousand dollars. Incredibly, Emmanuel raised the stated amount. On completion of the work, however, the bill came to two thousand five hundred dollars. The men of Calvary graciously assumed the additional five hundred dollar debt and saved the day for Emmanuel. There was also a new rectory built with the Bishop and Council advancing five thousand dollars. The church agreed to assume forty percent of the cost. The resultant modern brick rectory gave Emmanuel, not only a beautiful plant physically, but unquestionably raised the morale of the communicants and helped launch programs in which people of the community participated.

'For the next ten years under Father Simpkins' guidance, there was more involvement of the total membership than ever before in the history of the church. The programs of the Women's Auxiliary and the Altar Guild were revamped to be more inclusive. A Men's Club was organized and served to inspire greater responsibility in laity ministry. The establishment of the Youth Center provided leisure time activities for the children of the church and of the community. Several women of Emmanuel gave of their talents to that effort. Sunday School and Vacation Bible School provided channels for religious training for the young people. The Department of Christian Education of the Diocese selected Emmanuel for a demonstration program in religious education and related activities. A director was secured who continued in the program for two years. During this period, a community kindergarten was instituted.

'In 1954, structural change again became necessary. The Memphis Housing Authority had purchased and demolished all the houses surrounding Emmanuel in order to develop low income housing units. The question about Emmanuel remaining in the area became an issue because the church building did not conform to the developer's plan. The building was considered too old and outdated, architecturally. Lengthy discussions ensued and the National Church entered into the decision making. The National Church decided that the church should rebuild in the same location because Emmanuel would then have the greatest opportunity of any Episcopal church to assert itself in the spreading of God's Kingdom. Enormous growth was anticipated. If the church accepted the challenge, the National Church agreed to advance one-half of the estimated cost of ninety thousand dollars. Local Episcopal churches made pledges, the Diocese gave, and Emmanuel members agreed to give twenty thousand dollars. The completed cost was one hundred twenty thousand dollars. During the construction period, church services were conducted in a meeting room in the housing project. On completion, the new church was dedicated May 1956 by Bishop Theodore N. Barth. An English Gothic, brick structure, the new building was said to be one of the most liturgically correct churches in the Diocese. It faced, as we can see even now, in the right direction—east. The appointments, including altar and transepts were correct in design.

'After Father Simpkins moved from Emmanuel to Cincinnati, Ohio in 1957, Emmanuel maintained its activities and growth patterns, and when the Reverend Samuel D. Rudder assumed priest-in-charge responsibilities in 1958, he brought new dimensions. He was, indeed, a student of theology and Church history. He demonstrated sensitivity to the needs of individuals and the community as a whole; his help and advice were sought trustingly. Two young men served as assistants, the Rev. Robert F. Hunter from 1959 to 1960, and the Rev. Cecil Marshall, a deacon-in-training, from 1962 to 1964. Both men were ordained into the priesthood during their tenures. Father Rudder remained with Emmanuel until 1963.

'Father Marshall continued at the church after Father Rudder left and showed great leadership ability with the youth of the community. The Sunday School enrollment increased. In addition to his church duties, Father Marshall organized several social and athletic groups among both boys and girls of the community.

'Emmanuel had now attained one of its long dreamed goals: to have a priest-in-charge for pastoral duties and an assistant for outreach into the community. Housing for the next priest-in-charge was necessary, thus, another rectory was acquired in 1964 at a cost of thirteen thousand five hundred dollars. The Diocese advanced the money with repayment to be made monthly.

'This was the setting that the Reverend Jarrette C. Atkins entered when he came to Emmanuel as priest-in-charge in 1964. In the meantime, Father Marshall decided to leave. It should be remembered that most of Emmanuel's well-established programs were being continued. Several months after Father Atkins' arrival, some monies from the Diocese were withdrawn and the programs were curtailed. Although direct sponsorship of programs and activities proved impractical, the church facilities were made available for use by outside agencies. Head Start conducted the kindergarten. Nutrition and sewing classes, Scout troops, and similar groups meeting in the parish all gave impetus to the church's out-reach program. An outgrowth of the Wednesday evening Lenten devotions, the Home Communion enhanced the spiritual life of the communicants. Father Atkins started these services, which were held weekly in members' homes. This service continued for several years.

'Another of Father Atkins' unique contributions was his interest in the music. He insisted that hymns be selected and sung according to the church's liturgical seasons. Often for festival occasions, Father Atkins decorated the church himself. Many times he obtained the materials, particularly the palms for Palm Sunday, he wanted used. These touches certainly added to the worship services and were gloriously enjoyed by all. Father Atkins instituted a drive to raise money to install air-conditioning for the church plant. This project was completed in 1971, after Father Atkins left Emmanuel in 1970.

'In 1971, the Reverend M. Clark Baker assumed duties as part-time priest-in-charge by appointment of Bishop William Sanders. In the past few years, the church has been renovated at a cost of seven thousand dollars, and the next-door rectory has been rehabilitated at a cost of three thousand five hundred dollars. Both rectories are now rented and the income applied to the loan. Lay leaders have taken on a greater share of responsibility for the work of the church. A young man is being sponsored by Emmanuel as a candidate for Holy Orders. He is now in his first year of theological training. Emmanuel is again proud to give one of its sons to the priesthood. Father Baker had diligently and prayerfully sought to hold the church together. His main thrust has been to keep the people of Emmanuel headed toward their goal—to eventually obtain parish status."

At the Centennial Banquet held on November 21, 1975, Dr. James S. Barber was master of ceremonies; the invocation was given by the Rev. M. Clark Baker, Priest-in-Charge; remarks were made by the Rt. Rev. W. Fred Gates and by Blair T. Hunt. Addresses were given by Miss Roberta Church and the Rev. Canon St. Julian A. Simpkins.

The Rt. Rev. William E. Sanders preached the sermon at the anniversary services on November 23, 1975. Thus Emmanuel, Memphis ended its first century!

In 1898 there were, one hundred twenty seven communicants and in 1983 there are two hundred and one. Special annual events are the Mother's Day Fashion Show and the Father's Day Laymen's Sunday.

The Rev. Emery Washington has been rector of Emmanuel since 1976.

Kathryn Thornton (and the Author)

Church of the Good Shepherd, Memphis

Church Of The Good Shepherd, Memphis

The records of the formation of the Mission of the Good Shepherd in Chelsea are far from complete. The only official record is the Parochial Report of the Rev. James Junius Vaulx in 1866 to the Convention of the Mission Church which he had founded in Chelsea Community. The report is set out in full below:

> "Last autumn I began a mission in Chelsea. Mrs. Wood offered her house for me to hold services in. I began with Sunday School of four or five pupils. At first I held services but once every Lord's Day, having an attendance of about one-half dozen. In a short time with the assistance of certain devout church folks in Memphis we hired two small rooms where we have been holding services ever since, both morning and evening. To a large extent my labors have been among the strayed sheep of the fold. Many of these English people who have neglected the church since coming to this country or who have been repelled from the church by the actions of her ministers and members. Our congregation has constantly increased. We have purchased two lots for a school house, rectory, and other church buildings. The school house is now being built. Our Heavenly Father has wonderfully blessed our labor of faith and love."

The two lots which the Rev. Mr. Vaulx referred to in his report were conveyed to the Protestant Episcopal Church of the Diocese of Tennessee on February 1, 1866 for $3,750.00, $1,250.00 having been paid in cash and two notes of $1,250.00 executed for the balance. Default in payment resulted in a Trustee's Sale of this property on October 23, 1868 to John B. Leach who subsequently reconveyed it to the Church. Title was retained by the church until its sale in 1943. The Rev. James Junius Vaulx, a native of Jackson, Tennessee, had been ordained a deacon in 1860 and elevated to the priesthood in 1862. Establishing this mission in Chelsea Community was a major undertaking at this time. The sad condition of the whole Diocese of Tennessee would require a great volume of material which is encompassed in this study. The Rev. Mr. Vaulx remained as Priest-in-Charge of the Mission of the Good Shepherd until 1871. Statistics of the Church of the Good Shepherd for the period of 1866 through 1872 were: 138 Baptisms; 60 Confirmations; 4 Marriages; 27 Burials; and a total $8.80 for average weekly offering.

One of the most ambitious undertakings of the associate Mission of the Church of the Good Shepherd was the foundation of the Refuge of the Good Shepherd. The location of this mission was, first, near Gayoso Bayou and later, in part of the Old City Hospital at Front (Shelby) and Exchange Streets. This mission was a manifestation of the "social gospel" which had not yet become generally accepted. This was an endeavor which was to catch on and be worked much later by the Salvation Army, Hull House in Chicago, and other social settlement works.

The Refuge served immigrants to Memphis who were increasing in 1869. Many transients came to Memphis and the Rev. Mr. Vaulx found that a large number were sleeping around the retorts of the Memphis Gas Works. With Bishop Quintard's blessings he established the Refuge of the Good Shepherd on Main Street in an abandoned house boat, opening it on Ash Wednesday, February 8, 1869, approximately twenty years before the establishment of the Hull House in Chicago in 1889 by Jane Adams and Ellen G. Starr.

At the Episcopal Diocesan Convention held May 24, 1869, the Rev. Mr. Vaulx, in his parochial report, included a report of the Refuge as well as the Canfield Orphan Asylum and made a plea for assistance from the Diocese which was affirmed by the Bishop.

The Refuge of the Good Shepherd closed without funds or a home on April 27, 1870. The Journal of the Convention made no further reference to the Refuge subsequent to the parochial report on May 1870.

The cornerstone of a new church was laid August 24, 1869, and a day school with 32 pupils announced. In the Bishop's Journal an entry dated May 11, 1870, indicated that he visited "St. Savior's Mission Chapel" some eight miles east of Memphis under the supervision of the Rev. J. J. Vaulx. He also referred to "25 or 30 acres of land which had been presented to the church at this place for the benefit of the Mission of the Good Shepherd."

St. Andrew's was the fourth project of the Associate Mission of the Good Shepherd with Mr. Edwin Wickens, Lay Reader, in charge and Miss Worthington as teacher.

Following the tenure of the Rev. Mr. Vaulx at Good Shepherd the Rev. Charles Carrol Parsons served as Priest-in-Charge until July of 1872. The Rev. Mr. Parsons, a West Point graduate, served with distinction in the United States 4th Artillery during the Civil War, untimately attaining the rank of Lieutenant Colonel. He returned to his alma mater, West Point, and was an instructor there in 1868 when he determined to undertake the study of theology. He was ordained Deacon in 1870 and elevated to the priesthood in 1871. During his ministry at the Mission of the Good Shepherd the communicants submitted "Articles of Association of the Church of the Good Shepherd" to the Diocese of Tennessee and they were accepted with Good Shepherd being elevated to the status of a parish.

The Parish of the Good Shepherd Chelsea, was organized Easter Monday, April 1, 1872.

In August of 1872, the Rev. P. S. Ruth came to the parish and served through the yellow fever epidemic of 1873, resigning August 19, 1874. The Rev. T. C. Tupper became rector in September, 1874 and tendered his resignation on May 12, 1875. The Rev. Virginus O. Gee was rector from October 1, 1875 until September 30, 1878. On January 14, 1879, it seemed that the Bishop had suggested the Church of the Good Shepherd consider merely joining the St. Mary's Parish. In assessing the condition of the Memphis locality at that time it would seem that this might very well have been the only solution. However, it appeared that the people of this parish did employ another clergyman, the Rev. A. J. Yeater and managed in some way to carry on for another year, with the Rev. Mr. Yeater leaving sometime during early 1880. The Rev. George Moore was then rector from May 2, 1880 until Easter, 1881.

A well written history of the Church of the Good Shepherd is contained in the Canonical Register of the Church which deals with the period to the rectorship of the Rev. Arthur Howard Noll and which appears to have been written in the Rev. Dr. Noll's handwriting. It is not signed; however, Dr. Noll was a historian and published a history of the Diocese of Tennessee, which is referred to in other sections of this present history of the Church of the Good Shepherd.

The following is an excerpt from Dr. Noll's history:

> "In 1881 the parish was placed in charge of St. Mary's Cathedral under Father Klein until 1883; the Rev. H. A. Grantham having the services for that year, Father Klein himself having occasional services as his duties permitted.
> The Rev. J. A. Juny was rector from November 11, 1883 to 1885. The Rev. R. C. Young was rector from January 1885 to 1887. He had a great influence over the boys and young men of the parish and was greatly loved by them. In March, 1886, the Rev. Henry Dunlap came but his health failing him, he left for California in 1887. The Rev. George L. Neide, Jr., was placed in charge of the parish by the Rev. E. Spruille Burford, rector of Calvary Church April 1888."

The Rev. H. M. Dumbell succeeded the Rev. Mr. Neide, February 12, 1891. He resigned in April, 1893 to become Dean of St. Mary's Cathedral. The Rev. S. B. McGlohon held his first service as rector in 1893. It was during his rectorship that Bishop Gailor gave the Mass Lights to the parish, placing them on the Altar himself. They had been given to the Bishop and were memorials to

Bishop Hopkins, the first Bishop of Vermont, who consecrated Bishop Quintard in Christ Church, Philadelphia, at the General Convention in 1865. The Rev. Mr. McGlohon resigned in early fall of 1897.

The Rev. J. P. McCullough came to the parish in November, 1897. During Mr. McCullough's rectorship the old church was torn down and the present building erected, using the old lumber from the building. The ceremonies for the laying of the cornerstone for the new church were held by Bishop Gailor May 1, 1898, the Bishop making an address. During the summer services were held in a small Presbyterian Church several blocks nearer Chelsea on Fourth Street. The church was completed in the late summer and the first service held August 21, 1898. The Rev. Mr. McCullough resigned March, 1899.

The Rev. J. M. Northrop came the Sunday after Easter, April 9, 1899, leaving August, 1900. He organized the vested choir immediately with wonderful success, having about twenty-five members, most of which were boys. On September 30, 1900, the Rev. Thomas D. Windiate, Deacon, came to fill the vacancy left by the Rev. Mr. Northrop. He was ordained to the priesthood in St. Mary's Cathedral November 11, 1900 and became rector of the parish. In the summer of 1902 the Parish house was built with the assistance of the Bishop, Rector, various guilds, and friends.

On October 1, 1905, the church was declared free of debt and on Sunday, November 12th the same year, the building was consecrated by the Bishop Thomas F. Gailor, assisted by the Rev. James J. Vaulx, the founder of the parish, the Rev. Peter Wagner and the Rev. Thomas D. Windiate, who was rector at the time. Mr. Windiate resigned 1907. The Rev. R. W. Rhames became rector in 1907 leaving in 1911.

The Rev. G. L. Neide was again rector from 1912 until 1919. Dr. Arthur Howard Noll came in 1919, remaining ten years, the longest term of any previous rector. He resigned from active service September 1929. The Rev. Hiram K. Douglass came to Good Shepherd serving from 1930 until 1937. The Rev. Vernon W. Lane served from 1937 until 1940.

The Rev. Guy S. Usher came to Good Shepherd following Mr. Lane's rectorship in 1941. Father Usher was rector in 1943 at the time the old church at Fourth and Mill was sold. The residents had in great part moved from the homes near the Mill Street location, and the church was relocated at 1971 Jackson Avenue, a site which the Diocese of Tennessee had acquired on May 18, 1942. The cornerstone of the present church was laid in 1945.

Subsequent to the Rev. Mr. Usher's departure in 1951, the Rev. Charles Hamilton served for a short while as locum tenens from 1952 to 1954, after which there was a period when temporary supply priests filled in until 1955.

With the Rev. Homer C. Carrier's efforts through the years, membership expanded rapidly. The number of commuicants for 1964 was 426.

The Church was air conditioned in 1956, and with its encouraging growth came the need for expansion. In 1956 a new rectory was purchased at 2108 Hallwood Drive. The former rectory next to the church was converted, thus providing a parish hall, more Sunday School rooms, and a large kitchen.

Then in December, 1961, Carrier Hall, a new $30,000.00 Parish Hall, was completed and dedicated.

From its humble, but vigorous beginning Good Shepherd suffered a number of setbacks. It reverted to mission status following the yellow fever epidemic, but recovered itself substantially at the turn of the century and held that position for approximately eighteen years. It then fell into a gradual decline that reached its lowest ebb just prior to the time Father Carrier was called as its rector. Under his dynamic leadership, it recovered and progressed to a position far beyond the hopes of the Rev. James J. Vaulx, its energetic founder of one hundred years ago.

This sketch was taken from a pamphlet written by Edward Hoskins on the one hundredth anniversary of the Church of the Good Shepherd—1865-1965.

The Church of the Good Shepherd was served by the following: the Rev. David H. Plummer July 1972-July 1974; Canon George A. Fox served as interim preacher until the Rev. Charles H. Sykes came in October 1975 and remained until July 1982; the Rev. Robert D. Martin served as interim priest from June 1982 until July 1983 when the Rev. D. Barrington Baltus, present Rector, was called.

The Senior Warden is Donald E. Pearson. Mrs. Elliott L. (Margaret) Johnson is president of The Women of the Church. Mrs. Joanne (Robert D.) Martin serves as Organist. Mrs. Bernice P. Odom has served as church secretary since November 1981.

The Church of the Good Shepherd purchased a ten acre tract on Whitten Road in Shelby County, Tennessee. The rectory was relocated in 1976 to 5375 Wilton Avenue, Memphis, Tennessee 38119. A new Rodgers organ was purchased in 1979.

There are 132 communicants as of August 1983.

Information by Donald E. Pearson, Senior Warden

Grace-St. Luke's, Memphis

Grace St. Luke's Church, Memphis

The merger of the two historic churches, Grace and St. Luke's, in Memphis on November 28, 1940, was a most significant event in local Episcopal church annals.

In 1980 the Rector, Wardens and Vestry of Grace-St. Luke published a splendid history written by Martha Wharton Jones entitled, "The Story of Grace-St. Luke's Church"; Part One, Grace Church, 1852-1940.

Grace Church was started in 1850 as a mission of Calvary Church, reorganized in 1856, admitted to the Diocese in 1858 and had built the first church house in 1867. In 1850, the Rev. George Weller held services, followed by the Rev. David Page. Bishop Otey held the first service in Hightower Hall in 1852.

On March 28, 1853, Articles of Association were adopted, warden and vestrymen were elected. The Rev. George Schetky became rector on July 10, 1853 and served until 1859. Services had been moved from Hightower Hall to the second story of Hunt's China Shop on Main Street. The Rev. John Ambrose Wheelock was rector of Grace Church, 1865-1867.

Prior to 1891 Dr. E. Spruille Burford, Rector, Calvary Church held services on Idlewild. Later Bishop Gailor and Dr. F. P. Davenport, of Calvary, chose the original site for St. Luke at the corner of Idlewild and Union. St. Luke started in 1894, admitted to the Diocese in 1898. Bishop Gailor appointed a provisional vestry consisting of C. A. DeSaussure, Dr. T. R. Watkins, G. W. Reiter, A. B. Carter, W. S. Jett, A. J. Nolty, Sid Wheeler, J. J. Freeman, George T. Brodnax and J. C. French.

The first church was started in 1895 and consecrated on February 22, 1903. The first rector was the Rev. C. C. Crisman, 1897-1898, succeeded by the Rev. E. Baget Jones, March 1, 1898.

Rectors who have served Grace-St. Luke's since the merger have been: Dr. William G. Gehri, 1940-1946; Dr. Charles Hale, 1946-1955; the Rev. Malcolm Richard MacDonald, June 1, 1956-November 1, 1961; and the Rev. C. Brinkley Morton, 1962-1974, the Rev. William B. Trimble, Jr., since March, 1975.

The 1982 Church Directory carries the following: John Paul Jones, Jr., and Edward T. McNabb, Jr., Associate Rectors; Dr. James Pope McKnight and Anne S. Carriere, Assistants to the Rector. Dr. Sam Batt Owens as Director of Music. Edward E. Gamble as Headmaster of Grace-St. Luke School. Dr. H. David Hickey serves as the present Senior Warden. The president of the Women of Grace-St. Luke is Mrs. Martha M. Allen.

The present congregation consists of 1,708 communicants, adults and children.

Church of the Holy Apostles, Memphis

The Church Of The Holy Apostles, Memphis

Holy Apostles was a parochial mission of the Church of The Holy Communion. It is difficult to establish a precise date for the beginning of the Mission since it started as a group of interested persons gathering in homes in the Fox Meadows area. Holy Apostles as a community of faith "happened" more than it began. It is possible, however, to establish certain dates. The first Service in the Register is June 18, 1967, the Rev. Eric Greenwood officiated in the Evans School. The Record of Services is incomplete until December 10, 1967, though services were led by Messrs. Greenwood, Thomas, Lancaster, Hill and Behn and Lay Reader Hughes. Another way of dating the start of the Mission is through its petition to the Diocese of Tennessee and the filing of a Constitution and Bylaws for the congregation in January 1968. Still another way of dating the nativity of the Mission would be the purchase of the property at Hickory Hill and Knight Arnold Road. The date of this purchase is not clear, though there is a survey of the property dated, January 6, 1965.

The first Priest assigned to the Mission was the Rev. Bruce Green, who arrived November 15, 1968. The Rev. John Rice became the second Vicar in February 1971, and served through the building project ending his tenure in June 1975. The Rev. Allan Mustard served as the third Vicar from January 1976 through June 1979. The present Priest, the Rev. Bob Allen, came as the fourth Vicar on All Saints Sunday 1979, and was elected the first Rector following admission by the Diocese in January 1981. The Rev. Mr. Allen then called the Rev. Charles Galbraith to be his part-time non-stipendary Curate on February 1, 1981.

As is the case with many missions 'aborning', Holy Apostles has had its ups and downs. However, for the past three and a half years it has experienced an explosion of growth and a new commitment to the ministry of Christ in southeast Memphis and Shelby County.

The current staff and officers of Holy Apostles: The Rev. Bob Allen, Rector; The Rev. Charles Galbraith, Curate; Mrs. Marilyn Maddox, Parish Secretary; Mr. Bob Capra, Organist/Choir Master; Miss Rachel Mann, Assistant Organist; Mr. Bob Loos, Senior Warden and Mr. Jim Higgins, Junior Warden.

Robert E. Allen, Rector

Church of the Holy Communion, Memphis

Church Of The Holy Communion, Memphis

The First Thirty Years, 1950-1980, a booklet which admirably chronicles the history of the Church of the Holy Communion, Memphis, has been referred to in the compilation of this account of the Church and its growth. Points added since 1980 have been derived from other available sources.

A gift of $10,000.00 by Mrs. Emma Denie Voorhies to Dr. Charles F. Blaisdell, Rector of Calvary Church, played a most significant role in the establishment of Holy Communion. The money was given to Dr. Blaisdell to use as he saw fit. Immediately he said, "There's my chapel!" With the money he bought land on Poplar and Perkins. A sign was erected:

"Future Site, Chapel of The Holy Communion of Calvary Episcopal Church."

It was named for Dr. Blaisdell's former parish, the Church of the Holy Communion, St. Louis, Missouri.

The first service in the small gray wooden chapel was held on January 1, 1939. As clergy of the mother parish, Calvary, were from time to time available, occasional services were held, but during World War II a small church school meeting each Sunday was established. During this time, under the leadership of the Reverend Dr. Theodore Nott Barth, rector of Calvary, plans were developed for the new chapel to be erected on a twenty-acre tract on the corner of Walnut Grove and Perkins Road. The plan envisioned the project as a whole, of which the chapel was the first unit.

On October 24, 1948, the ground was broken for the new, larger chapel. $200,000.00 had been raised by the mother parish, Calvary. The first service was held on January 1, 1950.

The chronology of "firsts" as applied to the Church of the Holy Communion covers interesting and important historical facts related to this remarkable Church.

Only three Rectors have served the thirty-three year old church: the Rev. Eric S. Greenwood, January 1950-January 1971; the Rev. Harold Barrett, September 1971-November 1980 and the Rev. Reynold S. Cheney II, since September 1, 1981. Presently serving with Mr. Cheney are Duncan M. Gray, III, Associate and Lewis K. McKee, Assistant.

Among the many significant "firsts" in 1950 were the first confirmation class in February; the first guilds—Barth and Greenwood; the first visit by Bishop Barth, May; the first Young People's

Service League, September and the Inauguration Dinner, Claridge Hotel, Bishop Barth, speaker and Dr. Donald Henning, master of ceremonies, December.

On January 24, 1951 the Church was admitted to parish status by the Diocese. In Janaury five guilds were organized: Elizabeth Barth Guild, Calvary Guild, Barth-Greenwood Guild, Emma Denie Voorhies Guild and Charles F. Blaisdell Guild—business and professional women.

During the years which followed there were numerous constructive activities which caused the Church to continue a broad service to its congregation and to the surrounding community.

In January 1961 Holy Communion hosted the Tennessee Diocesan Convention for the first time. In May 1962, the Church jointly hosted with St. John's the 75th Annual Meeting of the Episcopal Church Women of the Diocese of Tennessee. Dr. Nathaniel Hughes became the new headmaster of St. Mary's School, June, 1962.

Groundbreaking for Holy Communion's first mission—Holy Apostles, corner of Hickory Hills and Knight Arnold Roads, was held in November 1972. An unencumbered deed to their property was presented to Holy Apostles dated January 1, 1981.

In October 1977 the Peggy Lucas Barrett Memorial Library was dedicated.

There were 580 names on the Church directory in October, 1979.

In April 1980 the Church had collected $88,375.00 for Venture-in-Mission, the important church outreach campaign. In May 1980, on Palm Sunday, the first public use of the beautiful new organ was shared.

The Women of the Church number about 200. Guilds, other than those already named are: All Saints Guild, Dandridge Guild, Gailor Guild and Vander Horst Guild.

The organists-choirmasters who have served Holy Communion have been: Harry J. Steuterman, John Murry Springfield, Kenton W. Stellwagon (acting), E. William Brackett, David Carl Ramsey, Eric Greenwood, Jr. (part-time) and James Brinson who began on July 1, 1976 and continues presently.

In 1983, Ben Ward serves as Senior Warden and Mike Saliba as Junior Warden. Mrs. Leonard (Aleine) Hansen has been the able Parish Secretary since 1969.

The recent installation of a sound system in the Church will be of great value.

The communicants to date number approximately 1700.

This sketch of history of the Church of the Holy Communion is concluded by this prayer from the Church's first bulletin:

> "Our first prayer is that all new beginnings and new undertakings which this first page symbolizes may, under God, prosper mightily, and that this chapel and its people may labor abundantly now and for many generations bringing forth much good fruit."

Compiled by the Author

As Christ said, "It is more blessed to give than to receive," "O God, give us grace today to think not of what we can get but of what we can give."

—The Prayers of Peter Marshall

Holy Trinity, Memphis

The Church Of The Holy Trinity, Memphis

The first service of the congregation to be known as the Church of the Holy Trinity was held in the home of F. D. Talley, 1081 McLemore, on August 11, 1901. The first building was erected at the corner of Cummings and Talley. The cornerstone was laid on March 31, 1902 by Bishop Gailor. On May 6, 1909, Holy Trinity was admitted as a parish of the Diocese of Tennessee.

The organizing members of the Mission in 1902 were: Mrs. C. W. Richmond, Mrs. F. D. Talley, Mrs. I. N. Chambers, Mrs. B. H. Wailes, Otey S. Hutton, Mrs. Henry Lenow, H. H. Cannon, H. E. Cannon, Mrs. E. B. Causey, Mrs. G. H. Batchelor, E. Juliette Stowers, and Mrs. G. A. Robinson.

In 1958 the present property on Kimball Avenue was purchased. This consisted of 5½ acres on which was located a large ante-bellum house (built 1853) and a swimming pool.

St. Edward's Chapel, a mission church, located on Lowell St., had been started with the assistance of the Rev. George Hale of Grace-St. Luke's Church in 1946. Among the first members of St. Edward's were Mr. and Mrs. Charles M. Scott, Mr. and Mrs. E. E. McCartney, Mr. and Mrs. Robert Robinson, Mrs. A. A. Mahoney, Mr. and Mrs. Henry Boyd, and Mrs. Ruby Mitchell. This small mission congregation merged with Holy Trinity in 1958 when the new property on Kimball was purchased. The cornerstone of the present Church building was laid by Bishop Barth on June 14, 1959.

Ministers who served Holy Trinity are: the Rev. Peter Wagner 1901-1905; the Rev. Prentice A. Pugh 1905-1915; the Rev. George Watts 1915-1917; the Rev. Alexander Rich 1917-1918; the Rev. Martgary Smith 1918-1921; the Rev. Martin Luther Tate 1922-1936; The Rev. Charles W. Seymour 1936-1940; the Rev. W. Pipes Jones 1940-1943; the Rev. Malcolm McMillan 1945-1949; the Rev. Porter Florence 1950-1962; the Rev. Paul Shields Walker 1962-1969; the Rev. H. Eugene Haws 1969-1975; the Rev. Charles M. Galbraith 1975-1978; the Rev. David R. Hackett 1978-. The Rev. Curtis Luck, Perpetual Deacon, was ordained 6/3/49. The Rev. Edgar E. Ince, Jr., Perpetual Deacon, was ordained 12/21/62.

Among the Organists/Choirmasters have been: Richard White (now at St. John's); Mrs. Anita Lofton; Mrs. Evelyn Scoby (presently).

The longest tenured Senior Warden of Holy Trinity has been Arthur B. Chambers who also served as Church School Superintendent for forty years.

Two unusual activities have been a project during the 1960's sponsored by Holy Trinity which raised money throughout the city to straighten the teeth of needy children. For years during the Rectorship of the Rev. Paul S. Walker, the Trinity Follies were held annually. This musical review was widely acclaimed.

Due to the excellent physical facilities of the swimming pool and athletic field, Holy Trinity has a strong outreach to the community. It is the location of numerous Scout Day Camps, of Day Camps for Underprivileged Children. The swimming pool is used by the YWCA, the Southeast Memphis Mental Health Center, Memphis House, and the Holy Trinity Neighborhood Parents' Association.

At present there are 430 communicants in good standing.

Arthur B. Chambers,
Parish Historian

The Christian Hope

Q. What is the Christian hope?
A. The Christian hope is to live with confidence in newness and fullness of life, and to await the coming of Christ in glory, and the completion of God's purpose for the world.

Q. What do we mean by the coming of Christ in glory?
A. By the coming of Christ in glory, we mean that Christ will come, not in weakness but in power, and will make all things new.

Q. What do we mean by heaven and hell?
A. By heaven, we mean eternal life in our enjoyment of God; by hell, we mean eternal death in our rejection of God.

Q. Why do we pray for the dead?
A. We pray for them, because we still hold them in our love, and because we trust that in God's presence those who have chosen to serve him will grow in his love, until they see him as he is.

Q. What do we mean by the last judgment?
A. We believe that Christ will come in glory and judge the living and the dead.

Q. What do we mean by the resurrection of the body?
A. We mean that God will raise us from death in the fullness of our being, that we may live with Christ in the communion of the saints.

Q. What is the communion of saints?
A. The communion of saints is the whole family of God, the living and the dead, those whom we love and those whom we hurt, bound together in Christ by sacrament, prayer, and praise.

Q. What do we mean by everlasting life?
A. By everlasting life, we mean a new existence, in which we are united with all the people of God, in the joy of fully knowing and loving God and each other.

Q. What, then, is our assurance as Christians?
A. Our assurance as Christians is that nothing, not even death, shall separate us from the love of God which is in Christ Jesus our Lord. Amen.

The Book of Common Prayer, 1977
Catechism—Pages 861 and 862

St. Elisabeth's, Memphis

St. Elisabeth Church, Memphis

St. Elisabeth's Episcopal Church is located in the old community of Raleigh in Shelby County, Tennessee. The address is 4780 Yale Road, Memphis.

In what was called a "resort" Chapter meeting of St. Mary's held at Sardis, Mississippi on April 1959 was the time the idea of a mission being supported by the Cathedral was first discussed officially. At this meeting Dean William E. Sanders suggested the name "*St. Elisabeth.*" In the issue of the *Chimes*, which told of Canon Dimmick's coming, the name was announced.

The group called "Mission Investors" which gave the five acres of land as a site for St. Elisabeth were: B. C. Adams, William Barr, William Deupree, S. R. Donelson, W. P. Embry, Sam B. Hollis, W. R. Hudgins, Dr. W. F. Morse, Miles Nevin, the Rev. M. C. Nichols, William Lea, J. M. Patten, Jr., A. Woodside, Hollis Rogers, Dr. W. L. Whittemore.

Members of the first Council were James Scheibler, Warden; Frank Howell, Treasurer; David Cushing, Clerk; Luther Heinz, Earl Suddoth, Guy Richardson and R. T. Pheifer, members.

The first meetings of the congregation were held in former residence on the property. The first building dates from July 3, 1960. By October 14, 1962 the present church had been completed and was dedicated by Bishop John Vander Horst on that day. The Education Building was completed in May 1967 and the Chapel adjoining the sanctuary was finished in 1982. The total value of the church property at present is $665,000.00.

The following clergymen have served St. Elisabeth: the Rev. John Walter Thomas, July 3, 1960 to November 30, 1962; John Turner Whaley, May 1963 to August 1967; Duff Green, September 1967 to April 1973; Nick Gill, April 1973 to September 1974; Joe Ted Miller, September 1974 to August 1981; Laurence Packard, July 1979-July 1980; John Abraham, September 1980 to October 1982. The Rev. Paul Dickenson, retired, willingly assists when needed for services. The Rev. Orion W. Davis, the present rector, began in May 1982. The Rev. H. Bruce Lederhouse became associate rector in January 1983.

In 1964 there were 114 communicants; in 1983 there are 684!

The present Senior Warden is Bob Jones; Frank Curd, Jr., Junior Warden; Mrs. Andrew (Roberta) Bush is President of the Women of St. Elisabeth and Curt Knight is the leader of the Men's Club.

St. James', Memphis

St. James Church, Memphis

St. James Episcopal Church is located at 1440 Central Avenue, Memphis, on one acre of land purchased for the site.

The Church was organized on January 29, 1939 and admitted to the Diocese during that year. There were 107 men as organizing members. The Church-house dates from 1942.

The clergymen who have served St. James:

>Dean Israel Harding Noe, 1939-1960
>The Rev. Warren H. Steele, 1961-1968
>The Rev. Julien Gunn, 1969-1971
>The Rev. Frank Crenshaw, 1971 and

continues as the present Rector.

The present organist is Richard Hicks. Among the choir leaders at St. James are Mrs. Barbara Hamner, Dr. David Weaver and Charles Overfield.

Jere McAdams serves currently as Senior Warden and Annette Rippee is the present President of the Women of St. James.

An annual project is the Fall Bazaar.

There are sixty-eight communicants at present.

In the Centennial Edition of the *Commercial Appeal*, January 1, 1940, the Rev. Mr. Noe recorded this statement:

> "The Diocesan Convention (1939) granted 107 men the right to start a parish where they might find a true church home and live a full, free life in Christ . . . St. James regards itself as a pioneer unit to help in ushering in the universal Church."

Compiled by Irma Kramer
(and the Author)

St. John's, Memphis

St. John's Church, Memphis

St. John's, a small Episcopal Mission was started in the Buntyn area in the early 1870's, but was destroyed twice by fire. Finally, in 1878, services were again held in a white frame building at Semmes and Spottswood, with the Rev. Peter Wager, a former vestryman at St. Mary's Church, Memphis, acting as Priest-in-Charge. Others followed him in the same capacity until 1926, when the Rev. Alfred Loaring-Clark was assigned to be in charge of the Mission Church.

On January 18, 1928, Articles of Association for St. John's Episcopal Church were accepted by the Diocesan Convention, meeting in Nashville, and Mr. Loaring-Clark, affectionately known to his flock as "Tib", was called as the first Rector of the Parish. The single, frame building grew to three, and the walls were bulging as new families moved into the fast growing area. Mrs. Walter E. Lott became the first parish secretary, and the Rev. Henry Nutt Parsley the first Assistant Minister.

Mr. Frederick Smith gave the land at the corner of Central and Greer for a new church building, and the cornerstone was laid on January 31, 1948. The first service in the new church was held on Palm Sunday, 1949, and on May 24th the new church building was consecrated, debt free. Church school classes and other activities continued to take place in the buildings on the corner of Semmes and Spottswood until 1951, when an additional building was added to the church at Central and Greer. The buildings at Semmes and Spottswood were sold, and from that date on, all of St. John's activities took place at Central and Greer.

This new church plant had been the dream of early members of St. John's, who had stoked fires, laid linoleum, painted walls and done much more in order to make possible the ongoing life of the parish. A Sunday School had been built, and the Choir, Altar Guild, Women's Auxiliary, Men's Club and Young People's group had all been established. Among these early, devoted and staunch pioneers were Mr. and Mrs. Harry A. Ramsay, Jr., Judge and Mrs. Charles N. Burch, Mr. and Mrs. T. K. Robinson, Sr., Mr. and Mrs. Palmer Farnsworth, Mr. and Mrs. Shubael T. Beasley, Mr. and Mrs. Walter E. Lott, Mr. and Mrs. Kit Williams, Sr., Mr. and Mrs. C. B. Rutledge, Mr. and Mrs. Ben H. Shawhan, Mr. and Mrs. John T. Tyler, Mr. and Mrs. L. M. Woolwine, Mrs. Laura C. Sharpe, Mr. and Mrs. Augustus Cummings, Mr. and Mrs. William Lytle Nichol, III, Mr. and Mrs. John Franklin.

The design of the new church building was patterned after Bruton Parish Church in Williamsburg, Virginia, by the architect, Lucian Minor Dent, a parishioner of St. John's. The style of architecture as expressed in St. John's Church is Georgian, characterized by the use of the Basilican floor plan and ornamentation typical of the Georgian style. The floor plan of the Church is based on the cruciform plan of the old St. Peter's Basilica in Rome. St. Peter's, a wooden structure, included a wide center aisle leading up to the High Altar and contained two side aisles, a transept, and two chapels. It is interesting to note that the architect chose three basic shapes: the square, the arch, and the circle, and has used them throughout the church in various forms, and by so doing has achieved a strong expression of unity. The floor plan of the Tower Room is a perfect square. The doors and windows are arched, while the chapel windows are complete circles.

In October of 1950, the Rev. Wallace M. Pennepacker, Rector of St. Bartholomew's Church, Ho-Ho-Kus, New Jersey, was brought to St. John's by Mr. Loaring-Clark as the Associate Rector. Together, these men sought to minister to a growing congregation in the suburbs of Memphis.

On February 21, 1952, the parishioners were saddened by the sudden death of their Rector, who had worked long and hard with them in their part of the Lord's vineyard, and he was laid to rest under the church chancel. Three weeks later on March 12, 1952, the Vestry called Mr. Pennepacker as the second Rector of St. John's Church.

Shortly before his death, Mr. Loaring-Clark had interested several parishioners in giving as gifts and memorials eight murals to be put on the walls of the church, and Mr. John De Rosen, an internationally known artist and native of Warsaw, Poland, was commissioned to do these paintings. It took him almost two years to complete his work, and it has been said of these murals that nothing in America can equal them, and nothing in Europe can surpass them.

The mural over the High Altar, called "Christ Triumphant", was given by Mr. and Mrs. Norfleet Turner and Mr. and Mrs. J. Bayard Boyle in memory of Mr. and Mrs. Samuel Ragland, the parents of Mrs. Boyle and Mrs. Turner. The mural at the west end of the church, called "Christ, The Judge", was given in memory of Mr. Alfred Loaring-Clark by his friends. The three murals in the Chapel of The Holy Spirit, "The Baptism of Jesus by John the Baptist", "The Baptism of Priscilla by St. Paul", and "The Baptism of

St. Augustine of Hippo by St. Ambrose", were given by Mr. and Mrs. Herbert Humphreys. In the Lady Chapel, the mural over the Altar is called "The Mother Enthroned", and was given in memory of James Swearengen by Mr. and Mrs. Jules Rozier. The one called "The Annunciation" was given in memory of Gertrude Alcorn Russell by her children, Mrs. Percy Wood, Mrs. Giles Coors and Mr. Edward Russell. The third one, called "The Visitation", was given by Mr. James D. Robinson in honor of his mother, Myriam Dinkins Robinson.

To add to the richness of services at St. John's, a bell for the steeple was cast in France and brought over here as a gift by Mr. and Mrs. J. Richard Walker in memory of his parents, Mr. and Mrs. James M. Walker and her father, John P. Bullington. The bell rings before services, after weddings and tolls at funerals.

One of St. John's finest assets is the magnificent pipe organ begun in 1949 and added to over the years by Mr. and Mrs. Herbert Humphreys in memory of his parents, brother and sister. The first organist and choirmaster to use this organ was Mr. Fergus O'Conner. He was followed by Mr. Richard T. White, who came in September of 1950. Mr. White's skill as a musician and his dedication to his work have brought to the parish the best in church music and the finest of volunteer choirs.

The walls of the church buildings continued to bulge until the final addition was completed in 1957. St. John's consists of four brick buildings surrounding a rectangular, cloistered garden. In the center of the garden is a sculptured statue of a clergyman in his cassock, made and given by Mrs. Phoebe Dent in memory of the first Rector of St. John's, "Tib" Loaring-Clark. Between the church building and the parish hall, by the baptismal shell and in the midst of an azalea garden is the statue of a child, given by Mr. and Mrs. J. Richard Walker in memory of her mother, Dora A. Bullington and her niece, Mary Pauline Schas.

When the new church building was erected in 1949, it consisted mainly of brick walls, but down through the years appointments in the nave, chapels and three chancels have been given in honor of or as memorials to loved ones, resulting in a church of great beauty. In addition to the murals are the needlepoint kneelers, first conceived by Mrs. Richard Doughtie, designed by Mrs. Indie Cockerham and stitched by women of the congregation and their friends. Mrs. Cockerham also designed, and this same group of women made, gold and white festival eucharistic vestments, processional cope, and an embroidered festival set which consists of chasuble, two stoles, burse and veil, markers, antependium and superfrontal. These works of art have been displayed at Diocesan and General Conventions.

In 1978 and 1979 the Parish Hall and Library were completely renovated and beautifully furnished. The exquisite work done in both is the result of the time and talent given by Mrs. Herbert Humphreys. Such an undertaking was made possible by memorials and other special gifts.

It was not long after Mr. Pennepacker took over the helm at St. John's, that Herbert P. Jordan, a communicant, wondered how he could best serve his church and Rector. His decision was to study and be ordained a Perpetual Deacon, and so he became the first to serve his church in this capacity. A second man, Frank T. Donelson, has followed in his footsteps.

The first and only missionary to go forth from St. John's Parish was Dr. W. B. R. Beasley, who served in Liberia and is now in Indonesia.

From 1952 through June of 1978, nine young men from St. John's have been ordained into the ministry. They are: William Jones, Albert Brown, Jack Arthur, Ben Shawhan, Frank McClain, David Babin, Craig Casey, James Curtis and Joe Alford. Of particular note, William Jones, son-in-law of Mr. Loaring-Clark, is now the Bishop of Missouri.

In 1978, St. John's celebrated its Centennial Anniversary, beginning with the Service of Worship on Sunday morning, April 16th, followed by a week of fellowship and festivities, and culminating in the morning Worship Service on Sunday, April 23rd. Just about all of the parishioners took part in one way or another during that week and the spirit of fellowship prevailed long afterwards.

From 1949 until the mid-sixties, St. John's was a suburban parish, meeting the needs of many young families with many children. But the suburbs are now far beyond the area of the parish, and St. John's has become a mid-town church, assuming new challenges along with the old. It now reaches out into the community more so than in the past, and is noted for the caliber and number of parishioners representing St. John's in a wide variety of endeavors. The educational program of the parish encompasses all ages and many subjects and is a vital part of the life of St. John's. Spiritually, there has been the need for a Sunday evening service in addition to the other three held on that day, as well as a 5:30 service on Tuesday evenings in addition to the regular Wednesday morning mid-week service. The communicant strength of approximately 1,000 and a total membership of 1,400 remains fairly stable, but there is more of a changing congregation than there was in earlier years.

From 1979 through 1983, there has been an influx of young couples at St. John's. Once again there is a growing Church School.

The latest property acquired by St. John's on December 7, 1979, is a cemetery, near the church on Central. The donor was James D. Robinson, a parishioner. Bricks for the wall around the cemetery were brought from Virginia and match those in the church buildings. The earliest burial date identified by existing markers was 1877. The beautiful wooded grounds have been completely restored by the Church.

St. John's Church is very unusual in that there have been only two Rectors throughout the life of the parish. However, on May 18, 1983, the following letter was read by the Senior Warden, W. Seldon Murray, III, to the Vestry at the regular monthly meeting and to parishioners on the following Sunday at all four services:

> TO: THE WARDENS AND VESTRY OF ST. JOHN'S CHURCH,
>
> It is with mixed emotions that I tender my resignation as Rector of St. John's Church, effective December 31, 1983.
>
> It has been my privilege to have served as your Rector for over thirty-one years, and before that as Associate Rector for sixteen months. On June 1st I will have been in the ordained ministry for forty-one years, and the time has come to retire.
>
> I have given you time to find a new Rector to be ready to step in on January 1st, so that the parish will not go through a period of having no Rector at the helm. My prayers will be with you in your endeavor to find the right man, and I have every confidence that you will.
>
> During the next seven months let each of us do all in our powers, to see that St. John's goes forward and continues to meet the daily challenges that come our way.
>
> God Bless You All,
> (signed) Wallace M. Pennepacker

Mr. Pennepacker's letter of intent to retire was very reluctantly accepted by a stunned and saddened Vestry.

Thus, on January 1, 1984, a new era will begin for St. John's Church. May God's Blessings continue to be with the new Rector and his flock as they continue to carry on the work begun in His Name so many years ago.

Frances Roome (Mrs. Wallace M.) Pennepacker,
Parish Historian

St. Mary's Cathedral, Memphis

St. Mary's Cathedral, Memphis

The day which St. Mary's Cathedral observes as its founding date is Ascension Day, May 13, 1858, the day on which the Church was consecrated by the Rt. Rev. James Hervey Otey. The following excerpt from the Bishop's Journal of 1858 gives authenticity to the date:

> "With the rites and solemnites prescribed, I this day set apart and consecrated to the service of Almighty God, St. Mary's Church, Memphis, according to the order and usages of the Protestant Episcopal Church in the United States. Morning Prayer was read by the Rev. Messrs. Harrison (St. Luke's, Jackson), and Schetky (Grace); the lessons by the Rev. Dr. White (Calvary); Ante-Communion by myself; the epistle and gospel by Rev. Mr. Wheelock (St. Mary's, Covington); the sermon by Rev. Mr. Pickett (St. James', Bolivar), and the communion was administered by Rev. Mr. Hines and myself. Thus has a work begun by a few ladies of Calvary Church a few years ago in faith and humble reliance upon divine help, by God's blessing, been brought to a most happy and successful conclusion. The seats are all free and the minister's support is provided out of contributions of the congregation, aided to a small extent this year by the Domestic Committee on Missions."

The Centennial History, 1858-1958, St. Mary's Cathedral, Memphis, so coveringly written by Dr. John H. Davis stands as a marvelous record of the founding and life of the Church for its first one hundred years. In 1965, *A Continuation 1958-1964,* was written also by Dr. Davis. Therefore, the writings of Dr. Davis have served as the authentic source for much of the content covered in this manuscript. Only the seemingly most essential facts related to the Church's history have been sifted and recorded in this writing. For the full story the reading of Dr. Davis' histories is quite necessary and a fascinating experience in familiarizing oneself with local Episcopal Church history.

St. Mary, the second mission founded by Calvary Church (Grace Church was the first) was a needed effort to reach the inhabitants of the then east Memphis, the area of Orleans and Dunlap. The official notice of the formation of St. Mary's may be found in the *1857 Tennessee Diocesan Journal* in Bishop Otey's address:

> "The Ladies Education and Missionary Society at Memphis have continued to prosecute the objects of their association with praiseworthy energy. They have recently served by donation from Col. Robert Brinkley a lot suitable for the site of a small church, and have through the assistance of some friends, made a contract for the erection of a building,

the sittings in which are to be free for all who will choose to avail themselves of the opportunity thus furnished for the public worship of God. So far, their enterprise affords an encouraging example of what the devotion of a few apparently weak instruments, may be God's blessings on their persevering efforts, accomplished for the promotion of Christ's cause among us. In the midst of very much to depress and discourage when I look at the state of the Church and of religion in this diocese, nothing has occurred for years past that has so filled me with thankfulness and hope for the future, as the inception and progress of this work."

Robert Campbell Brinkley who gave the land for St. Mary's Church in 1856 was a close friend of Bishop Otey. The first Chapel was erected in late 1857. The *Appeal* for November 22 made reference to the "Mission Church on Poplar." Again on November 29 an article signifies that Thanksgiving Day was the actual day of the organization of St. Mary's and possible the day it received its name:

"The Mission Church on Poplar Street. This Church which has been erected by the pious zeal of the ladies belonging to the Episcopal Church of this city, was organized Thanksgiving Day by the election of wardens and vestrymen. The Church is called St. Mary's, and the Reverend Richard Hines has been chosen rector. Mr. Hines has arrived in the city and will preach at St. Mary's this morning. The seats are all free, the expenses of the Church are defrayed by the offering of the congregation."

Three lots on Poplar played a great role in Episcopal Church history during the years—the Bishop's lot, the Church lot and the property of the Sisters, who came from St. Mary's, Peekskill, New York.

St. Mary's Church was presented to the Diocese at the Convention which met at LaGrange, May 26-28, 1858. The Rev. Richard Hines, D.D., served the Church from May 26, 1857 to 1871 then became the first Dean of the Cathedral 1871-1872. St. Mary's became the Cathedral of the Diocese of Tennessee on January 1, 1871. On January 19, 1926 the Cathedral was completed as "Gailor Memorial."

The Rt. Rev. William E. Sanders, Dean of St. Mary's Cathedral from 1948 to 1962, once wrote in the *Chimes* and explained little known activities of the Cathedral staff:

"During one week activities such as the following are being encouraged by your church: a night literacy study program, and evening discussion group called Recovery, Inc., designed as support and therapy for those who have suffered from nervous or emotional problems; an International Relations group meeting every Saturday night, extending a welcome and communal life to the many newcomers and visitors . . . from foreign lands. Community committees meet on such things as pre-school children, Girl Scouts, and a monthly meeting of the Transatlantic Brides and Parents Association, made up of people from England . . . one of the most exciting works carried on by a group of our Cathedral women is a monthly visitation to Bolivar."

Following the centennial celebration by the Cathedral, the most important project was the successful sponsorship and launching of its parochial mission, St. Elisabeth, Raleigh, Tennessee.

St. Mary's broad program of Christian service symbolized through the years continues vibrant and meaningful in the Memphis community and the surrounding environs. The Very Rev. Charles Edward Reeves, Jr., Dean, has as his associate the capable Dr. Frank M. Cooper, IV. Also on the Cathedral staff are the Rev. Canon George A. Fox, the Rev. Donald E. Mowery and the Rev. Joseph M. H. Gohn, Ph.D. Joe A. Morrow serves as Organist and Choir Director. Mrs. Lee Chadwick is president of the Women of the Cathedral. W. Lewis Wood serves as the Bishop's Warden.

By their determined dedication these able gentlemen give extraordinary meaning to the work of the Cathedral.

The Cathedral Chimes, published weekly by St. Mary's, is a splendid church publication. The schedule of services, memorials and important announcements are carried. On the front of each bulletin a timely article appears written either by Dean Reeves or one of his associates, each of which is an inspiration to read.

This account of the history and life of the mission of Calvary—named St. Mary, which became a Cathedral is concluded with these writings from *The Chimes:*

By Dean Reeves, March 13, 1983:
"It is said that when Henry David Thoreau was approaching death, his Calvinistic aunt asked the timely question, "Henry, have you made your peace with God?" Thoreau is reported to have answered: "I didn't know we had ever quarreled, aunt!" That is a good story and may have been appropriate for the famous poet-naturalist, but most of us are all too familiar with the deep need for reconcilation. So much of the distress which we experience is caused by alienation: we are separated from God, from other people, and from ourselves. The most wonderful thing that could happen for us would be to have the barriers broken down and the bad feelings removed.

Well, why don't we just "bury the hatchet" and be in love and charity again? The reason, of course, is that reconciliation is too costly. Somebody always has to pay a price or absorb the pain. Deep hurt just isn't easily healed. Even God couldn't do it without the Cross. This is what St. Paul was talking about when he said: *For our sake he made him* to be sin who knew no sin, so that in him we might become the righteousness of God.

Our essential job as Christians is to share, to make real and available, that reconciliation to this broken world. It is still costly as the late Mahatma Gandhi knew so well, even though he was not a Christian. Gandhi struggled to rid Hinduism of the pain of untouchability. He once said, 'I do not want to be reborn, but if I have to be reborn I should be reborn as untouchable so that I may share their sorrows, sufferings, and the affronts leveled against them in order that I may endeavor to free myself and them from their miserable condition.' Jesus calls you and me to join him in the costly ministry of reconciliation."

By Dr. Frank Cooper, October 10, 1982:

"What must I do to inherit eternal life? "This question asked by a rich young man was one of many our Lord sought to answer in bringing the Good News of salvation to humanity. As we shall hear this Sunday, Jesus' reply to the question is penetrating, unequivocal, and personal. Unfortunately the young man asking the question cannot bear the answer. Perhaps he looks for the easy way of salvation and fails to see he is a prisoner of his own needs and riches.

yank me off the treadmill of self-pity
pull me out of my failure into your future
I'm a prison of my own needs
and fed up with chasing empty illusions. . .
woo me to a new way
catch me off guard with forgiveness
stub my toe on your patience
free me from the tyranny of wanting approval. . .
dust me off—save me
    from aimlessness, mean ambition
    cheap pleasure, empty leisure
and thank you
    for strength I didn't know I had
    for confidence when things didn't go my way
    for not going to pieces when everything got shaky
and when I'm feeling sorry for myself again
because I've struggled much and achieved little
then I'll turn to you for another
    yank. . . .

—*Unknown*"

The Author.

The Peace of Meditation

"So we may know God better
And feel His quiet power,
Let us daily keep in silence
A *meditation hour*—
For to understand God's greatness
And to use His gifts each day
The soul must learn to meet Him
In a meditative way,
For our Father tells His children
That if they would know His will
They must seek Him in the silence
When all is calm and still. . .
For nature's greatest forces
Are found in quiet things
Like softly falling snowflakes
Drifting down on angels' wings
Or petals dropping soundlessly
From a lovely full-blown rose,
So God comes closest to us
When our souls are in repose. . .
So let us plan with prayerful care
To always allocate
A certain portion of each day
To be still and meditate. . .
For when everything is quiet
And we're lost in meditation,
Our soul is then preparing
For a deeper dedication
That will make it wholly possible
To quietly endure
The violent world around us—
For in God we are secure."

—Helen Steiner Rice

St. Paul's, Memphis

St. Paul's Church, Frayser, Memphis

Soon after the Frayser community became a part of Memphis in 1958, the Calvary vestry began to think about an Episcopal Church in Frayser. Frayser was first a railway stop, the first outside Memphis on the Illinois Central Railroad. Dr. J. W. Frayser was a long time resident of Shelby County. His home was just north of the present M. L. G and W. station in Frayser.

Miss Mary G. and Miss Octavia Love, long time members of Calvary Church donated 4 acres of land at Georgian Hills and Steele Rd. to the Diocese of Tennessee. Calvary was encouraged by this act of generosity by the Love sisters and more determined to plant an Episcopal church in the Frayser area.

At a Calvary vestry meeting May 12, 1959, it was decided to do some extensive research in forming an Episcopal Church in Frayser. The vestry under the direction of the Rev. Donald Henning formed a committee to explore the possibility of a church. They hired a young seminarian, Paul Pritchartt, to contact people in the Frayser area. It was hot work in the mid-summer of 1959 going from door to door talking to people about a new church. Young Pritchartt contacted about 80 people. The response was very favorable. Dr. Don Henning and Paul Pritchartt decided to call all the people contacted to a meeting. Letters were sent and on July 15, 1959 at 7:30 p.m. the first meeting was held at Holiday Inn on North Thomas. Dr. Henning spoke and acted as chairman. He said he could visualize a great new church of modern design in the Frayser area. He was pleased with the response as about 75 people were present.

A second meeting to organize was called. On July 27, 1959, the second meeting was held at the Holiday Inn on North Thomas. Dr. Henning again acted as chairman. He said the first order of business would be to select a name for the new church. He said since St. Paul was quite a traveler and since the Calvary influence had traveled to the Frayser area, why not name the new church "St. Paul." The Love sisters, both present, agreed as well as the other members of the meeting. So the name of *St. Paul* was given to the new church in Frayser.

The next order of business was to appoint a council for the new church which now must be called a Chapel. The new council members were Ira Knox, John Philipps, L. M. Smith, John Atkins, Sumner Baker, and Jack Poteet. The first council meeting was held August 23, 1959. Mr. Knox was elected council chairman.

St. Paul was now ready to begin regular church services. Calvary Church was taking care of all the finances. The money collected by St. Paul was turned over to the Calvary treasurer. Arrangements were made with Holiday Inn to hold services there at eleven o'clock on Sunday mornings. A portable altar was built. The altar was set up at the Inn the night before services and taken down and stored after each service. Several other Episcopal churches helped St. Paul by donating a missal stand, a processional cross, vestments and altar hangings. The first service was held on Sunday, August 2, 1959. The service was morning prayer and the sermon was conducted by Paul Pritchartt.

In September 1959 the time had come for Mr. Pritchartt to return to the seminary in Sewanee. Calvary again came to St. Paul's aid. Mr. Ed Boldt, a lay reader from Calvary, volunteered to conduct services at St. Pauls until a vicar could be found. Mr. Boldt took over the services at St. Paul from September 3, 1959 until September 1, 1960. From time to time in 1959 and 1960 a few ordained ministers conducted services at St. Paul and gave communion. The first communion service at St. Paul was conducted by Dr. Don Henning on September 13, 1959.

At this time the Calvary vestry and Dr. Henning were seriously looking for a vicar for St. Paul. They also had hired an architect from Calvary to prepare preliminary sketches for a contemporary church building.

Church services were going well at St. Paul. A choir had been formed by Mr. and Mrs. Paul Kernodle. Sunday School classes were formed and were meeting at Holiday Inn. An Altar Guild was organized and headed by Mrs. Calvin and a nursery was available. All these services were still performed at Holiday Inn.

The first confirmation for St. Paul was held at Calvary Church December 20, 1959. The first wedding for St. Paul took place at St. Ann Church June 25, 1960. In December 1959, Mr. Kenneth Orgill of Calvary donated a small portable organ to St. Paul.

The Calvary vestry again came forward and rented a vicarage at 1850 Townsend Drive in Frayser for a new vicar. The Rev. Robert Lockard accepted the call as vicar and began his duties on September 1, 1960. The Rev. Lockard was St. Paul's first ordained minister. His first service at St. Paul was held at Holiday Inn September 11, 1960. St. Paul while still a chapel was growing and moving forward in 1960.

The young people of St. Paul's organized an EYC group in 1960 under the guidance of Mr. Lockard. The Holiday Inn location was getting too small. In late 1960 arrangements were made to hold services at the Frayser Community Center on Watkins Street.

Bob Felts, a charter member of St. Paul's, organized and trained an active group of acolytes.

Again with the help of Calvary and a new vicar, a new church building of contemporary design had been decided on at a cost of $135,000.00. Mr. Ira Knox, St. Paul's council chairman, also played a large part in the design of the new church building.

On Sunday, October 2, 1960 at 4:30 p.m. official ground breaking for the new St. Paul's Church was held at the Georgian Drive property. St. Paul's council and Calvary vestry were present led by vested choir and acolytes. Some 50 people were present for this important occasion. Construction of the new church building was started a few days later. In July 1961 the building was completed. The first service in the new building on Georgian Drive was held on July 9, 1961, 6th Sunday after Trinity. The Rev. Lockard conducted this service.

Under councilman Jack Phillips and Mr. Lockard a lively athletic program was started. Junior, senior and pee wee basketball and baseball teams were organized.

In April 1964 Mr. Lockard received a call to a church in Columbia, Mississippi. In May 1964 the Rev. Tom Hutson became vicar of St. Paul's.

On December 12, 1968, Senior Warden, Lloyd Partridge, Ira Knox, council chairman, and the Rev. Tom Hutson went before the vestry of Calvary and asked permission to become a self sustaining church. Permission was granted and later approved by the Diocesan Convention. At this time the Calvary vestry also deeded to St. Paul's the vicarage residence on Watkins Street, free of all debt.

By this time St. Paul's was in need of more space for office and Sunday School rooms. Mr. and Mrs. Ira Knox donated most of the money for a new wing for the church. On Sunday, October 3, 1971, Bishop Gates dedicated the new wing and named it Knox Hall.

On September 15, 1974 the Rev. Hutson left St. Paul's to become assistant Rector of the Church of the Ascension in Knoxville, Tennessee.

On March 23, 1975 the Rev. George Gibson became Rector of St. Paul's. He conducted his first service at St. Paul's on Palm Sunday 1975. Under Father Gibson's leadership a tabernacle was installed next to the altar. Father Gibson served as rector of St. Paul's until April, 1978.

The Rev. Julian Carr Lentz became rector of St. Paul's June 4, 1978. Under the Rev. Lentz an outdoor altar was built. The E.Y.C. members helped hand mix concrete to build the altar. Ronnie Vandervene, a vesteryman, and Jack Poteet helped with the laying of the field stone blocks and altar top. Mr. Lentz left St. Paul's June 15, 1980 to become rector of a church in Jackson, Mississippi.

Our present rector, the Rev. William L. Sharkey, came to St. Paul's December 10, 1980. Many new converts have been added to the church rolls under Father Sharkey. A new organization under Father Sharkey, called "The Secret Society", has been formed where the men come together once a month for a dinner and general conversation. St. Paul's is growing under Father Sharkey's leadership.

With the Lord's help may there always be a St. Paul's Episcopal Church in Frayser.

Jack Poteet
Charter member, St. Paul's

"And an old priest said, Speak to us of Religion.
And he said:
Have I spoken this day of aught else?
Is not religion all deeds and all reflection,
And that which is neither deed nor reflection, but a wonder and a surprise ever springing in the soul, even while the hands hew the stone or tend the loom?
Who can separate his faith from his actions, or his belief from his occupations?
Who can spread his hours before him, saying, "This for God and this for myself; This for my soul, and this other for my body?"

All your hours are wings that beat through space from self to self.
He who wears his morality but as his best garment were better naked.
The wind and the sun will tear no holes in his skin.
And he who defines his conduct by ethics imprisons his song-bird in a cage.
The freest song comes not through bars and wires.
And he to whom worshipping is a window, to open but also to shut, has not yet visited the house of his soul whose windows are from dawn to dawn.

Your daily life is your temple and your religion.
Whenever you enter into it take with you your all.
Take the plough and the forge and the mallet and the lute,
The things you have fashioned in necessity or for delight.
For in revery you cannot rise above your achievements nor fall lower than your failures.
And take with you all men:
For in adoration you cannot fly higher than their hopes nor humble yourself lower than their despair.

And if you would know God be not therefore a solver of riddles.
Rather look about you and you shall see Him playing with your children.
And look into space; you shall see Him walking in the cloud, outstretching His arms in the lightning and descending in rain.
You shall see Him smiling in flowers, then rising and waving His hands in trees."

> On Religion, pages 87, 88, 89.
> *The Prophet*—Kahlil Gibran
> Knopf, 1923

St. Anne's, Millington

St. Anne's Church, Millington

St. Anne's Church was organized in 1897 after a series of meetings under a "brush arbor" on Seven Hills Plantation, (The Rembert Place) two miles north of Woodstock. Episcopal services had been held on the Rembert Place some 60 years earlier when Bishop Otey spent the night on the Rembert Plantation in 1834. Samuel Rembert was one of the founders of Calvary Church, Memphis.

Over 40 persons were confirmed after these meetings. The original members were Dr. David M. Saunders and his two daughters Letitia S. Ward and Eliza (Lyde) Branch, Col. and Mrs. Henry Douglass, Dr. and Mrs. William Henderson, members of the Rembert family, the Steeles, and a few others. Services were held in the old Rembert Town school. The first building was built on land given by Benjamin Hawkins and was consecrated in 1906.

The church flourished until the 1920's when many of the older members had died and the younger members of their families had moved to the city. Services were held irregularly during the 1930's.

About 1940, Calvary Church, Memphis started to provide clergy for St. Anne's on a regular basis. In the 1950's the church was assigned a full-time Priest, the Rev. Lee C. Balch. The church made tremendous strides under his leadership, a Parish Hall was built and running water was installed. Later another church was built in the vicinity (Frayser) and St. Anne's was suddenly reduced to a mission station by Bishop John Vander Horst; however with the assistance of the Rev. Homer Carrier, chairman of the Dept. of Mission, regular services were maintained with Layreaders and available clergy. Later, the Rev. Peter Keese came as Priest in Charge. It was during this time that a new church was built on Sykes Road. St. Anne's received a $14,000 grant from the National U.T.O. fund. This was done largely through the efforts of the Rev. Sheppard Crim, a Navy chaplain, who came to St. Anne's on a regular basis during his tour of the Naval Base, Millington.

In 1982, stained glass was installed in all the church windows. These windows depict the life of Christ and are done with symbols.

The present membership is about 100 active communicants. The Rev. Ralph W. Smith is the present rector. There are a number of members who are descendants of the original founders, a number of fourth, fifth and sixth generations.

Rembert Williams

Grace Church, Paris

Grace Episcopal Church, Paris

The oldest Church building in Paris and one of the richest in interesting tradition is Grace Church, which stands at 109 South Poplar Street.

The origin of the building is unique in two ways—first it was built mainly by the efforts of women at a time when a woman's place was in the home; and second, that J. P. Morgan, the great financier, contributed $250.00 to put a roof on the new building. The three founders were: Mrs. F. H. Upchurch, Mrs. J. N. Thomason, and Mrs. Thomas P. White.

In 1895, construction of the Church was begun with funds that were raised by subscriptions from friends abroad, while every effort was made by the women at home to raise the desired amount of $3,500.00 to erect a building that would not only serve as a place of worship, but one which also would be a monument to the swiftly growing town.

The new building was consecrated on November 10, 1895 by Bishop Thomas F. Gailor.

The complete record of the struggle to establish the Church was left in the form of a letter written by Mrs. Thomas P. White. Following are some of the most relevant excerpts:

> "On a bitterly cold afternoon in February 1854 a man on horseback rode up to the main hotel in Paris—his long beard and clothes frozen from his long ride in the rain and snow from Bolivar, Tennessee, where he had been holding service. That man was the Rev. Mr. Gray, afterwards Bishop of Florida. Being so cold and stiff, he had to be helped from his horse, taken into the hotel where he received every attention from the clerk and gentlemen stopping there, hot coffee prepared, clothes supplied him while his were dried. His horse also was given good attention.
>
> Afterwards Mr. Gray asked if there was any place he could hold an Episcopal service that evening. The Court House was suggested. Notwithstanding the severe weather some of the gentlemen boarding at the hotel volunteered to go around the square and notify the businessmen. A fair size crowd attended that evening, who were very much impressed by the young minister.
>
> Three women (Mrs. Upchurch, Mrs. Thomason, Mrs. White) feeling deprived and at a loss without their church, decided that, if humanly possible and with God's help, the Cross of Christ would be lifted over an Episcopal Church in Paris."

Evidently there was no effort to establish a Church until 1894. And with God's help, so it was done. In 1895 they bought a lot from the Anderson heirs, enlarged by a gift of a certain W. B. Jones of a few feet of land "wide enough for a two horse carriage" to draw coal to the furnance.

> "In the erection of the Church . . . we worked in every way to make money for its building, wrote hundreds of letters asking for subscriptions, held suppers, bazaars, benefits, etc., being very grateful to ladies of other denominations for their assistance. The building was erected under the supervision of the three trustees, with the advice and assistance of Mr. Wm. Stalls, a builder and carpenter who became interested in the Episcopal Church from 'your zealousness' and 'books loaned me'."

Early records reveal that in 1888 the first Episcopal marriage took place in Paris, Eva Harvey and Thomas Porter White, April 25th, as well as the first service of Holy Baptism according to the rite of the Episcopal Church, the eldest child of Col. and Mrs. Thomason.

The Church was complete and out of debt by November 10, 1904, and named Grace Church. Col. Thomason presented it from the Trustees, who had been appointed by Bishop Quintard, in the year that the Church lot was bought. The same Trustees were that day appointed by Bishop Gailor for their life-time with his commendation and appreciation for the work done and the ultimate spread of the Gospel of the Church in Paris.

> "Mr. Stalls did the fine workmanship of the Chancel, which with its seven arches was designed by Mrs. Thomason. Bishop Quintard donated the windows. After his death the willing workers unders Mrs. Upchurch's supervision made money and paid for the Chancel window, in memory of Bishop Quintard."

Throughout the years many people have admired the beautiful windows of Grace Church. Behind each window lies an interesting history.

The large window over the Altar is a symbol of Christ Jesus at His Second Coming. It is a Tiffany planned window and was made at the Tiffany plant in Versailles, France. Each piece was separately wrapped in straw and placed in wooden kegs for shipment to Philadelphia. From there they went by horse-drawn wagon to the Berghause Company in Lancaster, Pa. where the window was constructed as we now have it. Once completed, it was suspended on steel rods in a vertical position, wrapped in very heavy sheets of wool, and put on horse-drawn wagons and taken to Pittsburgh, where it was put on a flat car to be brought to Paris. It was then suspended on a rope-made bed drawn by six horses and brought to a location of Blythe and Fentress Streets—and finally carried for two and a half blocks by employees of the Berghause Company to be installed. This was done in 1895 at a total cost of $1,800.00 and five working days for installation!

The other windows are "lancet windows," also designed and executed by Tiffany. They reflect four colors from top to bottom. There are the blue of Lapis lazuli for the heavens, the golden ember of the sun, the natural green of the earth, and the blood red of the fires inside the earth. These windows were set in place in 1895. They were shipped to Paris at the same time as the Window of the Second Coming, as well as the original Rose Windows at the West end of the Church. The latter, however, were of inferior quality and faded in the direct sunlight from the West. In 1966, they were replaced by the present Rose windows as a memoriam to Mrs. Margaret Weber Trevathan by her children. They are among the finest anywhere in the South. The individual pieces of these two Rose windows were gathered from the Cathedrals of Europe that were destroyed during the first and second World Wars, and are dating from the 15th century.

The general lines of architecture of Grace Church are similar to the famous little church "Wee Kirk o' the Heather", surrounded by Forest Lawn Cemetery in Hollywood, California. As dictated by Church tradition, Grace Church faces East, so that the rays of the rising sun fall upon the Altar.

In the years following the Consecration (1904), Church services were held rather irregularly by various visiting clergymen. It was not until nine years later on April 6, 1913, that Harry L. Keller, a missionary, was sent to Grace Church. He continued his ministry until August 9, 1914.

During the early Nineteen hundreds the Rev. Prentiss A. Pugh served Grace Church for a short time as its first resident priest, with travels to other Mission Churches in Upper West Tennessee at the direction of Bishop Gailor. (Exact dates unknown.).

The history of Grace Church is sketchy from 1917 through 1953. Throughout these years we find only excerpts from the Church history. They are as follows:

On a hot summer day, June 2, 1924, sixteen Communicants greeted the Rev. George L. Whitney. He served until October 26, 1930, at the direction of Bishop Maxon. The largest recorded attendance at any service was during the Bishop's visit on Sunday, March 30, 1930, at Evening Prayer with 92 persons present.

During the periods of 1930-34 services at Grace Church were conducted by ministers of local surrounding Churches, with the Rev. James A. Sharp coming at the direction of Bishop Maxon.

On March 1, 1934, the Rev. G. W. Goodson came to Grace Church, holding services on alternate Thursdays and Fridays. In addition, there was Holy Communion on Feast Days.

During the Depression Years the congregation dwindled. On one occasion there were only two members in attendance. It was during this time that the Mission began the practice of collecting a weekly offering. The first recorded offering was $3.75 on a Thursday when there were only five people present. The years of Mr. Goodson's ministry marked a period of decline in the Church. It was in October of 1941 that his work at Grace Church came to a close. During the following interim Bishop E. P. Dandridge held services with the assistance of Lay Readers, David T. Oakley and Charles Gouffon.

The Rev. Leslie A. Wilson served Grace Church regularly from Quinquagesima Sunday 1942 until May 1944. He was followed by the Rev. Charles B. Romaine of Union City, who held regular services at 5:00 p.m. each Sunday from 1945 until January 1950. Then, in subsequent years, the Revs. Alfred De Forest Snively, Cecil Woods, Jr., and interim visits of Bishop Theodore N. Barth held regular services.

On January 23, 1953, the Rev. John G. Arthur assumed the ministry of the Mission at Grace Church. The first Midnight Mass, a beautiful candlelight Service on Christmas Eve, was held on December 24, 1956. With pride Mr. Arthur wrote of the Sunday School, begun only a year and a half before, 'Hosanna!, twenty at Church School from nothing in a year and a half!'. Also, a youth choir had its beginning in 1957.

In August 1958 there were Lay Readers which held Grace Church together for ten ensuring months. They included R. B. Carothers, Jr., Dudley Peel, Canon Rue Moore, Campbell Rhea, and H. T. Vogel.

Then came the Rev. W. Harold Pauley, who served Grace Church from June 23, 1958 to January 1, 1963. He changed the services to include Holy Communion each Sunday, a new idea for Grace Church. During this time, in 1960, a Parish Hall was built. It was dedicated to the three original founders: Eva Harvey White, Frances Harvey Thomason, and Dora Howard Upchurch. In 1960, Grace Church purchased a home on Whitehall Circle at the cost of $6,500.00, to be used as a Vicarage.

The Rev. R. W. Clark of Union City came to Grace Church each Sunday at 9:00 a.m., following Mr. Pauley's departure, along with regular visits of Bishop Wm. E. Sanders. On June 23, 1963, the Rev. Franklin C. Ferguson became the new Vicar. He showed a great interest in young people and it was during his time that the "Dead End Cafe" was organized as a place for young people to go on Saturday nights. Held in the Parish Hall, it served as a local coffeehouse. After Mr. Ferguson ended his ministry at Grace Church in September, 1966, the Rev. Mr. Clark resumed the 9:00 a.m. services. Assisting Lay Readers at this time were: Rainey Reynolds, Arky Fayette, R. B. Carothers, Jr., and C. Frazier Cravens.

The next resident pastor came on July 17, 1967. He was the Rev. J. Lee McLean, Jr. The Vicar was ordained to the priesthood while at Grace Church. Mr. Dan Nealon donated a magnificent Mason and Hamlin reed organ to the Church on October 8, 1967. Christmas 1968 marked the first time a Christmas tree was erected in the Church. The Rev. Mr. McLean preached his last sermon in Grace Church on October 25, 1970.

Early in 1971 it was realized that the property at Whitehall Circle had become too small and outmoded for use as a Vicarage. It was sold, and in the summer of 1971, a lovely new Vicarage was purchased at 401 Jerome Drive, at a cost of $26,000.00. The double carport was enclosed and redecorated for use as a den, study, and meeting room.

In June 1971 the Rev. William T. Patten came to serve Grace Church. On August 25, 1971, he held his first planning meeting. In the course of the meeting a new goal was set for the Church, namely to raise Grace Church from its Mission status to that of a self-supporting Parish. If so, Grace Church would no longer be dependent on the Diocese for financial aid. In addition it would also gain the right to elect and call a rector instead of being dependent on a Diocesan appointment for a vicar.

Due to this initiative, financial support increased from $4,000.00 to $11,000.00 in the first year, and indeed to $21,000.00 in the second year after the appeal. On January 19, 1973, Grace Episcopal Church in Paris was welcomed as a new Parish of the Diocese of Tennessee. Since that time Grace Church has been active in Diocesan affairs. Mr. Robert Cockroft of Grace Church has had the honor of being a member of the Bishop and Council of the Diocese of Tennessee, which consists of six priest and six laymen—an unusual and far-reaching Christian service indeed!

In the fall of 1971 the Herman R. Cravens Memorial Library Fund was begun with a gift from the Cravens family and other donations from both friends and parishioners. In shortly over five years the library has grown to over 300 volumes, and is quite unique for a Parish Library.

In 1973 Mr. Dan Nealon gave to the Church a lovely Estey Reed organ, which was built in 1913, but completely renovated before being brought to Paris. It was originally presented as a Memorial to a small Roman Catholic Parish in Indiana. The old Mason and Hamlin organ was presented to the School of Theology of the University of the South as a gift from Grace Church.

In 1974 a Chime System was installed in the steeple of the Church at a cost of $2,500.00; this was a gift to Grace Church by Frances and Carson Alley, communicants of the Parish. The system is set with an automatic time clock to play at designated times, making lovely background music for downtown Paris at proper and vital hours.

In September of 1974 the Rev. William T. Patten left Grace Church for new work in Fort Oglethorpe, Georgia. His successor, the Rev. Phillip G. Houghton, arrived on February 1, 1975, but stayed only a few months. As in the past, an excellent group of Lay Readers held the Church together during the following interim: David Hessing, Tom McCutcheon, Rainey Reynolds, Frazier Cravens, and Dr. Larry Long.

Finally, and bringing this outline of the history of Grace Church to the present time, the Rev. John G. J. van Moort held his first service on the Second Sunday after Trinity, June 27, 1976. Both he and his wife came to Tennessee from the Diocese of Arizona, both originally having come from the Netherlands.

The past but serves to instruct the present and to lay out hope for the future. From the faithful beginnings of three devout Episcopal women has grown an Episcopal Parish, and may God bless all who are called to bear witness to our Lord and Saviour, Jesus Christ.

In 1981 the Church purchased the two story building next door. The first floor now renovated provides space for the Rector's and Secretary's offices and classrooms for the Church School program. A new Parish Hall will be developed in the new building.

The Rev. William L. Winston presently serves as Rector of Grace Church.

Compiled by
C. Frazier Cravens

"Then a priestess said, Speak to us of Prayer.
And he answered, saying:
You pray in your distress and in your need; would that you might pray also in the fullness of your joy and in your days of abundance.

For what is prayer but the expansion of yourself into the living ether?
And if it is for your comfort to pour your darkness into space, it is also for your delight to pour forth the dawning of your heart.
And if you cannot but weep when your soul summons you to prayer, she should spur you again and yet again, though weeping, until you shall come laughing.
When you pray you rise to meet in the air those who are praying at that very hour, and whom save in prayer you may not meet.
Therefore let your visit to that temple invisible be for naught but ecstasy and sweet communion.
For if you should enter the temple for no other purpose than asking you shall not receive:
And if you should enter into it to humble yourself you shall not be lifted:
Or even if you should enter into it to beg for the good of others you shall not be heard.
It is enough that you enter the temple invisible.

I cannot teach you how to pray in words.
God listens not to your words save when He Himself utters them through your lips.
And I cannot teach you the prayer of the seas and the forests and the mountains.
But you who are born of the mountains and the forests and the seas can find their prayer in your heart,
And if you but listen in the stillness of the night you shall hear them saying in silence,
"Our God, who art our winged self, it is thy will in us that willeth.
It is thy desire in us that desireth.
It is thy urge in us that would turn our nights, which are thine, into days which are thine also.
We cannot ask these for aught, for thou knowest our needs before they are born in us:
Thou art our need; and in giving us more of thyself thou givest us all."

On Prayer, pages 76, 77, 78.
The Prophet—Kahlil Gibran
Knopf—1923

Immanuel, Ripley

Immanuel, Ripley

In noting the significant facts related to the establishment of Immanuel Episcopal Church in Ripley, Lauderdale County, Tennessee, bits of history of the setting, the town and the county are interesting and totally worthy of consideration.

Ripley was named in honor of General E. W. Ripley, who distinguished himself in the War of 1812. It is the seat of Lauderdale County, established by the Legislature in 1835 and named for Colonel James Lauderdale who won fame in the Battle of New Orleans. Ripley was first chartered in 1838.

Located eight miles east of Ripley and about twelve miles from Brownsville, Haywood County, was Eylau Plantation, comprised of 10,000 acres, the magnificent estate of Dr. Samuel Oldham. The splendid colonial mansion on the land was completed in 1835.

Records reveal evidence of the devotion of Dr. Samuel Oldham to the Episcopal Church. In 1841, Dr. Oldham was a delegate from Zion Church, Brownsville, to the Diocesan Convention held in Columbia. In 1844, Bishop Otey reported to the Convention "On the 11th—etc. left next A.M., for Dr. Oldham's at Eylau, near Woodville. 1846, "The report of the Parish includes the family of Dr. Oldham of Eylau. 1850, Zion was in charge of the Rev. Cyrus Waters . . . also in charge of the congregation at Ripley."

Records show that when the lots were sold in Ripley, Dr. Samuel Oldham brought lot 40 for $190.00. Goodspeed's *History of Tennessee* makes reference to this lot:

> "The Episcopal Church erected in 1858 was of frame and and cost $1,500.00. It was standing upon a lot donated by Dr. Samuel Oldham."

The Church was consecrated by Bishop Charles Todd Quintard on the "Third Sunday after Easter, 1874." The present building dates from 1930 and the Parish House, 1961. The total property value in 1983 is $76,000.00.

Clergymen who have served Immanuel have been: the Rev. Cyrus Waters, Charles Francis Collins, Charles Weller, Paul Sloan (1936-1950), Robert A. Tatum, Sam A. Boney, Robert Rickard (1960-1962), Wayne Kinyon (1963-1966), John Sterling (1968-1972), George Hart. The Rev. Richard M. Flynn, since 1980, is the present Priest-in-Charge. Senior wardens: Dan Wells, Frank Keefe and Randy Winslow. Peggy Crutcher presently heads the Women of Immanuel. There are approximately 37 communicants.

The Author.

St. Thomas' Mission, Somerville

St. Thomas, Somerville

St. Thomas is one of the oldest Episcopal churches in West Tennessee. It was organized in 1834 by the Rev. Samuel George Litton. Mr. Litton was a native of Ireland and a graduate of the University of Dublin. He was sent by Bishop Otey, the first bishop of Tennessee, into this newly settled area of the state known as the Western District.

St. Thomas languished in the next few years. Meanwhile at a point where Fayette, Haywood and Tipton counties meet, in 1835, a church was organized with ten communicants. This church was known as St. Andrew's. A house for worship was purchased in 1836, but after 1845 St. Andrew's disappeared from the records and the house used for worship was burned during the Civil War.

In 1839, the Rev. William Steel, who had been in charge of St. Andrew's revived St. Thomas Church in Somerville. Before the church building was erected, serviecs were held in the Masonic Hall, not in the present Masonic Hall, but in a Hall located somewhere near the corner of the Northwest corner of the square and Market Street, as the Masons once occupied a Hall on the corner and later a Hall lower down on Market Street and finally the present Masonic Building.

The church building was erected in 1858 and has been in continuous use since that time. It is not known who designed or built the church. In May 1861, the 14th through the 19th, the thirty-third annual Convention of the churches in the Diocese of Tennessee was held in St. Thomas and at that time the building was dedicated.

This was the last Convention that Bishop Otey attended and the last until after the Civil War. At that Convention it was reported the Church of Tennessee had 27 clergymen, 26 organized parishes and 1,506 communicants. It was further reported that three churches paid, or promised (as Rev. Arthur Howard Noll so aptly puts it) their Rector $2,000.00 a year, one $1,500.00 and four $1,000.00 a year. Among the latter, wrote Dr. Noll, were the two small towns of Columbia and Somerville. Columbia was not a small town for that period and St. Thomas, evidently, paid more than any other country parish.

The church grew and was vigorous in the period of 1838 to 1861. There are no written records of the period of 1839-1861 and only scant traditions. These were undoubtedly St. Thomas' greatest moments. The communicants of St. Thomas were among the very best families in the county, —families of affluence and culture.

During the time of the 1861 Convention held in Somerville, many of the Southern states had seceeded from the Union. Tennessee was still in the Union, but seceeded a few weeks later. There were, of course, differences of opinion as the delegates were from various parts of the state, but no definite stand was taken as to separating within the Church. However, it was left to the discretion of each Clergyman whether the prayer for the President of the United States should be read. Later that year at Columbia, South Carolina, the Protestant Episcopal Church in the Confederate States of America was organized and a Prayer Book adopted. In this Prayer Book, the Confederate States was substituted for the United States. There was one curious oversight in the printing of the Prayer Book. The Prayer at Sea continued to read as follows:

> "That we may be a safe guard to the United States of America and a security for such as pass on the seas on their lawful occasions."

That this prayer was not discovered until after the War, leads one to think prayers were not offered very often on Confederate ships!

Many of the prominent Episcopalians of this period joined the Confederate Army. Bishop Polk was a Lt. General in the Confederate Army and was killed during the War. Dr. Charles Todd Quintard (afterwards Bishop Quintard) was head of the Chaplains in Bragg's Army and other famous clergymen of the Church served as chaplains during the War.

Southern Dioceses were never dropped from the National Church and at the Philadelphia Convention in 1865, Southern delegates were admitted and resumed their place in the National Church.

The Civil War was disastrous and devastating to Fayette County and in an equal degree to St. Thomas Church. The county, from one of the wealthiest and most cultured counties of the state, became impoverished and left with problems not yet solved. St. Thomas declined in membership and wealth. There is little to record of its decline.

The Church Register from 1872 to about 1910 was in existence at the time of the depression in the 1930's. It is incomplete and scanty, but it was copied by WPA in the thirties and the copy is in the Archives of the State Library in Nashville. What became of the original is not known. J. D. Mosby of Nashville, formerly a communicant of St. Thomas, has furnished excerpts from it. From the record we learn that the window over the altar of the church was given in memory of the Rt. Rev. Davis Sessums, Bishop of Louisiana, by his family, some of whom formerly lived in Somerville.

The first window in the west wall is a memorial to the Rev. John Miller Schwrar, the rector in 1878 who was advised to leave but remained at his post and died of yellow fever during the great epidemic of that year. The marble cross on the altar is a memorial to his wife, Anna. The other memorial window was given by the family of John Cowan Humphreys, Circuit Court Judge before the Civil War. The baptismal font is a memorial to Mary Lewis Scott, and the baptismal shell to Mrs. Edna Penick. The altar, made of local cherry, is a memorial to Mrs. Jane T. Williams. The brass lectern was erected in memory of Col. Thomas S. Gallaway, Senior Warden, Supt. of Sunday School and a Lay Reader. The processional cross is a memorial to the Cocke and Juny families. Three Rev. Messrs. Juny served there, and Miss Margaret Juny was organist and choir director for many years. The organ is a bequest from Mrs. S. B. C. Bradford. The candelabra was donated by Mrs. Jennie Williams Bevan. The reredos was given by the family of General Joseph Williams. The altar vessels, the paten and chalice, in present use, were made from silver given by members of the Ladies Guild in the 1890's. The chalice is decorated with gems from the jewels of these same ladies. The great aunt of Mr. Mosby, Mrs. Flora Booker Scott, made a number of other contributions to the church and in her will, left St. Thomas a sum of money, known as the Scott Fund, which Mr. Mosby stated is still in existence. He did not say who had it.

The name of Col. Gallaway, who was a real Colonel having been Colonel of a North Carolina regiment in the Civil War brings to mind, Branch Maury. Branch was a former slave of the Maury family and served as Sexton of St. Thomas for many years. Branch, sometimes took a dram too many and neglected his duties. On one occasion of this kind, when Col. Gallaway had reprimanded him in language more suitable for a soldier, than a churchman, Branch said, "It's a pity that a man that preaches such a fine sermon as Col. Gallaway cusses so!"

Another excerpt from the Register shows that the Rector in the 1880's performed a marriage ceremony between two inmates of the poor house. This is one couple who found two could live as cheap as one, since the county furnished food, clothing and lodging. In a list of the members, a notation was made opposite the name of Mrs. Mattie Skipwith as follows: "Relapsed into Methodism."

From a manuscript in the hands of Miss Margaret Juny, it is learned that three clergymen of that name have held services in St. Thomas. The Rev. Frederick A. Juny, Sr., was born in France of a Roman Catholic family and was graduated at a French University. On account of his difference with his family in faith, he came to the United States and became an Episcopal clergyman. His son, the Rev. F. A. Juny, Jr., was a Rector of St. Thomas and was married in the church to Miss Eva Cocke of Somerville, of a family long prominent in St. Thomas. The ceremony was performed by his father, the Rev. F. A. Juny, Sr. The Senior Juny had another son, Edward S. Juny, who frequently conducted services at St. Thomas. The Rev. F. A. Juny, Jr., is the father of Miss Margaret Juny, church organist.

Other ministers of St. Thomas have been: the Rev. Messrs. Thomas Wright, missionary who organized churches in this area in 1832; George Litton; Dr. Joseph James Ridley; John Miller Schwrar, 1872-1878; George Moore, 1879; F. A. Juny, Sr., and F. A. Juny, Jr., early 1880's; Mr. Case, 1887; S. B. McGlohon; T. C. Tupper, 1896, Arthur H. Noll, 1897; James Craik Morris, 1902; Irenaus Trout, 1903; Alex Crawford, 1905; James Junius Vaulx, 1906-1908; Francis Moore, 1911; Grant Knauff, 1916; Mr. Bennett; Prentice Pugh; Archdeacon B. F. Root, 1923; Charles S. Ware, 1925; Lyle Kilvington, 1925; Archdeacon Charles K. Weller, 1925; Israel H. Noe; Thomas E. Dudney; James R. Sharp; J. F. Plummer, 1933-1937; Dr. W. J. Loaring-Clark; Alfred Loaring-Clark; Nicholas Rightor; Charles Woodward, 1940-1949; E. Dale Baker, 1951-1953; Robert G. Tatum; Robertson Eppes, Jr., 1954-1956; Sheldon Davis, George Elton Sauls, 1956-1960; Ben Shawhan, 1960-1962; Mr. M. C. Nichols, 1962-1964; C. J. Gregory, 1965; W. Joe Moore, 1965-1966; E. S. Ballentine, 1966-1970; T. Roberts, 1971-1977 and Dr. James P. McKnight, 1978-.

The Rector who succeeded Mr. Juny, the Rev. S. B. McGlohon, was married to a somerville girl in St. Thomas—Miss Pattie Thomas.

Additional excerpts from the Register show that the communicants were 54 in 1874, 46 in 1891 and 15 in 1903. Collections were at times fifty cents, sixty cents and $1.20. Sometimes however, $7.50 or $10.00. This was during the depression of the 1870's. On March 7, 1875, there were only two persons in the congregation.

At present, 1983, there are 5 communicants at St. Thomas: Paula M. Cima, Catherine C. Cima, Mrs. Dee Thompson, Mrs. Bessie Latta and Mrs. Mary Williamson.

Many years ago Mr. Charles Stainback, a veteran citizen of Somerville, although not an Episcopalian, wrote a very covering sketch of history of St. Thomas. This old writing given to the Author in 1982, by John Rosser, has been quoted freely in this account of St. Thomas. Mr. Stainback acknowledged the help of Miss Margaret Juny, J. D. Mosby and Miss Annie Moorman, of Somerville, for much material supplied for his paper.

The Author.

"What is a home without Bible?
 'Tis a home where daily bread
For the body is provided,
 But the soul is never fed."
C.D. Meigs
The Treasure Chest, p. 37

St. James', Union City

Saint James Church, Union City

General George Gibbs is generally given credit for being the "father" of Union City. The name, as some might suppose, has nothing at all to do with any partisanship in the war between the states, but derives from the fact that two railroad "unions" or intersections, lie within the confines of the city with a third close, but outside the city. Naturally, where "two or three are gathered" there should be a church. This fact is mentioned in the report of the Diocesan Missionary, the Rev. Robert W. Rhames to the Diocesan Convention of 1906. His principal point was that with all this available transportation the town is obviously an excellent place for the establishment of a mission.

When first laid out by General Gibbs in the 1830's, lots in the city were set apart for the use of Baptist, Christian, Methodist and Presbyterian churches. A Cumberland Presbyterian church already was located here. No provision was made for either the Episcopal or Roman Catholic Churches. This was rectified for the Episcopal Church in 1872 by Mr. and Mrs. Alexander Campbell (a daughter of General Gibbs). They provided a block on First Street (the main street of town) large enough for a church and parish house surrounded by trees. Many years elapsed with nothing done on the property. Bishop Gailor even tried to return the property but the Campbells would not consider it. The property eventually sold in 1894 for $1,000.

The first known Episcopal priest in the area was the Rev. Nathaniel Newlin Cowgill. The first Episcopal Church was St. Paul's Church, Hickman, Kentucky, which was established in the 1840's. In the 1890's the Rev. Mr. Irenaeus Trout received permission from the Waddell family to hold Episcopal services in the Swedenborgian Church in Union City. It is interesting to note that the site of that church is next door to the present church site of St. James.

In April, 1905, the Rev. Robert W. Rhames began holding services in Union City. Subscriptions were received for a building fund, plans were drawn for a church structure and on July 25, 1905, the corner-stone for the church was laid, with great ceremony. Participants in this grand occasion were the Rev. Robert W. Rhames, the Rev. Mr. Price of Hickman, Kentucky, and the Rev. Holly W. Wells of Saint Luke's Church, Jackson, who gave the principal address. Music was under the direction of Professor

Ownby, a local piano teacher. The newspaper report of the festivities stated that:

> "The address, which was made by the Rev. Wells of Jackson, showed him to be not only a forceful speaker, but a scholar as well. We trust that the people of Union City may have the pleasure of hearing this talented young clergyman address them on future occasions."
>
> The December 29, 1905 edition of the same paper stated:
>
> "The First service was held at St. James Episcopal Church last Sunday (Dec. 24, 1905). Service was conducted by the Rev. R. W. Rhames, assisted by Mr. George and Mr. Watts. The services for next Sunday are as follows: Holy Communion 10 A.M., Morning Prayer and Sermon 11 A.M., Sunday School 2:20 P.M."

The land upon which the church was built was donated by Dr. and Mrs. W. M. Turner. In 1941 an adjacent lot (and parish house) were given by the late Hugh Smith and Mrs. Laura Long Smith.

The Diocesan Journal of 1906 records that the building—heated by a stove, with electric lights, windows given by Trinity Church, Clarksville, and one window (over the altar, then) given by the descendants of Gus Herring, and chairs for the sanctuary given by St. Luke's Church, Jackson, Tennessee—had been opened. The total cost, including the architect's plans which were given to the Diocese, was $2,236.33!

Easter Day (April 15), 1906 must have been a great day in the life of the Episcopal Church of West Tennessee. "All the Episcopalians of Paris, Lexington, Humboldt, Milan, Huntingdon, Greenfield, Martin, Union City and Trenton" were invited to united services held in Jackson. Holy Communion was celebrated at 6:30 A.M., Morning Prayer at 11 A.M., Holy Communion at 12 Noon and a children's service at 1:30 P.M. Several mission Sunday Schools were represented by delegates and *all* by banners.

The Rev. Robert W. Rhames served the growing mission from 1905 to 1907; the Rev. Emile S. Harper of the Diocese of Quincy, in 1908; Archdeacon McCabe 1910-1917; Archdeacon Root, 1925-1929, and George W. Whitmeyer, 1929-1930.

A notice in the April 18, 1930 edition of The Commercial announced services at:

St. James Episcopal Church
"THE AMERICAN CHURCH"
Services every Sunday—11 A.M.

Later that year, the Rev. George W. Goodson, a graduate of the Dubose Memorial Church Training School, came on the scene. He stayed through 1941. His responsibilities included: St. Mary's,

Dyersburg; Holy Innocents, Trenton; Grace Church, Paris; and St. Ambrose, Milan; as well as St. James. During his tenure, St. Augustine's Church, a mission to the black community, was also established.

The Rev. Mr. Goodson was succeeded by the Rev. Leslie A. Wilson (1942-46) and the Rev. Charles B. Romaine (1946-55).

Under the leadership of the Rev. B. Sidney Sanders, who came to St. James as a Deacon and was ordained by Bishop Vander Horst in 1956, the old parish house (given in 1941) was torn down and a new parish hall constructed. His successor was Mallie Clark Baker, who also came as a Deacon and served from 1958 to 1961.

The Rev. Richard WIlliam Clark came to Union City as a Deacon in 1961. It was under his leadership that the mission more than doubled its communicant strength and attained parish status in 1965. Mr. Clark left for Christ Church, Whitehaven in 1969.

The Rev. Barclay Devere Wilson was called as rector later that same year and served through 1975. The current rector, the Rev. Lloyd E. Johnston, was called in 1976.

The rolls of St. James includes the greats, near greats, not-so-greats and the ordinary citizens of the community. It is a true community. As one recent guest of the community described it "It was not the way that I was treated that impressed me—it was the way they treated each other."

Lloyd E. Johnston, Rector
St. James, Union City

"O world, thou choosest not the better part!
It is not wisdom to be only wise,
And on the inward vision close the eyes,
But it is wisdom to believe the heart.
Columbus found a world and had no chart,
Save one that faith deciphered in the skies;
To trust the soul's invincible surmise
Was all his science and his only art.
Our knowledge is a torch of smoky pine
That lights the pathway but one step ahead
Across a void of mystery and dread.
Bid, then, the tender light of faith to shine
By which alone the mortal heart is led
Unto the thinking of the thought divine."
—George Santayana.
Leaves of Gold p. 64

CHAPTER 6

The Creation of the Diocese of West Tennessee

For more than a hundred years, there has been talk of dividing the State of Tennessee into more than one Diocese. In April, 1865,[1] the Convention met after several years in which there was no meeting, due to the War between the States. Bishop Otey had died, and the Rev. Dr. Quintard was elected to succeed him. Later in the session, the Rev. Dr. George White, Rector of Calvary, Memphis, introduced a resolution calling for the division of the Diocese and the establishment of what was called a "See Episcopate" with Bishops in Knoxville, Nashville, and Memphis. The Bishop-elect seconded this motion.

After the General Convention at which he was consecrated, and this plan for division was presented, Bishop Quintard reported back to the Diocese that the plan was not workable under existing canons. But he urged that it ought to be worked toward, and in order to move in that direction, he proposed the creation of three Deaneries, each with its own Rural Dean, appointed by the Bishop, and each responsible for the missionary work within its area. This was the beginning of the Convocation system. Evidently he hoped that these rural Deans would eventually be Bishops, but still part of some larger unity.

This idea was expressed in a lengthy report presented to the Convention of 1882. This proposed that the state be described as a Province, which would be divided into two or more dioceses. Each would elect its own Bishop and have its own convention once or twice a year, but all legislation would be up to the convention of the entire State or Province. This would replace the old Diocesan Convention and would assemble every year, or perhaps every two years. This plan, as was the case with the previous one, looked to a relative autonomy in the 'Grand Divisions,' but overall unity under one 'Provincial Synod.' The operational Convocation system was to prepare the way for this.

The Convention of 1883 once again petitioned the General Convention to divide the Diocese, beginning in West Tennessee. Once again the Convention refused the request, mainly because no adequate provision was made for the support of the Episcopate.

From this time on, Bishop Quintard's interest in dividing the Diocese seems to have waned, and he increasingly pressed for an assistant Bishop. But the Convention seemed set on division. Thus developed a tension between the Bishop and the Convention which from time to time voted for division. Bishop Quintard dutifully presented these petitions to General Convention.

The problem was money. Bishop Quintard was very inadequately paid, and was sometimes left in acute financial embarrassment. All efforts to raise an endowment for the Episcopate had failed. The General Convention of 1892 bluntly told Tennesseans that there was not enough money, and there were too few clergy and faithful to justify a division and suggested that some other means be found to secure assistance to the now aging and ailing Bishop Quintard. The Bishop in reporting this, once again pleaded for an assistant Bishop in lieu of further attempts at division. The Convention at last heard him, and Thomas Frank Gailor was elected assistant Bishop in 1893.

As futile as all this was, there was an idea of local autonomy within a larger unity, that was well in advance of its day. The Convocation system was a preparation for this. Originally the Convocations shaped the budget and the planning for advance work in the area. It was still the case, within the memory of this writer, that the missionary budget was proposed by the Convocation. Gradually, however, the Bishop and Council took over the functions of the convocations, until none remained. In the Episcopate of Bishop Vander Horst the whole plan was abolished, and replaced by the largely ineffective Mission Districts. Yet some still thought, when agitation for division began again, that this pattern had some answers to the problems which division was expected to solve. A strong central administration in Nashville, relatively autonomous Suffragans in Knoxville and Memphis; each planning and operating its own missionary strategy would have left a single vigorous Diocese, which would have overcome the weakness inherent in too small dioceses. Something like this was in the mind of Bishop Quintard and the early promoters of the 'See Episcopate' idea. One may be permitted to wonder if there was not great wisdom there.

After the consecration of Bishop Gailor, the whole subject of division was quiescent, although never completely forgotten. It was mainly in East Tennessee that the thought arose from time to time. Bishop Maxon, as Coadjutor, lived in Chattanooga, and was thought to desire independence for this section. However in 1930, Bishop Gailor asked him to select a committee of laymen to consider this matter. Upon due deliberation the committee reported to the Bishop and Council, that they felt that East Tennessee was the most likely section for early separation—but not yet. There the matter rested and Bishop Maxon seemed more and more inclined to maintain the single diocese.

Thus it was that from the time Bishop Maxon became the Ordinary in 1935, until the time Bishop Sanders became the Ordinary in 1977, there was nothing more about this other than informal, occasional talk, and strong indication that the intervening Bishops would not support such a move, a support which under canon was necessary.

In February, 1977, Bishop Sanders appointed an advisory Committee on Structure. Mr. Robert McNeilly of Kingsport was the Chairman. Its function was to look into the existing structure of the Diocese with reference to population trends, growth potentials and such, and to determine how the Church in Tennessee could best fulfill its mission. They met for two years, and in 1979 presented to the Convention a very full and detailed report. Recognizing that in the Catholic scheme of things, the Diocese rather than the Parish is the primary unit of Church life and that—"A Diocese is centered in its Diocesan Bishop. He is the chief pastor, spiritual leader, symbol of apostolic succession, prophet, priest, counselor, and administrator."—they recommended an eventual creation of three Dioceses in the State of Tennessee, corresponding to the 'Grand Divisions.' West Tennessee was to be detached first, and two years later East Tennessee, leaving the continuing Diocese in Middle Tennessee.

Bishop Sanders strongly endorsed the report, and the Convention acting as a committee of the whole took a straw vote on the proposal. The result showed that 56% in West Tennessee; 60% in Middle Tennessee; and 87% in East Tennessee supported the move toward three Dioceses. The Convention concurred in a delay, while committees in the three areas were set up, and regional meetings were held to explain, clarify, and refine the proposals.

In 1981, the West Tennessee committee reported favorably, as did the committees from Middle and East. The vote was decisive (344-44) for division, and there seemed no need for further delay. Eighteen months would elapse, before the action of General Convention in 1982 and this would be spent in preparation, for January, 1983, when the Diocese of West Tennessee would come into being.

The action of the General Convention meeting in New Orleans

in September, 1982, was favorable to the plan as sent to it from the Diocese of Tennessee. Anticipating this, there had been a meeting in June, 1982, representing the Churches in West Tennessee at St. Mary's Cathedral. Obviously this meeting had no authority to act, but the stage could be set, by tentative setting up of plans, organizations, etc. which would be adopted by the Primary Convention assembling after the General Convention and becoming effective in June 1983. For instance the June meeting reviewed proposals for the canons of the new Diocese. These were studied and refined, and accepted by the Primary Convention.

The Primary Convention met on October 21, 1982 at St. Mary's Cathedral. The Diocesan structure was approved and put in place, ready for January 1, 1983, when the new Diocese came into existence. The Rt. Rev. W. Fred Gates, Jr., retiring Suffragan of Tennessee was asked to become the 'Interim Bishop' until such time as an Ordinary for West Tennessee could be consecrated. An episcopate committee had been set up to decide methods, and receive names for election of a bishop for the new Diocese.

When the first annual Convention assembled at the Cathedral January 20-22, 1983, most of the routine business, such as elections for standing committee, Bishop and Council, appointments of Diocesan officers, had already taken place at the Primary Convention, so that the main business in hand—the election of a Bishop—could proceed. On the 33rd ballot the Rev. Alex D. Dickson was elected. The next day he came to Memphis and met with the officers of the Diocese. At an impromptu Eucharist celebrated in the Chapel of the Cathedral he announced his acceptance of the election, dependent, of course, on the canonical consents of the Bishops and Standing Committees throughout the American Church. When these consents were obtained, the Primate—Bishop Allin—took order for the consecration on the Saturday in Easter week, April 9, 1983. This event taking place in the Memphis Civic Center, completed the creation of the Diocese of West Tennessee.

In 1985, the division between East Tennessee and the continuing Diocese will take place, and so the plans, and hopes of more than a hundred years will become concrete facts of history.

The Rev. Canon George A. Fox, Archivist
The Diocese of West Tennessee

CHAPTER 7

The Election of the First Bishop of the Diocese of West Tennessee

On November 4, 1981, Bishop William E. Sanders appointed the Committee on the Episcopate and requested it "to establish a process to assist the Church in West Tennessee in the election of a bishop for the Diocese of West Tennessee." This is the first time in the history of the Diocese of Tennessee that such a committee had been appointed to assist the Convention in the election of a bishop.

The membership of the Episcopate Committee[1] represented a broad range of experience in the Church in West Tennessee. Many of its members had served various diocesan and area-wide responsibilities prior to the appointment. Liaison with the West Tennessee Committee on Structure was maintained through the Chairman of the Structure Committee who was an ex-officio member of the Committee on the Episcopate.

Bishop Sanders asked that the Committee seek the broad involvement of the clergy and laity of the Church in West Tennessee in carrying out its responsibilities. He charged the Committee as follows:
 1. To examine and define the office and ministry of the bishop, specifically as seen in the relationship to the development of the mission and life of the Diocese of West Tennessee.
 2. To describe the characteristics and qualities sought in the person to fill that role.
 3. To develop a process through which persons might be nominated and considered by the Church in West Tennessee for that position.

Theological Statement

For the first few months, the Committee saw itself principally as a study group. It spent a considerable amount of time attempting to develop a rational system to assure that all clergy and laity had input into the three responsibilities outlined by Bishop Sanders. However, early in its work, the Committee developed a Theological Statement upon which all of its future deliberations were to be based. The importance of the Theological Statement cannot be over-stated and, therefore, it is stated in its entirety as follows:

> The election of a Diocesan Bishop is always a major event in the life of God's people. The Church has affirmed the Episcopate as the continuing preservation and renewing empowerment of mission and ministry as received from the ancient Church, enabling us as the people of God to fulfull our respective callings.
>
> Historically, we believe in a God who works with and through the normal everyday routines and processes of the lives of individual human beings. We should not be surprised then that the same God works with and through the normal routines of a structure created and called by Him to be faithful. The "nomination" and "election" process of the Episcopal Church is simply one of the ways in which we order our lives together. The "political process" of this Body is the manner in which we work together for the common good, and we believe that the Holy Spirit is at the center of our organizational life, directing and moving us, as we open ourselves to Him and seek His guidance.
>
> We affirm that the Holy Spirit of God is with us in the process of nominating persons to be considered for election as Bishop of the Diocese of West Tennessee. We prayed that the delegates to the First Annual Convention of the Diocese of West Tennessee may be open to be led by the Spirit both individually and corporately. We believe that as we are open to Almighty God, using all the resources at our disposal, He will work in and through us for the good for His Church in West Tennessee as we seek to choose Episcopal leadership.

Examination and Definition of the Office of Bishop

The Committee's examination of the Office of Bishop revealed, not unexpectedly, that many demands are made of bishops in our Church. The Committee prepared a draft of an outline of the different functions of a bishop. After some modification of the profile at a diocesan Convocation in June, 1982, the profile was prepared in final form and approved by the Primary Convention of the Diocese of West Tennessee.[2] Although the profile did not seek to prioritize different apostolic responsibilities (chief evangelist, chief steward of the sacraments, chief pastor, chief proclaimer of the gospel) and executive functions (President of the Convention, Chairman of the Council), it did establish as a principal objective of the Diocese of West Tennessee to make known the Good News of God in Jesus Christ. The profile further emphasized that the bishop is the successor to the apostles and his principal function should be to preserve and transmit the faith once delivered to the saints. Finally, the profile stated that the bishop should be a man of prayer and spiritual growth and that the apostolic office of the bishop should reflect a spirit of reconciliation made known by our Saviour in all matters.

Description of the Characteristics Sought in the Person to be Bishop

Although the Committee suggested this profile of the functions of the episcopate, no attempt was made to prioritize. It was felt by the Committee that all communicants in West Tennessee, not just a committee or even a convention of delegates, should express their attitudes as to the importance of different characteristics sought in a person to be bishop. Therefore, a congregational survey was developed and was distributed and answered by all confirmed members who attended worship services on April 25, 1982. The results of the survey questionnaires were tabulated and collated by experts and the final report gave a wealth of information about the direction that communicants in West Tennessee felt their Diocese should take and the qualities they would like to see most in their new bishop.[3] It allowed communicants in West Tennessee to voice an opinion as to whether they were for or against (or strongly for or strongly against) several outlined ministries and it gave important demographic information about the new Diocese. It revealed the following five qualities as the most important characteristics that the Church in West Tennessee would like to see in their new bishop:
1. Be readily available and reach out with pastoral concern.
2. Have a strong personal faith supported by disciplined prayer life.
3. Be able to listen with an open mind.
4. Be an effective administrator, able to motivate and delegate.
5. Be able to manage conflict with healing and creativity.

The Development of a Process

One of the most difficult responsibilities assigned to the Committee by Bishop Sanders was the duty to develop a process for the election of a bishop. The Committee spent a great deal of time researching the processes used in other dioceses and developing and refining a process that would be suitable for use in the new Diocese of West Tennessee.

The process developed by the Episcopate Committee and approved by the Primary Convention of the Diocese of West Tennessee included, among other things, the receiving of names for consideration as first bishop from all interested persons; the collecting of data from references on all persons whose names were submitted; the evaluation of such persons as were suggested; the making of nominations of a small number of persons at the First Annual Convention; the allowing of nominations throughout the election, but the disallowing of any nominating speeches.[4] Finally, the process developed by the Committee and approved at the Primary Convention resolved that voting should follow Article XI of the Constitution of the Diocese of West Tennessee (and Tennessee), that is a two-thirds majority of each order on the same ballot required to elect.

In early January, 1983, the Episcopate Committee issued its final report to all registered delegates to the First Annual Convention of the Diocese which was scheduled for January 20, 21, and 22, 1983. By the time of its report, the Committee had received suggestions of 47 names of potential nominees. Eighteen of these had withdrawn from consideration, however. The Committee reviewed information on the remaining 29 persons, including letters of recommendation, Church Deployment Profiles, telephone interviews and visits by three-member teams to a limited number. In its report, the Committee submitted the six nominees considered most able to offer distinguished spiritual, pastoral and executive leadership as the First Bishop of the Diocese of West Tennessee. The six priests nominated by the Episcopate Committee were as follows:

(a) The Rev. Edward C. Chalfant
   Rector, St. Mark's Episcopal Church,
   Columbus, Ohio, Diocese of Southern Ohio
(b) The Rev. C. Allen Cooke
   Rector, St. George's Episcopal Church
   Germantown, Tennessee, Diocese of West Tennessee
(c) The Rev. Alex D. Dickson, Jr.
   Rector & Headmaster, All Saints' Episcopal School
   Vicksburg, Mississippi, Diocese of Mississippi
(d) The Rev. George L. Reynolds
   Rector, St. Stephen's Church
   Edina (Minneapolis), Minnesota, Diocese of Minnesota
(e) The Rev. William B. Trimble, Jr.
   Rector, Grace-St. Luke's Episcopal Church & School
   Memphis, Tennessee, Diocese of West Tennessee

(f) The Rev. R. Stewart Wood, Jr.
   Rector, Christ Church
   Glendale, Ohio, Diocese of Southern Ohio

During the election, the following priests and bishop were nominated from the floor of the convention:

(a) The Rt. Rev. Robert P. Atkinson
   Bishop, Diocese of West Virginia
   Charleston, West Virginia
(b) The Rev. David R. Hackett
   Rector, Holy Trinity Episcopal Church
   Memphis, Tennessee, Diocese of West Tennessee
(c) The Rev. Daniel P. Matthews
   Rector, St. Luke's Church
   Atlanta, Georgia, Diocese of Atlanta
(d) The Rev. Joe Ted Miller
   Rector, St. John's Church
   Norman, Oklahoma, Diocese of Oklahoma
(e) The Rev. W. Theodore Nelson
   Rector, Church of the Resurrection
   Dallas, Texas, Diocese of Dallas
(f) The Rev. Wallace M. Pennepacker
   Rector, St. John's Church
   Memphis, Tennessee, Diocese of West Tennessee
(g) The Rev. Canon Robert G. Tharp
   Canon to the Ordinary of the Diocese of Tennessee
   Knoxville, Tennessee

On the 33rd vote of the convention, the necessary two-thirds majority in both orders was obtained, and The Rev. Alex Dockery Dickson, Jr. was elected. The election was then made unanimous. The delegates sang the Doxology and ended the Convention in a standing ovation of thanks and praise.

M. Anderson Cobb, Jr., Chairman
Episcopate Committee

The Diocese of
Tennessee

The Diocese of
West Tennessee

CHAPTER 8

A Bishop is Consecrated[1]

The consecration of a Bishop is one of the most significant events in the life of a Diocese in the Episcopal Church. The Bishop is the symbol of unity, not only between the diocese and the parishes and mission churches, but also between the diocese and the Episcopal Church in the United States of America, and also with the Anglican Communion throughout the world. The office of the Bishop also symbolic in that it defines the nature of this branch of Christ's One, Holy, Catholic and Apostolic Church as one whose chief pastor is a bishop . . . *Episcopos* . . . from the Greek word meaning 'overseer'.

The Book of Common Prayer is quite definite as to the order of service for the ordination or consecration of a Bishop in the Church. The Rubric on page 511 is quite specific as to the details of service. Paragraph 2 states as follows:

> "When a bishop is to be ordained, the Presiding Bishop of the Church, or a bishop appointed by the Presiding Bishop, presides and serves as chief consecrator. At least two other bishops serve as co-consecrators, representatives of the presbyterate, diaconate, and laity of the Diocese for which the new bishop is to be consecrated, are assigned appropriate duties in the service."

Each of these representatives of the various orders of ministry symbolizes the unity of the episcopate with the people and the heirarchy of the church. It is worthy of note to mention that a Bishop is not a member of the Diocese which he serves, but rather is a member of the House of Bishops, again symbolizing the wider and more interlocking of the various areas of the Church.

The consecration of Alex Dockery Dickson, Jr. as First Bishop of the Diocese of West Tennessee took place on April 9, 1983, being the Saturday in Easter Week. As we might consider appropriate for the ordination of the first bishop of a diocese, many other first time events marked the occasion. In order that as many of the episcopal community in West Tennessee, as well as visitors from the Bishop's home diocese of Mississippi and representatives from other communions and dioceses might be accommodated without crowding or being separated, the service was not done in St. Mary's Cathedral. Rather it was held in the Cook Convention Center. As a result of this change of venue many who otherwise would have been denied being present were able to attend.

The choir, directed by Dr. John Hooker, organist and choirmaster of Calvary Episcopal Church, and Dr. Sam Batt Owens, organist and choirmaster of Grace-St. Luke Episcopal Church, consisted of over two hundred voices from all the choirs and congregations of all the churches in the new Diocese. The remarkable blending of so many voices, most of whom had never sung together before, was most impressive. The musicians who, with only one rehearsal on the morning of the consecration, were able to bring together so many groups of varying degrees of proficiency are to be commended. No doubt this was one of the largest choirs for an Episcopal service ever assembled in Tennessee.

Another 'first time' for the consecration of a bishop in Tennessee was the television coverage on such an extensive basis. Not only were the commercial stations represented by their cameras for the news programs, but video tapes were made to provide a permanent visual record of all the service. The taping was made possible by the generosity of The Federal Express Company. The tapes were replayed by the public television and local stations at times advantageous for those who were not able to be present. They were also made available for use in the parishes and missions. This will prove a valuable historical record in years to come.

The Rev. Francis Marion Cooper, Ph.D. of the staff of St. Mary's Cathedral and also Secretary of the Convention of the Diocese of West Tennessee, was the Master of Ceremonies. So efficient was he in planning and rehearsing the numerous participants ranging from the acolytes to the Presiding Bishop that everything moved with dispatch. Indeed, the efficiency rather intimidated at least one Bishop who on overhearing Dr. Cooper instructing the acolytes as to their movements and saying in a firm tone that if they moved before the signal was given almost certain death awaited them responded; 'I wouldn't dare'. Nevertheless, it was because of such meticulous attention to detail that this unfamiliar and impressive service was able to move without confusion from beginning to end.

The procession was formed in a space adjacent to the area set apart for the service. When everybody was in place, the Crucifer and Torches began moving toward the altar. They were followed by acolytes representing many churches in the Diocese, each bearing a banner symbolic of his own parish. The choir followed and took its place on the risers provided for it in the rear of the building.

When all were in place a fanfare was sounded by the Shelby State College Brass Quintet. This was followed by the stirring notes of the hymn, "St. Patrick's Breastplate", #268, tune, "Deidre". The long procession entered as the choir and people sang.

The procession followed the first crucifer and accompanying torches. First in order of precedence came the civic and academic representatives, members of the House of Young Churchmen, Lay members of the Bishop and Council, Lay members of the Standing Committee of the Diocese of West Tennessee, the presenters of the Episcopal Regalia, the Lectors and the Litanist. There then followed a Cross with torches leading the Ecumenical representatives (clergy); then came a seasonal banner carried before the Episcopal clergy from other Dioceses. The next processional Cross and its accompanying torches led the Diocesan clergy by orders and in order of precedence to their places. The fourth Cross and torches preceded the Registrar of the Episcopal Church in the United States of America, the Rev. Canon James Richard Gundrum, D.D., the Presenters, the Attending Presbyters and the Bishop-Elect.

As the procession neared its end, yet a fifth processional Cross and torches led the Bishops of the Church who were present, the co-consecrators to their place near the High Altar. Then came the Primatial Cross followed by the Chaplain to the Presiding Bishop, and finally in the place of highest honor at the end of the procession, the Presiding Bishop, the Most Reverend John Maury Allin. As the Presiding Bishop ascended the steps to the Cathedral the hymn came to a close in perfect time.

THE PRESENTERS

Mrs. Charles L. Clarke
Mr. Theodore B. Sloan
Mr. Elijah Noel, Jr.
Mr. Richard O. Wilson
Mr. John R. Moss
Mr. George C. Jackson

The Rev. Richard M. Flynn
The Rev. Lewis K. McKee
The Rev. Donald E. Mowery
The Very Rev. C. Edward Reeves, Jr.
The Rev. Anne S. Carriere
The Rev. Douglass M. Bailey, III

ATTENDING PRESBYTERS

The Rev. Frederick J. Bush
The Rev. Emery Washington
The Rev. L. Noland Pipes, Jr.
The Rev. Clifton J. McInnis, Jr.
The Rev. John M. Barr
The Rev. Duncan M. Gray, III

The Rev. Ernest W. Saik
The Rev. Wofford K. Smith
The Rev. C. Osborne Moyer
The Rev. Reynolds S. Cheney, II
The Rev. Martin L. Agnew, Jr.
The Rev. James B. Roberts

CONCELEBRANTS

The Rev. C. Allen Cooke
The Rev. William B. Trimble, Jr.
The Right Reverend Duncan Montgomery Gray, Jr.
The Right Reverend William Evan Sanders

Bishop Allin began the Eucharist for the Consecration of a Bishop with the Easter Acclamation; *"Alleluia, Christ is risen!"* to which the congregation gave the thundrous response which rolled forth from more than twenty-four hundred people present; *"the Lord is risen indeed, Alleluia".* At long last the event so long awaited with fervent prayer and great hope was underway. By the grace of God the Diocese of West Tennessee was consecrating its first bishop according to the ancient practice of the Anglican Communion of the One, Holy, Catholic and Apostolic Church.

Again the meticulous planning of the Diocesan Liturgical Committee, the Rev. Robert Allen, Chairman, was evident. Each participant moved forward without delay starting with the presentation of the bishop-elect, and followed by the reading of the required testimonials as follows:

> The Certificate of Election—The Rev. Francis M. Cooper, IV, Ph.D.
>   Secretary of the Convention of West Tennessee
> The Canonical Testimonial—The Hon. Charles M. Crump,
>   Chancellor of the Diocese of West Tennessee
> The Evidence of Ordination—The Rev. Robert M. Watson, Jr. Ph.D.
>   Chairman, Commission on Ministry, Diocese of West Tennessee
> The Consents of the Standing Committees—The Rev. Wallace M. Pennepacker
>   President of the Standing Committee of West Tennessee
> The Consents of the Bishops—The Rt. Rev. Furman Charles Stough
>   President of the Fourth Province, The Episcopal Church

The Bishop-elect then signed the Declaration of Conformity in the sight of all present and the official witnesses added their signatures as the people gave vocal approval. The litany for Ordinations was then read by the Rev. Laurence K. Packard, Vicar, St. John's Church, Martin, Tennessee.

Following the Litany the old Testament Lesson (Isaiah 61:1-8) was read by the President of the House of Young Churchmen, West Tennessee, Mr. James R. Crumrine. The gradual Psalm (100) was sung by cantor and congregation. Next Mrs. R. Lee Winchester, Jr., Chairman of the Ecumenical Commission read the Epistle (Hebrews 5:1-10). This reading was followed by the hymn "Alleluia", text and tune by Donald Fishel (1973). The Gospel was then read (Luke 24:44-49a) by the Rev. Robert Bartusch, Perpetual Deacon at Calvary.

The sermon was preached by the Most Reverend John Maury Allin, Presiding Bishop of the Episcopal Church, Primate and Chief Pastor. The sermon took a conversational form in that Bishop Allin addressed his remarks to the Bishop-Elect granting the congregation permission to listen. The sermon dealt essentially with the temporal responsibilities of a bishop which must be grounded in a firm spiritual foundation.

Following the sermon a hymn ("For All The Saints") 126 was sung and the Examination of the Bishop-Elect by those Bishops appointed was made. The Ecumenical Question was asked by the Most Reverend Joseph B. Brunini, Bishop of the Roman Catholic Diocese of Jackson, Mississippi. The Presiding Bishop then invited the Bishop-Elect to lead the congregation in the Nicene Creed, our statement of the universal faith of the Church.

The Bishop-Elect still vested only "in rochet, without stole, tippet, or other vesture distinctive of ecclesiastical or rank or order", ascended the steps where he knelt before The Primate, the other Bishops present standing to the right and the left of Bishop Allin. The "Veni Creator Spiritus" was sung, followed by a period of silence.

The people stood as the Presiding Bishop began the ancient Prayer of Consecration. At the proper moment the Chief Pastor and all the other Bishops laid their hands on the head of the Bishop-Elect as the Presiding Bishop continued the Prayer. At the close of the Prayer, the Bishop-Elect became the First Bishop of The Diocese of West Tennessee.

The new Bishop remained kneeling, still simply vested. He was then vested according to the manner of the order of which he is now a member. The Pectoral Cross was presented by the Rt. Rev. Duncan M. Gray, Jr., Bishop of Mississippi, on behalf of the Trustees of

All Saints School, Vicksburg, Mississippi, of which the new Bishop was Headmaster and Rector for 16 years prior to his election. The Rev. Frederick J. Bush presented Bishop Dickson with the Episcopal Ring, a gift from the Clergy of the Diocese of Mississippi.

The Stole, Cope and Mitre were presented by Mrs. Byron M. Hutchison, Mr. Robert S. Cockroft and Mr. H. Clark Doan on behalf of the Laity of the Diocese of West Tennessee. The Presiding Bishop presented The Holy Bible, symbolic of the Bishop's "role as teacher and protector of the faith" as handed down from the Apostles. The pastoral staff, made of local wood and designed by a local craftsman in the form of a simple shepherd's staff, was presented by the Rev. Robert E. Allen on behalf of the clergy of West Tennessee.

The Presiding Bishop then presented Bishop Dickson to the people who offered their acclamation and applause. The new Bishop then made his first public utterance as Bishop of The Diocese of West Tennessee. The words presage and era of good feeling in the Diocese

"The peace of the Lord be always with you"
The huge assembly responded enthusiastically in word and action
"And also with you"
Following a brief time in which the exchange of the Peace was made throughout the congregation the offertory sentence was said. As the offering was received the Choir sang the anthem "All Creatures of our God and King." The alms were presented after the announcement that they would be given to feed the hungry and to Bishop Dickson's Discretionary Fund.

The Great Thanksgiving was according to Rite II of the Book of Common Prayer, 1979, Eucharistic Prayer "A". The Concelebrants were the Rt. Rev. William E. Sanders, Bishop of the Diocese of Tennessee, the Rt. Rev. Duncan M. Gray, Jr., Bishop of Mississippi, the Rev. C. Allen Cooke and the Rev. William B. Trimble, Jr., of the West Tennessee Clergy. The Bishops were the first to receive the elements, followed by the clergy of the Diocese of West Tennessee. The Bishops and clergy then moved to their appointed stations at strategic locations around the hall to assist in administering to the people. Again the masterful planning, especially the work of the marshals, the Rev. Scott Davis and Mr. Roy Wittman made the process move quite rapidly. The provision made for the vessels and linens by the Diocesan Altar Guild was most helpful. More than two thousand people received the Body and Blood of Christ on this occasion with their new Bishop.

During the Communion of the people the choir led the congregation in singing hymns both old and new. Most impressive was the anthem composed by Dr. Sam Batt Owens for Dr. John Hooker and the Choir of Calvary Church with words by J. R. Peacey called "Go Forth For God". It was done beautifully, especially considering the wide variance in the members of the choir.

Following the Communion the Rt. Rev. Maurice M. Benitez, Bishop of Texas and classmate of Bishop Dickson offered the Post Communion Prayer. The new Bishop then gave the people his Episcopal Blessing. The hymn sung following the Dismissal was "Praise to the Lord, the Almighty". The bishops, clergy and visiting dignitaries moved from their places. It was done! The Rt. Rev. Alex Dockery Dickson, Jr., was now the First Bishop of West Tennessee.

Following the Service a reception was held in a space prepared and beautifully and tastefully decorated at the Convention Center for Bishop Dickson, his family, the Presiding Bishop and other participants. Many in the congregation were able to greet their new Bishop for the first time, old friends were seen, acquaintances were renewed, and so the great occasion came to a close and the general concensus was that it had been well done. Every phase of the life of the Church from the smallest mission to the largest parish had been a part of the event. In was a day to remember with joy and thanksgiving. Even the drenching rain and the lowering clouds could not dampen the enthusiasm of the people of the Diocese of West Tennessee who were now well embarked on a new journey in the Mission of the Church, a journey firmly rooted in our historic past and with eyes firmly fixed in hope toward the future.

> Gordon Bernard, Vicar
> St. Philip, Davieshire, Brunswick

Consecration of the Bishop
Cook Convention Center
April 9, 1983

The Rt. Rev. W. Fred Gates, Jr., Suffragan Bishop of Tennessee, The Presiding Bishop, The Most Reverend John Maury Allin

Mrs. Alex D. Dickson, Jr., Cassandra Earhart Dickson (Mrs. Charles W.), Charles Wicks Dickson, Charles W. Dickson holding Jennifer Faye Dickson and Stephanie Nell Dickson (standing)

Mrs. John Maury Allin and Mrs. W. Fred Gates, Jr.

The Rev. Frank M. Cooper, IV

The Rt. Rev. W. Fred Gates, Jr., Charles M. Crump, Mrs. R. Lee Winchester, Jr.

The Most Reverend and Mrs. John M. Allin

A Bishop Is Consecrated

The Rt. Rev. Alex D. Dickson, Jr.
The Rt. Rev. E. Paul Haynes,
The Rt. Rev. W. Fred Gates, Jr.

Choirs, Led by Dr. John L. Hooker and Dr. Sam Batt Owens, Mrs. Timothy Sloan, Organist

Acolytes

Procession Beginning

Paul Wilson, Paul A. Calame, Jr., James R. Crumrine, Mrs. R. Lee Winchester, Jr., Mrs. Byron M. Hutchison

The Ministers of Consecration: The Rt. Rev. Duncan Montgomery Gray, Jr.; The Rt. Rev. William Evan Sanders; The Most Rev. John Maury Allin; The Rt. Rev. W. Fred Gates, Jr.; and The Rt. Rev. Herbert Alcorn Donovan, Jr.

Canonical Testimony, by Chancellor, Mr. Charles M. Crump

274　　　　　　　　Heirs Through Hope

Laying on of Hands

The Most Reverend John Maury Allin, Sermon—"A Charge for All of Us."

The Epistle—
Mrs. R. Lee Winchester, Jr.

The Rt. Rev. Alex D. Dickson, Jr. immediately after Consecration

Communion Served to some 2000 in 15 minutes,
The Rev. Gordon Bernard, The Rev. Ralph Smith, and Bishop Sanders.

Recessional

A Bishop Is Consecrated

The Rev. Frank M. Cooper, IV, The Rt. Rev. Alex D. Dickson, Jr., The Very Rev. C. Edward Reeves, Jr.

The Rev. Robert M. Watson, Jr., The Rev. Wallace M. Pennepacker

The Rev. Robert E. Allen and guests

Paul Calame, Jr., holds the brown bag (offering collected), William Mackey, Mr. and Mrs. William Lea

The Rev. Frank M. Cooper, IV; M. Anderson Cobb, Jr., John Peyton

Worship

"God made my cathedral
Under the Stars;
He gave my cathedral
Trees for its spires;
He hewed me an altar
In the depth of a hill
He gave for a hymnal
A rock-bedded rill;
He voiced me a sermon
Of heavenly light
In the beauty around me—
The calmness of night;
And I felt as I knelt
On the velvet-like sod
I had supped of the Spirit
In the Temple of God."

—Ruth Furbee.
Leaves of Gold p. 187

CHAPTER 9

The Welcoming and Seating of the Bishop

Since Bishop Dickson was consecrated in the Cook Convention Center rather than in St. Mary's Cathedral, a special service was held in the Cathedral on Ascension Day, Thursday, May 12, for the purpose of installing the new Bishop in his Cathedral Church. The service is entitled "The Welcoming and Seating of the Bishop."[1]

Adding to the significance of this occasion was the fact that on this same date St. Mary's Cathedral observed the 125th anniversary of its founding. The Cathedral was consecrated on May 13, 1858, Ascension Day. That same year Bishop Otey moved to Memphis and lived in a house next door to St. Mary's. A few years later St. Mary's Church became the Cathedral of the Diocese of Tennessee.

At the service for Bishop Dickson the congregation gathered prior to the beginning hour of seven o'clock in the evening. The doors were then opened, and the Bishop was met by a respresentative group which included the Very Rev. C. Edward Reeves, Jr., Dean of the Cathedral, the Rev. Frank M. Cooper, IV, Associate at the Cathedral, W. Lewis Wood, Bishop's Warden of the Cathedral Chapter, Charles L. Chavis, Chapter's Warden of the Cathedral Chapter, Paul P. Wilson, Treasurer of the Diocese, the Rev. Wallace M. Pennepacker, President of the Standing Committee of the Diocese, and Mrs. Charles L. Clarke, President of the Episcopal Church Women of the Diocese of West Tennessee.

At the door the Dean welcomed Bishop Dickson as "our Bishop" to his Cathedral Church, "the symbol and center of your pastoral, liturgical, and teaching ministry in this Diocese." The Bishop responded by promising to be "a faithful shepherd and servant among you." He then requested that he be seated in the Cathedral, the Bishop's Chair, which is the symbol of his office.

During the singing of the stirring hymn, "Crown Him with Many Crowns," a procession of a crucifer and two torch bearers, the welcoming group, and Bishop Dickson made its way to the Chancel, and Bishop Dickson was escorted to the Cathedra. The Bishop was greeted with applause, which was followed by a fanfare consisting of organ, trumpets and bells, ending with the singing of the "Te Deum."

The ceremony continued with the celebration of the Holy Communion. Bishop Dickson was the celebrant and the preacher.

In his sermon, the Bishop used as his text the incident whereby Elijah cast his mantle over Elisha, as leadership in ancient Israel was transferred from one to the other. Bishop Dickson urged the new Diocese to move forward in new directions, and to be engaged in total ministry.

The service music was performed by the Cathedral Choir, led by Joe A. Morrow, Organist and Choirmaster of the Cathedral. The Prelude and Postlude were performed by Dr. John David Peterson, Organist and Choirmaster of Christ Church, and Chairman of the Organ Department of Memphis State University.

The service in the Cathedral was followed by a gala reception in the Parish Hall.

W. Fred Gates, Jr., Retired
Suffragan Bishop of Tennessee

THE WELCOMING AND SEATING OF THE BISHOP 279

Seating of the Bishop
May 12, 1983
St. Mary's Cathedral

The Right Reverend Alex Dockery Dickson, Jr., First Bishop of West Tennessee

Canon George A. Fox

Canon George A. Fox, the Rev. Donald E. Mowery, Bishop Dickson

Canon George A. Fox, Bishop Alex D. Dickson, Jr., the Rev. Donald E. Mowery

The Altar

Bishop Dickson knocking at Cathedral door

Bishop Dickson administering Communion

Canon George A. Fox, Bishop Dickson and the Rev. Donald E. Mowery

Bishop Dickson and the Rev. Donald E. Mowery

The Right Reverend Alex Dockery Dickson, Jr.

CHAPTER 10

Time Is Postlude
The Challenge of Tomorrow

> "They reap not where they labored;
> We reap what they have sown;
> Our harvest may be garnered
> By ages yet unknown.
> The days of old have dowered us
> With gifts beyond all praise;
> Our Father, make us faithful
> To serve the coming days. Amen."[1]

And what does the future hold for the newly created Episcopal Diocese of West Tennessee?

What are the objectives, the anticipated service, the crowning rewards for the conspicuous groundwork which is presently evident on which the accomplishments of the future must be based? The whole answer can come only after a careful study, evaluation and adaptation of the "Then, Now and Yon" of the Episcopal Church. The assimilation of past endeavors coupled with new ideals and determination can project a pattern to guide future achievement. Abundant faith and prayer are necessary with which we pave the road to tomorrow. Imbued, as free heirs in hope these tools—faith and prayer—must ever be ready for dedicated employment.

A favorite bit of verse comes to mind which seems to best express the efficacy of the tools of faith and prayer:

> "If radio's slim fingers can pluck a melody
> From the night, and toss it over land or sea . . .
> If the petalled white notes of a violin
> Can be heard across a mountain or a city's din;
> If songs like crimson roses can be culled from thin blue air
> Why should mortals wonder that God hears and answers prayer."[2]

The organization of the work of the new Diocese reveals a number of essential committees, each with a specific responsibility to work now and to meet the challenge of the future. From the list as recorded in the 1983 Diocesan Journal, several division Chairmen have been chosen to express opinions of their work as they foresee its relation to the uncharted future. To these very special Churchmen and Churchwomen hearty thanks are sincerely given for their cooperation and timely inspiring comments! By their accounts we shall receive a bold peep into the full meaning of the challenge of tomorrow.

University Ministries in Memphis

Quintard Foundation (named for Bishop Quintard), serving the University of Tennessee Medical Units (since renamed the University of Tennessee Center for the Health Sciences) has been operational since 1952. Begun under the auspices of St. Mary's Cathedral, its directors have been canons of the Cathedral. They have been H. Sheldon Davis (1954-1956), Rue I. Moore (1957-1963), and Robert M. Watson (1962-1978). Housed initially in a converted dwelling adjacent to the medical center, then in a rented office suite in Goodman House Apartment-Hotel at 22 N. Manassas. Quintard Foundation has since 1970 shared the occupancy of the University Interfaith Center, 740 Court Avenue, toward the construction of which the Diocese of Tennessee contributed $33,000 realized from the sale of a parcel of real estate purchased for projected Episcopal student center, the construction of which was deemed impractical in the light of developing plans for an ecumenical building at much less cost to our church. Our medical center ministry was subsequently integrated in many areas with that of the ecumenical University Interfaith Association, which holds title to the center building; and whose program and costs of operation we share with the Roman Catholic, Methodist and Presbyterian judicatories. A distinctively Episcopal Mission to the health-care education-and-delivery enterprise is conducted concurrently.

The University Interfaith Center building was constructed on land owned by the Methodist Church, valued at $35,000. The Roman Catholic Bishop of Nashville donated $10,000, while the Presbytery of Memphis and a fund-raising drive helped make up the balance of the $256,375 needed to erect the building, which was completed and dedicated in January 1970.

A second significant ecumenical venture which has been a fruit of our medical center ministry was the *Memphis Institute of Medicine and Religion*, charted in November 1967. Quintard Foundation and the Diocese of Tennessee were the prime mover in this undertaking. The Diocese provided the initial funding with a $10,000 grant, and has supported it with annual subsidies since. The Institute is an academically-accredited clinical pastoral training program providing chaplaincy services to patients in the City of

Memphis Hospitals and the Memphis Medical Center. Thus, our medical center ministry has two thrusts, one aimed at those in the healing professions, and the other to those who come to receive treatment.

Barth House, serving Memphis State University, had its formal inception in 1958, when a frame dwelling at 409 Patterson Street, adjoining the campus, was purchased and converted into a student center. Approximately two years later, a garage on the premises was converted into a chapel, and the facility was named St. John Chrysostom's Chapel—Barth House. Regular worship was offered beginning October 15, 1958, and in January of the following year Canon Robert W. Knox was assigned as first chaplain-director (part-time). After Canon Knox's departure in August 1960, Canon Rue I. Moore, Quintard Foundation director, supplied chaplaincy services until September 1962, when Canon W. Carson Fraser assumed the part-time directorship. In May 1963, Chaplain Edwin L. Hoover was appointed first full-time director, and began his duties in September of that year, serving through January 1972. Under Fr. Hoover's administration, the present St. Theodore's Chapel—Barth House was constructed on the site formerly occupied by the old buildings. The following sketch appeared in the *Order of Science* for the consecration of the new facility, which took place on May 5, 1968:

> "...The ministry of Barth House has been richly blessed, temporally and spiritually, during its decade of life. As Chaplain, I want to express my thanks to the Board, and for the Board, to all of you for your concern and interest. We bid your thanksgiving with us in our joy today, and your prayers that Barth House may give vision to the University, and in turn be a place where the University can challenge and renew the Church.
>
> Faithfully and affectionately,
> Edwin L. Hoover, Chaplain"

Upon Fr. Hoover's acceptance of a call to another diocese in 1972, various priest supplied services until the appointment of the Rev. H. Edwin Caudill as director on 1 August 1972. Fr. Caudill served until October 1976, when Canon Robert M. Watson was asked to assume this responsibility in addition to the Quintard Foundation directorship at the University of Tennessee Center for the Health Sciences, in order to cut operating costs. Dr. Watson has held the dual post since, assisted during 1977-78 by a semi-retired priest, the Rev. George C. Gibson.

The dual board-and-budget administrative structure proved increasingly cumbersome and inefficient, leading to a consolidation of the two campus ministries into one administrative organization, the Memphis Episcopal University Ministry, effective 1 September 1978. With a single budget and board, centered at Barth House, but retaining an office at the University Interfaith Center, this new structure has more flexibility and the capability of working with all persons involved in any way in higher education in the city. Dr. Watson is director, assisted by Mrs. Marianne Williams.

Barth House as prescribed by Canon 22, 1983 Journal of the Diocese of West Tennessee is a Mission Station. Therefore, it functions as such and is neither a Parish nor an Organized Mission.

The Reverend Robert M. Watson, Ph.D

The Tennessee Churchman

In the spring of 1963 the Rt. Rev. John Vander Horst asked Mrs. Louis Baumgartner (Isabel), a communicant of St. Timothy's in Kingsport, if she would be willing to start a diocesan newspaper for Tennessee. Prior to that time Mrs. Wells Awsumb had edited an occasional news publication which included the two Bishop's journals, a message from the Diocesan, and news of the national Church. The publication, *Forward in Tennessee,* appeared four or five times a year and came out of the Bishop's office in Memphis.

Mrs. Baumgartner met in the summer of 1963 with Bishops Vander Horst and Sanders, the presidents of the Episcopal Church Women and the Episcopal Young Churchmen, and representatives of the Diocese's department of promotion. A policy statement was written and final plans were made for the new diocesan newspaper, *The Tennessee Churchman.* The first issue was printed in Elizabethton and mailed in October to all communicants in the Diocese of Tennessee.

In its first year of publication The *Tennessee Churchman* won the Presiding Bishop's award, a national award for the most improved diocesan newspaper. Under the editorial hand of Isabel Baumgartner the *Churchman* became one of the most admired and respected of all diocesan newspapers. Isabel, as she is known amongst her colleagues, was instrumental in the formation of the Episcopal Communicators, a nationwide professional organization of Episcopal journalists. *The Churchman's* first editor also has covered more House of Bishops meetings than any other church journalist. During the 1982 House of Bishops meeting at General Convention in New Orleans, it was noted that only three bishops present on the floor had been to more House of Bishops meetings than had Mrs. Baumgartner.

Mrs. Baumgartner retired in March of 1982 and the Rev. Joseph S. T. Alford became the Diocese's first full-time communications officer with the responsibility of editing and publishing *The Tennessee Churchman*. This position was made possible by a three-year grant of funds from Venture in Mission. During that same year, with division of the Diocese imminent, Mr. Bill Givens of Memphis became the part-time communications officer for the new Diocese of West Tennessee and associate editor of the *Churchman*.

During 1983, the first year as two separate dioceses, all Tennessee Episcopalians continue to receive the *Churchman*, which strives to cover the news of both the Dioceses of Tennessee and West Tennessee. When planning for division the structure committee and Bishop and Council considered that *The Tennessee Churchman* might continue to serve the two, then three, dioceses in Tennessee because of our long history together. The two dioceses are cooperating presently in the publication of the *Churchman* but both dioceses are open to the possibility that each new diocese might need its own separate publication. The forward look for *The Tennessee Churchman* is that it may remain one publication serving all Tennessee Episcopalians who share a common heritage, but it may well become three new and distinctive publications.

Joseph S. T. Alford, Editor
The Tennessee Churchman

Communications Outlook

In 1981, the Diocese of Tennessee made a giant step in increasing the level of communications among its members, as well as to persons outside the faith, when it set up an Office of Communications, funded by a VIM grant. The grant enabled the Diocese to hire professional Communications Officers for the three grand divisions, which were destined to become self-standing Dioceses.

While the Diocese of West Tennessee was in the formative stages, the Communications Officer worked through the area commission, the Episcopal Metropolitan Ministry—later becoming a part of the Diocesan House staff when Bishop Dickson was consecrated.

The first year of the operation was a busy one, since there were many facets of the organization of the Diocese and election of a Bishop that needed to be communicated to the various congregations and to the general public. New programs and procedures had to be developed, and new opportunities to increase the level of awareness of Diocesan affairs arose frequently. Many congregations sought the aid of the Communications Office in strengthening their own information—dissemination programs in their local communities.

The structure of the new Diocese of West Tennessee offers an excellent opportunity for communications programs to continue and to grow. Since most of the Diocese is within the Area of Dominant Influence (ADI) of the Memphis media, excellent vehicles for communication are available to us. But we also have to work with the major media in all of the metropolitan areas, especially those in Jackson and in the northern part of the Diocese.

While we should continue to work diligently with the print media, we must increase the exposure of our people and programs through the electronic mediums available to us. Already, we have an increased awareness of these facilities, and the election and consecration of our Bishop led to some excellent television and radio coverage. We also have begun to look seriously at the communications phenomenon of the decade, cable television. Through the kindness of civic spirit of Federal Express, we were able to videotape the consecration for a series of several broadcasts on cable systems in Memphis and in other parts of the Diocese. Videocassettes of the consecration have been made available to the various congregations and to individuals for program and private viewing.

As technology moves in that direction, we must become increasingly aware of the powers of the video image and to use it to further our communications efforts. The larger congregations are beginning to install video recording and viewing equipment, and it is hoped that more and more will follow their lead as video begins to replace the traditional movie projectors and filmstrip equipment for program uses. We must develop ways to use this equipment and technology on a Diocesan level, hopefully at some point in the future having production facilities to provide programming to Diocesan congregations. We should also increase the awareness of the video program materials available to us through the national communications office of the Episcopal Church, as well as other denominational and secular sources.

We must also begin to examine how he will develop our internal communications among individual members of the various congregations. Through seminars and other methods, we hope to assist and strengthen the communications efforts of the churches through their bulletins, newsletters, brochures, and through increased use of community news media.

Also, we must determine if and when we are to move to a Diocesan newspaper, or if we will continue to share a newspaper with the other two Dioceses of Tennessee. This will require much study and deliberation, both in the determination of the role and scope of the publication, as well as its funding and day-to-day operation.

Presently, the Communications Office is a part-time effort. However, there are enough opportunities for communications to make it a full-time staff position—especially if a West Tennessee diocesan newspaper comes into being. We should look toward increasing and strengthening the Communications Office as our Diocese grows, using it as a valuable and effective tool for outreach, both from the Diocese to the congregations, and from the congregations to their members and to the communities which make up the Diocese of West Tennessee.

Bill Givens
Communications Officer

The Development Office
The Diocese of Tennessee—The Diocese of West Tennessee

The Development Office of The Diocese of Tennessee was activated on July 15, 1982 by the employment of Glenn N. Holliman of Bell Buckle, Tennessee, as its first director. With the division of the Diocese, Mr. Holliman came to serve both the Diocese of Tennessee and the Diocese of West Tennessee. Mr. Holliman had previously served as headmaster of Cambridge Academy, Greenwood, South Carolina and Assistant Headmaster and Director of Development at The Webb School, Bell Buckle, Tennessee.

The purpose of the Development Office is to encourage Planned Gifts for the parishes, dioceses, and the national church. A Planned Gift is a bequest in a Will, a charitable remainder trust, participation in a pooled income fund, a charitable lead trust, a gift of life insurance, a life estate, personal or real property, and a gift of stocks and bonds. These gifts are encouraged for the purpose of building endowment. The First Annual Convention of The Diocese of West Tennessee passed a resolution:

1. Affirming Planned Giving as an appropriate statement of Christian stewardship.
2. Encouraging all Episcopalians to consider a Planned Gift to their church, and
3. Encouraging income from endowments established to be used for Christian outreach and building the Kingdom of God.

The Director of Development speaks to vestries, councils, Sunday Schools, ECW's, Men's Clubs, and parish events and provides information about Planned Giving and the outreach work of the Diocese. Literature and personal counseling is provided. By the end of the first year, two-thirds of all parishes and missions in the Diocese had initiated or had scheduled Planned Giving activity.

Of particular note was an Estate Planning Seminar held at Holy Communion, Memphis, on April 25, 1983. Bishop Alex Dickson spoke on the theology of Christian stewardship. Mr. Roy Bell, chairman of Holy Communion's endowment committee presided. Speaking to the need of endowment for Christian outreach was the Rev. Lewis McKee of Holy Communion.

A much respected Memphis business leader and banker, the Rev. Mr. McKee entered the ministry late in life. A dedicated Christian, his warm personality has brought comfort to many in time of crisis. His organization skills and business acumen have served the church well. A leader in the Venture in Mission drive, Mr. McKee urged the establishment of a diocesan-wide planned giving program and now serves as chairman of the Development Committee. Also serving from West Tennessee on that joint diocesan committee is Joseph Orgill, III, Memphis.

In 1983, a West Tennessee Development Committee was appointed. The Reverend Mr. McKee and Mr. Orgill serve as do the Reverend J. Kelly Avery, M.D., Union City; Mr. Henry Morgan, Memphis; Mr. Peter Wilmott, Memphis and Mr. Frank Caldwell, Jr., Jackson.

The support and encouragement of this program by Bishop Fred Gates cannot be overlooked. He has observed many times that as gifts and bequests for endowments are received, additional resources will become available "to expand the Kingdom of God and to build His Church in this world."

Although still a young program, many caring Episcopalians have made changes in their Wills and have included a bequest for their parish or diocese. Because of the nature of this program, it will be many years before these gifts are realized. Yet, the generous spirit exhibited now by West Tennessee Episcopalians will strengthen the church for generations to come. Thanks be to God!

Glenn N. Holliman
Director of Development

Episcopal Church Home

The Church Home was founded in 1865 by a group of Episcopalians from the four Episcopal parishes in Memphis. The Institution Board consisted of the Rector and one layman from each. The Home would serve the many Civil War orphans and widows roaming the streets.

The Home has had many locations from 100 Market Street to Dunlap Street, then to the Buntyn Station location where it burned in 1871. At this time the treasury went down to ten cents.

In 1874 the Home was moved to Jackson Avenue and was located there for sixty-four years.

On November 1, 1872, the Sisters of St. Mary from Peekskill, New York, consented to undertake the work for the Church Home in Memphis.

The devoted and heroic work of the Sisters during the yellow fever epidemics in 1873, 1878 and 1879 saved the lives of many children. On August 26, 1878, Sister Amelia moved children of all races and creeds to Canfield Asylum on the outskirts of town as it was not as near the infected area as the Jackson Avenue location. The Jackson Avenue location was then used as an infirmary. Many children were moved to Huntsville, Alabama. In May 1880, the Home was placed entirely under the care of the Sisters and remained until 1929.

Sister Anne Christine served as the efficient director for the Home for over thirty-five years. Sister Anne is still lovingly remembered by two wings of the present Home that bear her name "Anne Hall" and "Christine Hall."

In 1929 the Sisters of St. Mary decided to leave Memphis.

The order of St. Anne sent three Sisters who were installed on November 2, 1929, by Bishop Gailor in the Chapel of the Holy Spirit. The Sisters gave up control of the Home in 1936.

Bishop Maxon ordered the Diocese of Tennessee to take over the management of the Church Home. At this time the Home was caring for about one hundred children.

In 1938 the Home moved to Oakville, Tennessee, on Lamar Avenue and was located there for twenty-two years.

In 1941 a Board of Trustees was formed, composed of the Bishop, seven men, and a Board of Directors, composed of one woman from each parish in Shelby County.

In the thirties and early forties at the Lamar location the Home served boys and girls. Later the program changed to the care of dependent or neglected girls, or girls from broken homes.

The Chapel of the Holy Spirit was consecrated June 22, 1941 by Bishop Maxon. The beautiful windows, old brass and other memorials are still in use at the Bishop Otey Memorial Chapel.

In 1961 land was donated and in May of 1962 the new facility at 3232 E. Raines Road opened.

In 1974 the program changed with the needs of the city. A contract was entered into with the Tennessee Department of Education. This contract was for one year.

In 1975 a contract was signed with the Memphis City Schools as a Residential Training Center for autistic-like children. In the contract the Church Home agreed to provide all maintenance of buildings and grounds, vehicles for transportation, a house-keeping staff and a manager who oversees this staff.

The Church Home programs are for children with severe behavior and communication disorders. These disorders warrant individual attention in a structured environment. Programming emphasis include speech and language skill development, selfcare, socialization, functional pre-academics living skills, pre-vocational skills and lecture time training. An individualized education program is developed for each child.

There is also an extended day program for children between the ages of four and eight, who are at the Home for several hours each day with training in the same areas as above.

The Division of Special Education, Memphis City Schools, have in the past used one wing of the Home for behavioral disordered children. The funding for this program was cut several years ago. In the fall of 1983 the Home will again have short term residential placement in the area of behavioral disordered with the Church Home supplying ninety percent of the funding. This is a one year contract.

For the future the Trustees and Board of Directors visualize expanding the residential component for autistic children.

Our work has been nationally recognized.

It is our prayer to provide the equipment and furnishings that enrich the learning experience and enhance the living environment for these children, that they may reach their maximum potential.

Mrs. Ralph (Ida Lee Manns) Scott, President
Board of Directors, Church Home

Episcopal Churchmen of Tennessee

The Episcopal Churchmen of Tennessee was organized 1947. It was designed to bring laymen throughout the Diocese together once a year for a meeting to enrich their spiritual life and for fellowship. West Tennesseans played an important part in organizing the Laymen. The third president of the organization was Burnell Stevens, a West Tennessean. The meetings are always held at DuBose Conference Center at Monteagle, Tennessee.

The Laymen are organized into four divisions: Upper East, Lower East, Middle and West Tennessee. While all of the divisions support the organization the largest number of attendants has always been from West Tennessee. Each year an award (an oak bucket) is given to the parish and mission with the largest attendance. Calvary, St. Mary's, Grace St. Luke's and Holy Communion have won this "bucket" more than all other parishes in the diocese and St. Anne's, Millington always took home the mission award until they became a parish.

The Churchmen is solely for laymen and no clergy attend except by special invitation. Even the Bishops have to be invited although there has never been a meeting without them.

Attendance at these meetings exceeded 600 laymen in the middle sixties and for the past several years has been about four hundred.

The presidency of the Churchmen is rotated among the four divisions and each division has an area vice president. Among the West Tennessee presidents have been Bob Ruch, Ewing Carruthers, Joe Patten, Shep Tate, Sam Hollis, Bob McRae, Charles Crump and Fred Cochran.

The format of the program is to have an outstanding keynote speaker, usually a nationally known layman, for the Friday night opening session. On Saturday morning a report is made by the Bishop (or Bishops as is presently the situation). Saturday afternoons are free time and laymen enjoy golf, tennis, tours of The University of the South or just visiting with each other. The Saturday night session is highlighted with another outstanding speaker.

Communion services are held Saturday and Sunday mornings with the Saturday service in the DuBose pavillion and the Sunday service in All Saints at Sewanee. Each evening session is concluded with the Service of Compline. Singing is a large part of the program and it is indeed a thrilling experience to hear four hundred men singing "Rise Up O Men of God."

With the creation of the Diocese of West Tennessee it was decided to continue the Churchmen in the same format as before, and the Episcopal Churchmen of Tennessee will involve both Dioceses. This meeting is one of the largest regular meetings of laymen in the Anglican Communion and its thirty-six year history will continue with the support of all Tennessee Churchmen.

George Clarke

Episcopal Churchwomen

The Episcopal Churchwomen of the new Diocese of West Tennessee held their first annual meeting on January 27, 1983, at St. Mary's Cathedral, Memphis, with the Right Reverend W. Fred Gates, Jr., installing the officers. There was a good attendance and much enthusiasm and all seemed delighted to see the new Diocese off to such a good start.

Since the women of the original Tennessee Diocese had been divided into Districts with separate organizations in each, it simplified our converting from the District of West Tennessee to the Diocese of West Tennessee. We have 34 churches and 31 of these have organized groups of Churchwomen. The other three are small missions that we certainly hope can grow. I have been able to visit all three of these. We feel that in having the Diocese smaller we may be able to know each other better and work together, not only in our own Churches but in activities of the whole Diocese.

There are plans for an altar at St. Columba and our Altar Committee expects their first project to be obtaining hangings and linens to be used there. As our main Mission work we have undertaken to assist Father Emmanuel Twesigye of Uganda in completing his education. We expect to participate in the Diocesan Christian Education Workshop in the fall of 1983 to stimulate continuing education. Many of our women are involved in the four year Education for Ministry course sponsored by Sewanee. Of course, we will always continue the excellent work of the United Thank Offering and its many projects. Most of our Churches have representatives who participate in the Churchwomen United. We also hope to re-establish an interest in the Church Periodical Club, which for many years was well supported, but recently has been dropped in many Dioceses.

Here in the Diocese we have the Church Home which is doing a most creditable job with autistic children. Youth Service, whose programs have spread throughout the United States, is outstanding. The progress they make with underprivileged children and young adults is remarkable. St. Augustine's Guild is an organization to assist in supporting this fine work. Our Churchwomen contribute both donations and service to each of these organizations.

We are looking forward to progressing steadily under the excellent leadership of our Bishop Alex D. Dickson, Jr.

> Jane Alvis (Mrs. Charles L.) Clarke, President
> Diocesan Churchwomen of West Tennessee

Episcopal Young Churchmen

The Episcopal youth in West Tennessee have fashioned a reputation of steady support for their Church over the years. Even though a great distance from the Dubose Conference Center in Monteagle, camps and conferences and conventions have all been heavily represented by the West. Such a strong tradition provides a reliable foundation upon which development of youth ministry in the Diocese of West Tennessee will continue.

Certainly a general hope shared by all in the new Diocese is that we will form our current strength so as to produce a greater sense of Episcopal community throughout the entire Diocese. It is no less a goal of Youth Ministry in the new diocese to see the activity of faith consistently shared between urban and rural youth groups.

Future developments should also see a balance between programs designed for the intake of Christian renewal and the outreach of Christian mission. The former provides a vision or a "taste" of the kingdom without the sense of purpose perishes in the heart. On the other hand, attention to Christian outreach and mission projects are needed to offer actual "hands on" experience. These mission efforts keep our Christian vision from dwindling into mere wishful thinking.

I believe the development of youth ministry in the 1980's will go well provided they continue to be blessed with caring adults who offer their time and energy to the support of the young people. There is certainly a strong heritage from which youth ministry can proceed. We are also in a time where many young people are truly sifting through the things of this world in search of spiritual reality. The youth of the 80's are also more and more willing to commit themselves to the search, although depth of commitment is becoming increasingly difficult to establish. Our young people face a world in which the trauma of rapid change is one of the few consistent realities they can easily perceive. To us, no less than the youth, comes the increased challenge of learning how to stand with the steadfastness of God's love in the midst of the whirling world. However, I also believe the Holy Spirit has become no less adept as a teacher and I look forward with eagerness to the days ahead for youth work in the Diocese of West Tennessee.

Edward T. McNabb, Jr.

Episcopal Youth
The Church of Tomorrow—Today!

Today in the Diocese of West Tennessee the youth movement is growing and expanding to meet the needs of its area at a rate previously unknown. As a smaller diocese, the youth are able to concentrate their efforts in West Tennessee thus yielding higher participation than was given in the former diocese or in the district system.

The diocesan youth structure in West Tennessee is the Fellowship of Episcopal Youth, FEY. Under the present constitution the FEY is composed of all Episcopalians in the Diocese in the seventh through the twelfth grades. "The purpose of the Fellowship of Episcopal Youth shall be to provide an organization to foster and promote channels through which Episcopal Youth may actually share in the experience of Christian living and so come to know Christ through a balanced life of worship, study, fellowship, service and therefore further His kingdom in the Diocese, the Nation, and the World." (Constitution, Article 11)

The structure of a diocesan youth organization was provided for as the diocese was being set-up. In the first budget the Department of Youth Ministry was one of the largest line items. The Department was first defined as an acting committee to keep youth work going during the interim period until the new Bishop arrived. After Bishop Dickson was consecrated, the Department consisted of: Ted McNabb, Don Brooks, Marshall Scott, Jim Crumrine, Mary Jo Parnell, Diane Riggs, Velma Hughes, Ronald Canter, and James Morris. The Department is now the body that oversees all the Episcopal Youth work in the diocese.

Given the strength of the youth program in the Diocese of Tennessee it was inevitable that everyone would be anxious to begin West Tennessee. In August of 1982 a Convocation of the youth was held at St. Mary's Cathedral in Memphis. Ed Wills chaired the planning committee and with the committee arrived at "Hopes and Fears in the New Diocese" as a topic. Kit Crighton chaired the Convention.

In December of the same year a "Pre-Convention" was held at St. Columba Retreat Center. There the program was entitled "Being the Church in West Tennessee." The thoughts of the youth, where they want to go and how to get there, were discussed. The "Pre-Convention" was chaired by Jim Crumrine. Both "Pre-Convention" and the Convocation provided the Department and the youth leaders with ideas necessary to begin to plan the first year of youth work in the new diocese.

Beginning with a strong "Youth Presence" at the First Annual Convention of the Diocese of West Tennessee the 1983 program has run well. In March the youth gathered at St. Luke's in Jackson for their Primary Convention. This convention covered the elections of Karen Clay as Chairman, Nancy Dilts as Associate Chairman, and Merideth Cisel as Communicator for the Summer Convention in West Tennessee. The standard term of office in youth work runs from Summer Conventions, but for the first term a group of officers were elected for only five months (March to August).

The Convention was also broken into caucuses to discuss summer convention, fall retreat, and bike-a-thon.

April was a high month for youth work in the diocese. Jim Crumrine read the Old Testament lesson and Karen Clay and Nancy Dilts represented the youth at Bishop Dickson's Consecration. The West Tennessee bike-a-thon was held three weeks later. This year the money was used to aid youth work in West Tennessee (previously the money has gone to the Diocese of Costa Rica). The week before six representatives from West Tennessee traveled to the annual youth meeting of Province IV. The Province consists of twenty-three dioceses of which West Tennessee is the youngest.

Camp Gailor-Maxon is a long-time favorite of the youth. Open to fourth graders through college freshman during specified weeks of June and July. Camp Gailor-Maxon in 1983 was again a success.

A large number of youth from West Tennessee attended these camps. Camp is one of the programs that encourages continuing unity between the dioceses.

With a smaller diocese the focus of youth ministry can become more specialized. In the first year the youth have worked in Youth Service, Inc., tutoring ministeries, Clown Ministry, and the food bank. Much thought and time is being put into inner-city projects also.

Also under the Department of Youth Ministry is the Clown Ministry program. "Clowning" is a ministry which depicts the clown as a "fool for Christ's sake." Presently under the direction of Mary Jo Powell, Jim Crumrine, and Marshall Scott the program has held two workshops, five Sunday services, and several charity projects. The ministry has grown quickly and is flourishing in the new diocese.

Another youth project that the Department is considering is "Happening." The Happening movement is very popular in the Diocese of Tennessee and continues to be of great interest in the new diocese. "Happening" is an intense retreat and renewal weekend for sophomores through services in high school and adults.

The summer FEY Convention and fall retreat will round out the first year of youth work in the new diocese. Ted McNabb chaired the Department until summer convention when Duncan Gray took over the position. The second year looks even more promising. As the youth grow and expand so will their out-reach through-out the diocese.

James R. Crumrine

Episcopal Schools

The future of society and of the Church is in large measure to be determined by the education of today's children and young people. Will the children be complacent adults? Will they be believers in God and in themselves? Will they be caring people who contribute to their society, their church and their fellow men? Will they have the knowledge and wisdom to make the best use of their talents?

These are all questions vital to the future of the Episcopal Church in West Tennessee. They lead directly to an examination of how we educate our children and to the conclusion that the Church has an interest in establishing, maintaining, and nurturing schools of quality where academic, personal, and spiritual standards are highly valued.

West Tennessee is fortunate to have a number of fine schools that have an orientation toward the Episcopal Church, each offering a unique educational opportunity. The Episcopal Day School in Jackson offers innovative education in grades Kindergarten-9. In Memphis, St. George's Day School in suburban Germantown and Grace-St. Luke's in midtown provide outstanding coeducational elementary education. St. Mary's Episcopal School in east Memphis is for girls in Kindergarten-12 and is recognized as one of the leading academic programs in the mid-South.

Obviously, the schools share the common traditions of the Episcopal Church. What will they be in the future? In looking at the present and future of the Episcopal schools, it is essential to understand the premise that they do not represent an attempt to segregate children socially, religiously, or racially. On the contrary, the Episcopal schools must be voices of responsible leadership among other independent schools in promoting cultural, religious, and racial diversity. The schools must stand for a superior quality of life that is rooted in concern and service to society.

As stated in the "Report of Social, Economic, and Racial Mix in Episcopal Schools" by the National Association of Episcopal Schools, "we maintain that our schools should seek to be inclusive rather than exclusive, that our schools should be broadly representative of the social, economic, and racial groups which reside within their reachable communities. . . . No matter what the content of education may be, the process of education is enhanced through the diversity which students and teachers bring to it. Dialogue, not monologue, fosters learning."

In recent years private education in the South has often been viewed as promoting social, economic, and racial exclusion. The Episcopal schools, however, must provide sound leadership for justice and social responsibility.

Another objective of the Episcopal schools should be the teaching of respect and appreciation for religious diversity. It is an interesting fact that Episcopal schools throughout the country attract a majority of their students from outside the Episcopal Church. Our schools are heavily populated with children from the other Protestant denominations as well as Catholic, Jewish, Moslem, and Hindu students. While it is testimony to the educational quality that attracts such diverse enrollment, it is also an opportunity for all the students to enrich their lives.

For the Church, this diversity presents an enormous opportunity to communicate with hundreds of young people that would otherwise have no contact with the Episcopal Church. It remains to be seen whether or not the Church can take constructive advantage of this unique opportunity.

With the creation of the Diocese of West Tennessee, the likelihood of closer communication between the Diocese and the schools is increased merely by proximity. Furthermore, it may encourage a closer working relationship among the several Episcopal schools within the area.

However, the development of improved communication in this regard should not preclude the continued participation in the Episcopal Schools Commission which currently certifies eleven Episcopal schools in the state. The continuation of a statewide network of Episcopal schools crossing diocesan lines is no less desirable than before.

If we expect our schools to educate future leaders, then the schools themselves must be leaders to the future. They must stand for progress rooted in the experiences and wisdom of the past and in the teaching of love for all men.

> Geoffrey Butler, Headmaster
> St. Mary's Episcopal School, Memphis

St. Columba Episcopal Conference Center

On the afternoon of May 2, 1982, the St. Columba Episcopal Conference Center, located at 4577 Billy Maher Road, northeast of Bartlett, in Shelby County, Tennessee, was dedicated. Appropriately by these prayers were invoked the blessings of the day:

> "Almighty and Everlasting God, grant to this Center the grace of your presence, that all who come here may by your grace know you better...
> Give your blessing, Lord, to all who come here, that they may be knit together in fellowship here on earth, and joined with the communion of your saints in heaven, through Jesus Christ our Lord. Amen."

In 1964 and 1965, James E. Scheibler, Jr. and his sister, Beatrice Scheibler Gerber, conveyed to the Diocese of Tennessee 77 acres of the 140 acre tract now designated as St. Columba Episcopal Conference Center and agreed to leave to the Diocese the remaining acreage. This tract of virgin timber on rolling hills with lake and meadowland had been owned by the Scheibler Family for more than 80 years, having been purchased by Mr. Scheibler, Sr. on recommendation of Billy Maher.

In providing that the tract should be used as a whole and recognizing that this might appear as an extravagant use of land, Mr. Scheibler, explaining that there are examples of extravagance in church design, stated:

> "Nature should be permitted the same chance we extend to architects to create something to the Glory of God."

In 1971 when the Conference Center was formally organized, Bishop W. Fred Gates chose the name 'St. Columba' in recognition of the lovely countryside . . . as a refuge for reflection and prayer . . . a place where modern-day Christians can renew their spirit and faith and go forth with new zeal for ministry.

The name chosen by Bishop Gates for the Center had a decidedly historical background and was entirely meaningful for the particular project. St. Columba (c.521-597) was an abbot and missionary. He was of royal blood and came from a powerful Irish family. He was known as Colum, the dove, but his physical appearance would indicate that he was more like an eagle—tall, broad, vigorous, tempestuous, with a voice of thunder. Distinguished as a monk and founder of monasteries in Ireland, he moved to the island of Iona off the coast of Scotland. There he developed a flourishing monastery and went forth for missionary labors among the Picts who occupied the northern two-thirds of Scotland. As Columba went on his travels he found the powers of the druids strongly entrenched but with the cry of 'Christ is my Druid' he began to build on the sure faith of Christ and the pagan clans were gradually brought within the fold of the Christian Church. Iona soon became a center from which missionary journeys were undertaken throughout the country-side. To Iona also came many who were sick in body or troubled in spirit.

The Conference Center lodge was named the *Scheibler Lodge* and was dedicated to the Glory of God and in thanksgiving to James E. Scheibler, Jr. and his sister, Beatrice Scheibler Gerber. The generosity and foresight of these Donors, their love of God and of this small portion of his creation prompted their generous gift to the Diocese of Tennessee. The purposes for which the facilities were constructed have made the property available for use by the people. The resident manager is Ed Wills.

In conclusion—

"Jesus, our good Companion, on many occasions you withdrew with your friends for quiet and refreshment: Be present with your servants in this place, to which they come for fellowship and recreation; and make of it, we pray, a place of serenity and peace; in your Name we ask it. Amen."

Lewis K. McKee, Chairman
St. Columba Conference Center
(and the Author)

Stewardship

The most concise and complete definition of Christian Stewardship is: "the systematic and proportionate giving of our time, talents, and treasure based on the conviction that these are a trust from God to be used in His Service, in grateful recognition of His redeeming love." The First Annual Convention of the Diocese of West Tennessee passed a resolution pertaining to stewardship entitled "On The Tithe As The Standard of Giving, numbered C1-2." A complete resolution and explanation may be found on page 59 of the Journal of the First Annual Convention.

With this definition and resolution as a basis, I would like to make some personal observations regarding stewardship in the new Diocese of West Tennessee.

As chairman of the Department of Stewardship my first objective will be to broaden the understanding of stewardship in the Parishes and Missions of the Diocese. Stewardship is NOT just one's money; stewardship is time, talent and treasure.

Second, I will encourage each Parish and Mission to develop a year-round stewardship program. The primary purpose of such a program should be to teach the concepts of Christian Stewardship as related to living the Christian life. Because of its importance Stewardship emphasis should be a year-round educational process. It is essential that all clergy and lay leaders practice and teach the aspects of Christian Stewardship throughout the year.

Third, it is my opinion that the Department of Stewardship should be a source of information for Parishes and Missions. The exchange of information, especially successful results, should be encouraged and facilitated by the Department.

As we grow in our understanding of these three aspects of Christian Stewardship, we realize that the sharing of our talents and money also involves the sharing of our love, friendship and concerns for others inside as well as outside our Church. This is what Christian Stewardship is all about: it is the reaffirmation of our baptismal commitment to proclaim the good news of God in Christ in the church and outside.

>Paul Calame, Jr.
>Chairman, Department of Stewardship

The University of the South Sewanee

The University of the South at its founding in 1857 was the culmination of plans begun twenty-five years before for an Episcopal institution to be located in Tennessee "west of the Tennessee River," which would provide a "classical and theological seminary" for the diocese of Tennessee, Mississippi, and Louisiana. The Panic of 1837 brought an end to those plans which had advanced as far as naming the institution Madison College for its location in Madison County. Arthur Howard Noll in his history of the Diocese says that "Perhaps the hand of Providence" was in the failure to establish Madison College. Had it succeeded "it might have diverted and absorbed the attention that was destined for The University of the South, which was the fuller embodiment of Bishop Otey's educational scheme."

Bishop Otey, Leonidas Polk then a young clergyman at Columbia, Tennessee, and Francis B. Fogg of Nashville, principal workers in the 1830's enterprise, found themselves reunited in a larger educational proposal in the late 1850's, when Polk, by then Bishop of Louisiana, issued a letter to the bishops of the Episcopal Church in the South and Southwest, calling for an interdiocesan university. Bishop Otey as senior bishop in the Episcopal Church between North Carolina and Texas presided at the founding meeting of the Board of Trustees at Lookout Mountain on July 4, 1857, when it was decided to establish a university under the sole and perpetual direction of the Episcopal Church. The years between 1857 and 1861 were devoted to selection of a name,—The University of the South, which denoted an advanced level of education not then existing in the region; selection of a site at a height of 2,000 feet atop the Cumberland Plateau where the Sewanee Mining Company and Franklin Countians had provided nearly 10,000 acres; preparation of the organization scheme which anticipated thirty-two schools in that many branches of knowledge; and securing pledges for an endowment of $500,000, the largest sum raised up to that time in one effort by an American institution of higher learning. No permanent buildings were built and no classes begun before the Civil War came in 1861. At its end, only the Domain remained, and title to the land was in jeopardy unless school opened by September 1868.

First of the trustees to visit the site after the War was the new Bishop of Tennessee, Charles Todd Quintard, medical professor at Memphis before his ordination by Bishop Otey. He established his home at Sewanee in 1866. He raised the funds, principally in England after his attendance at the first Lambeth Conference of Anglican bishops, which made it possible to open the University in 1868 with nine students and four professors, securing the title to the land. As the first Vice-Chancellor or president, he saw work begun at the university level, including theological courses, before retiring from the vice-chancellorship in 1872. His succesor as Bishop of Tennessee, Thomas F. Gailor, had served nearly his entire ministry at Sewanee as chaplain, professor and vice-chancellor before his election as Bishop Coadjutor in 1893. Bishop Gailor served the longest period as Chancellor or chairman of the Board of Trustees in the University's history, from 1908 to 1935. Bishop Maxon served as Chancellor in 1942-44. Bishop Dandridge became Dean of the School of Theology upon his retirement as disocesan. The last Bishop of the undivided diocese, the Rt. Rev. William Sanders, and the first Bishop of West Tennessee, the Rt. Rev. Alex Dickson, Jr. are graduates of the University's School of Theology.

Strong lay leadership from West Tennessee has often been present. Jacob Thompson of Memphis, prewar Secretary of the In-
Strong lay leadership from West Tennessee has often been present. Jacob Thompson of Memphis, prewar Secretary of the Interior, and A.T. McNeal of Bolivar, were trustees and prominent members of the University's Executive Committee during the last quarter of the nineteenth century. Thompson's bequest made possible the building now known as Thompson Hall which was used to house the University's medical school throughout its existence (1892-1909), while McNeal was dean of the law school during several years of its duration (1893-1909). During the twentieth century several members of the Snowden family of Memphis served as trustees and regents, and J. Bayard Snowden of Memphis took a leading role in the development of the department of forestry, whose building is named for him. Edmund Orgill of Memphis in the 1950s devised plans for parish support of University which

greatly increased that source of the University's financing. The University has been blessed by the gifts and services of many others from the Diocese of West Tennessee.

Memphis has been the origin of a substantial number of bequests to the University, culminating recently in the more than a one million dollar fund bequeathed by Suzanne Trezevant Little, whose brothers attended Sewanee. A dormitory is named for her family, while Bishop Gailor is honored in the dining hall-dormitory which serves both college and seminary and Bishop Quintard in the large dormitory of the former Sewanee Academy, now merged with St. Andrew's School just beyond the University gates. St. Luke's Hall at the School of Theology takes its name from the fact that Bishop Quintard was a physician before he became a priest.

The Diocese of West Tennessee became the twenty-sixth diocese associated with The University of the South, with Fort Worth the newest diocese. Together with the dioceses from East Carolina to West Texas and from Missouri to Southeast Florida, they own a university with its Domain of nearly 10,000 acres and endowment approaching $50,000,000. There are approximately 1,000 undergraduates in the College of Arts and Sciences, 75 seminarians in the School of theology, 35 students each summer in the Doctor of Ministry program, 200 young musicians each year in the Sewanee Summer Music Center, and an Education for Ministry enrollment of 4,000 throughout the country.

The University today takes seriously the words of one of its principal founders—Leonidas Polk, Missionary Bishop of the Southwest, former priest of the Diocese of Tennessee, and the University's second Chancellor: "It shall be an institution established for the cultivation of true religion, learning and virtue that God may be glorified and the happiness of man advanced."

The University's appreciation for and recognition of the importance of high standards in every area of life has been one of its distinguishing features. Its willingness to boldly proclaim the Gospel of Jesus Christ in a world searching for meaning has been and must always be its most significant contribution to the Episcopal Church.

As this University continues to be true to the mission set before it by its founders, it continues to grow in stature and service to Almighty God.

Robert M. Ayres, Jr.
Vice-Chancellor and President
The University of the South

Venture in Mission

The Committee on Venture in Mission in charge of this far reaching and worthy part of the work of the Diocese of West Tennessee as carried in the 1983 Journal follows: —COMMUNICATIONS—Howard K. McIntyre, Daniel Conaway, Mrs. Richard Briscoe, Eugart Yerian, Mrs. Arvelle Carey and the Rev. Douglass M. Bailey III. GRANTS—The Rev. David R. Hackett, the Rev. Lewis K. McKee, the Rev. William B. Trimble, Jr., Richard O. Wilson. Mrs. Thomas Tucker (Mollie), Treasurer.

Bishop Sanders reported at the 1983 Convention of the Diocese of West Tennessee that the Diocese of Tennessee currently had an approximate income of two million, two hundred thousand dollars from the Venture in Mission campaign. He reported the appointment of Glenn N. Holliman as Development Officer for the Diocese and urged the utilization of Mr. Holliman's talents and skills in promoting this new program.

Truly these beginnings will provide a sound and solid future for the Venture in Mission program and with dedicated determination will meet the challenge of tomorrow.

David R. Hackett

Youth Service

"March 30, 1922

My Dear Bishop Gailor:

At the February meeting of the local assembly of the Daughters of the King held in St. Mary's Cathedral, Mrs. J. H. Noe called attention to the fact that little or nothing was being done among the female delinquents in Memphis and suggested that an effort be made to organize a unit of Church Mission of Help in Memphis. A resolution to this purpose was presented and adopted, and Mrs. R. E. Mitchell was appointed chairman of a committee to secure an organization."

The above letter was written by Bishop Troy Beatty to his superior Bishop Thomas F. Gailor, seeking approval for establishment of Church Mission of Help in Memphis. Through the years, Church Mission of Help has evolved into what is today—Youth Service in Memphis, Inc.

Church Mission of Help was established in New York in 1911 to gain more information on the problems confronting young women especially those who had gone through Women's Court. It was incorporated in New York State in 1913. In 1919, a National Council for Church Mission of Help was formed and was recognized as an official agency by the General Convention of the Episcopal Church.

The Memphis organization began when the two ladies from Calvary Church mentioned in the letter above received official approval from Bishop Gailor on April 24, 1922. The agency worked through volunteers until raising $500 at which time they were able to hire a professional social worker. On October 1, 1924, Miss Therese de Birmingham took over as the first Executive Secretary. Miss de Birmingham stayed until May, 1925, when she was succeeded by Miss Agnes Grabau. Miss Grabau held the position until she retired in 1960.

In 1932, as a result of a study done by the National Council of the Church Mission to Help, it was decided to put greater emphasis on prevention. The agency decided to accept responsibility case work with white unmarried girls, residents of Memphis, between the ages of 16 and 25 and to put greater emphasis on preventive counseling for young adolescents.

At the Board of Directors Meeting, March 21, 1947, an important change became effective. The name was changed to Youth Service and in January, 1948, the program was for the first time to include boys so that a youth as a whole might be better served.

Youth Service incorporated in 1962, and became known as Youth Service in Memphis, Inc. In January, 1963, the Rev. Donald E. Mowery came from Nashville where he had been Rector of St. Andrews to take over as Executive Director. During his tenure, the Youth Service began a camping program for young people utilizing state parks. However, events necessitated a change of location.

In 1968, Father Mowery went to the Naval Air Station, Memphis, to request permission for Youth Service young people to use the installations recreational facilities. Permission was granted and a model program was established that has been replicated at some 100 military installations nationwide with over 300,000 young people having participated. Youth Service USA, Inc., was incorporated in 1970 to promote and coordinate this replication effort.

In January 1970, the radio program "Talk It Out" was first broadcast by WHBQ. Every Sunday night since, Father Mowery and his guests have entertained and informed their listeners.

The program at the Naval Air Station was shifting focus from recreation to vocational exposure. In 1973, working with the Navy the first Jobs Skills Training and Employment participants took part in an auto mechanics school. After certification of competency the graduates were placed with local auto dealers as entry level mechanics.

As part of the Bicentennial, Youth Service sponsored "Liberty Celebration" held in conjunction with the Liberty Bowl festivities. The program that featured former astronaut Maj. Gen. Thomas Stafford, USAF (Ret.), Charley Pride, and Miss America had a religious patriotic theme.

Funding from the Environmental Protection Agency gave the Youth Service Garden Project its start in 1977. Using land furnished by the Shelby County Correctional Center young people and their families have the opportunity to benefit from this learning experience.

Perhaps the most significant event came about in 1980 when as part of a Department of Labor (DOL) National Demonstration Project Youth Service in Memphis received funding that established the Job Skills Training and Employment Program as the model for the contract. Although the DOL contract has expired, the Jobs Program continues through various funding sources with participants in training at the Naval Air Station, Memphis, Defense Depot, Memphis, Tennessee Air National Guard and the U.S. Army Corps of Engineers.

The State of Tennessee has funded replication of the Jobs Program in Nashville, Knoxville, and Chattanooga. Youth Service in Nashville currently has participants in training with Knoxville and Chattanooga to begin their Youth Service programs in 1983. The Rt. Rev. William E. Sanders, Bishop, Diocese of Tennessee has been very active in establishment of the programs in these Tennessee cities.

Bishop of the newly formed Diocese of West Tennessee, the Rt. Rev. Alex D. Dickson, Jr., has been very active in agency activities. Shortly after election, Bishop Dickson, an ex officio member of the Youth Service in Memphis Board, accepted an invitation to join the Youth Service USA Board of Directors. Support such as this will keep Youth Service a viable part of the new diocese.

Plans to replicate this Memphis Model outside the State of Tennessee have the support of the Very Rev. John M. Allin, Presiding Bishop, Episcopal Church. Bishop Allin was instrumental in orchestrating a meeting between Father Mowery and George H. W. Bush, Vice President of the United States.

As for the future of Youth Service, with guidance from our

Board of Directors and assistance of volunteers such as St. Augustine's Guild, we hope to continue to assist young people in this area through Christian care and concern. We also hope to continue to maintain a level of quality that will make others across the nation want us to help them replicate what we are doing here in Memphis.

We have come a long way from the work those women of the Church envisioned long ago, but there is still much to be done.

Donald E. Mowery
Executive Director

The Challenge of Tomorrow

The challenge of tomorrow was charted in Tennessee when the first minister of the Episcopal Church rode his horse across the mountains and preached the gospel to those eagerly waiting to hear the Word; when the first convention of the Church was held in the State; when the first Bishop was elected and consecrated; when the first men-of-the-cloth were ordained; when the first dedicated laymen and laywomen labored to build the first houses of worship; when the first congregation gathered; when the first communion was celebrated; when the first baptism was administered; when the first marriage was solemnized; when the first child learned the salient words prescribed in the Catechism; when the first burial service was read in memory of a departed communicant!

Daily, tomorrow is challenged by every deed performed. As we begin anew in the Diocese of West Tennessee we are blessed with an eternal Hope which we share as Heirs of a goodly heritage. Unquestionably, before us looms vividly and determinedly the enduring sacred challenge of today continued tomorrow in His Service.

Time is Prelude.

Time is Postlude.

And Jesus said, "I am Alpha and Omega, the beginning and the ending, which is, and which was, and which is to come. . . ."

REFERENCE NOTES

DEDICATION

[1] Holy Bible, Titus 3:7

MESSAGE FROM BISHOP ALLIN

[1] Holy Bible, Psalm 16:6

AUTHOR'S PREFACE

[1] Book of Common Prayer, p. 339
[2] Holy Bible, Romans 8:17
[3] Holy Bible, Galatians 4:7
[4] Holy Bible, James 2:5
[5] Three volumes of Episcopal Church history written by Ellen Davies-Rodgers, published by The Plantation Press, Davies Plantation, Brunswick, (Memphis) Tennessee.
[6] On April 23, 1983, the author gave a "Cousins' Party" (a Tea) in her home, The Oaks, Davies Plantation, Brunswick, in honor of the Rev. Donald E. and Mrs. (Julie Bailey) Mowery. (Mrs. Mowery, a cousin of the author.) Their marriage was the first ceremony by Bishop Dickson after his consecration. The Bishop and Mrs. Dickson flew from Vicksburg, Miss., and were honored guests at the reception.
[7] Webster's Encyclopedic Dictionary of the English Language, 1970. p. 397.
[8] The American Heritage Dictionary, 1969. p. 611.
[9] Alfred Tennyson
[10] William Shakespeare, *"Love's Labor Lost."*
[11] Holy Bible, Romans 8:17
[12] "Sons of Hope," stanza 1, Mary Artemisia Lathbury.
[13] Holy Bible, John 14:2
[14] *Ibid*, John 14:18
[15] *Ibid*, John 15:12
[16] Ibid, John 3:15
[17] *Ibid*, Psalm 39:7
[18] *Ibid*, Psalm 71:5
[19] *Ibid*, Acts 2:26
[20] *Ibid*, Galatians 5:5
[21] July 28, 1863 was the birth date of Frances Ina Stewart (Mrs. Gillie Mertis) Davies, mother of the Author.

CHAPTER 1

[1] *Old Churches and Families of Virginia*, by William Meade, D.D., Bishop of Virginia, Vol. 1, p. 63.
[2] *The Founding of Jamestown and the Church* (a pamphlet) National Council of Episcopal Churches.
[3] *The Romance of the Episcopal Church in West Tennessee*, by E. Davies-Rodgers, see pgs. 26, 27, 28.
[4] *Ibid*, p. 29
[5] *Ibid*, p. 33
[6] *Ibid*, p. 34
[7] *Ibid*, p. 34
[8] *History of the Diocese of Tennessee*, by Dr. Arthur Howard Noll, p. 34, 35.
[9] The State Constitutional Convention of 1834 created three grand divisions in Tennessee —East, Middle, West. Tennessee State Constitutional Conventions have convened in the years 1796, 1834, 1870, 1953 and 1959. The author was a delegate from Shelby County to the 1953 and 1959 Conventions.
[10] *Constitutional History of Tennessee*, by Joshua W. Caldwell, 1907. pp. 130, 131.
[11] *The Romance of the Episcopal Church in West Tennessee,* 'p. 41.
[12] *Ibid*, p. 45
[13] *Ibid*, p. 49
[14] *The Great Book*, p. 99
[15] *Ibid*, p. 102
[16] *Ibid*, p. 103
[17] *The Romance of the Episcopal Church in West Tennessee*, p. 51
[18] *Ibid*, p. 52

CHAPTER 2

[1] *The Romance of the Episcopal Church*, p. 34
[2] *Ibid*, pp. 113-174 (The Bishops)
[3] *Ibid*, The Otey Family, pp. 203-213.
[4] *The Great Book, Calvary Protestant Episcopal Church, 1832-1972, Memphis, Tennessee*, p. 290.
[5] Dedication—*Heirs Through Hope*
[6] *The Romance of the Episcopal Church in West Tennessee*, p. 125
[7] *Ibid*, p. 130
[8] *Ibid*, p. 132
[9] *Ibid*, A Hymn, *Forward*, written by Bishop Gailor and printed on the program—"Fortieth Anniversary of the Consecration to the Episcopate of the Rt. Rev. Thomas F. Gailor, and the 25th Anniversary as Chancellor of the University of the South, Sewanee, Tennessee." (Tune—"There's a Long, Long Trail.")
[10] *The Romance of the Episcopal Church in West Tennessee*, p. 141
[11] *Ibid*, p. 152
[12] *Ibid*, p. 153
[13] *Ibid*, p. 155
[14] *Ibid*
[15] *The Romance of the Episcopal Church in West Tennessee*, was dedicated by the author in memory of Bishop Barth. (See p. 166, his interment at St. John's, Ashwood.)
[16] 1983 *Diocesan Journal, West Tennessee*, p. 9
[17] Author unknown
[18] *The Great Book, Calvary Protestant Episcopal Church 1832-1972, Memphis, Tennessee*, p. 72
[19] *Ibid*, p. 75
[20] *Noll*, p. 49
[21] *Ibid*, p. 75
[22] *Diocesan Journal*, 1982, p. 65
[23] *Noll*, p. 126
[24] *Ibid*, p. 204
[25] *Ibid*, p. 228
[26] *Ibid*, p. 65
[27] *Ibid*, p. 212
[28] *The History of the Episcopal Churchwomen in the Diocese of Tennessee* by the Rev. Al W. Jenkins, pp. 23, 158
[29] 1983 *Diocesan Journal, West Tennessee*, p. 18

CHAPTER 3

[1] *Historic Madison*, by Emma Inman Williams, 1946, p. 26
[2] *The Chickaswa Nation*, by James H. Malone, 1922, p. 314
[3] *Ibid*
[4] *Natural and Aboriginal History of Tennessee*, by John Haywood. Edited by Mary W. Rothrock, 1959, p. 364.
[5] Malone, p. 57
[6] *Ibid*, p. 58
[7] Williams, p. 43. (*Jackson Gazette*, 2/19/1825.)
[8] *The Romance*, p. 57
[9] *Ibid*, p. 50
[10] *Ibid*, p. 60 (f.n. 11, 12, 13)

CHAPTER 4

[1] *The Romance*, pp. 91, 92
[2] *Ibid*, p. 93
[3] *Ibid*, p. 94
[4] *The Great Book*, pp. 89, 90
[5] *Ibid*, p. 109
[6] *Ibid*, p. 111
[7] *Ibid*, p. 112
[8] *Ibid*, p. 113
[9] *Ibid*, p. 121
[10] *The Romance*, p. 96
[11] 1983, Jl., *Diocese of West Tennessee*, p. 3h
[12] Map of Counties of West Tennessee drawn by Flocene Strickland (Mrs. T. Velmer) Murphy, a former student of the author at Memphis State University

CHAPTER 5

[1] *The Great Book*, p. 118
[2] *Noll*, p. 105
[3] Shelby County, Tennessee, records
[4] *Dioc. Jl, 1976*, p. 44
[5] Program on file
[6] Elba Gandy, a foster daughter of the author
[7] Bible, in memory of T. Rivers Young
[8] St. Philip Mission Council, records
[9] Fishers of Dundee, Mississippi, friends of Ellen and Hillman Philip Rodgers. Met at Holly Hills Country Club opening, 1974
[10] Germantown—sketch of Scruggs and Hebron on file

Due to the fact that numerous references are included in the sketches of the Churches the listing of further references seemed unnecessary.

CHAPTER 6

[1] Noll, *(Division of the Diocese)* p. 155, 9/6/1865

CHAPTER 7

[1] The Members of the Episcopate Committee were as follows: Mr. M. Anderson Cobb, Jr., Chairman, Holy Trinity Church, Memphis; Mr. Robert S. Cockroft, Grace Church, Paris; Mr. Charles M. Crump, Holy Communion, Memphis; Mr. Loucas S. Dimou, St. George's, Germantown; the Rev. David R. Hackett, Holy Trinity, Memphis; Mrs. William W. Heiskell, Calvary, Memphis; the Rev. Lewis K. McKee, Holy Communion, Memphis; Mr. Elijah Noel, Jr., Emmanuel, Memphis; Mrs. J. M. Patten, Jr., St. Mary's Cathedral, Memphis; the Rev. Wallace M. Pennepacker, St. John's, Memphis; Mr. John B. Peyton, Grace-St. Luke's, Memphis; Mr. Theodore B. Sloan, St. Matthew's, Covington; the Rev. John C. Sterling, St. Mary's, Dyersburg.

Ex-Officio Members were: Mr. Richard O. Wilson, Chairman, Structure Committee; the Rt. Rev. William E. Sanders, Bishop, the Diocese of Tennessee; the Rt. Rev. W. Fred Gates, Jr., Interim Bishop, Diocese of West Tennessee.

[2] The Profile of the Office of the Bishop and of the Bishop outlines several apostolic responsibilities and executive functions of the bishop. A copy of the profile can be obtained from the Office of the Diocese of West Tennessee, 692 Poplar Ave., Memphis, Tenn. 38105.

[3] On June 5, 1982, Yacoubian & Associates issued its report of the survey questionnaires. The data in the report was based on 2,336 completed questionnaires. A copy of the full report can be obtained from the Office of the Diocese of West Tennessee, 692 Poplar Ave., Memphis, Tenn. 38105.

[4] The resolutions concerning the process for the election of the first bishop of the Diocese of West Tennessee which were approved at the Primary Convention were as follows:

WHEREAS, Bishop Sanders appointed the Episcopate Committee of West Tennessee in November, 1982, and charged it with the responsibilities of (1) examining and defining the Office of Bishop, (2) describing the characteristics sought in the person to fill that role and (3) developing a process through which persons might be nomenated and considered for the position, and

WHEREAS, the Episcopate Committee has outlined the functions of the Office of Bishop, such outline having been presented to the Convocation of the Church in West Tennessee in June, 1982, and

WHEREAS, survey questionnaires with respect to the characteristics sought for our Bishop were distributed to all communicants of the Church in West Tennessee in April, 1982, and the Episcopate Committee has collated and analyzed the data from the questionnaires, and

WHEREAS, the Episcopate Committee has developed a process for the nomination and consideration of persons for the position of first Bishop of West Tennessee which the Committee recommends to the Primary Convention of the Diocese of West Tennessee, and

WHEREAS, this Primary Convention desires to empower the Episcopate Committee to carry out the process recommended so as to assist in the selection of a Bishop for the Diocese of West Tennessee.

IT IS, THEREFORE, RESOLVED that the Episcopate Committee of West Tennessee be authorized to develop a process for the placing of names in nomination at the First Annual Convention of the Diocese of West Tennessee (January 21-23, 1983), such process to include, without limitation, the following:

- (1) The receiving of names for consideration as first Bishop of the Diocese of West Tennessee from all interested persons and the disclosing of the names periodically to the clergy and lay delegates to the electing Convention;
- (2) The collecting of data from references on all persons whose names are submitted, such data to be elicited from uniform questions asked of the references;
- (3) The evaluation of such persons as are suggested based on the information and recommendations obtained and the results of the data from the questionnaires;
- (4) The evaluation of a relatively small number based upon personal interviews by at least three members of the Committee;
- (5) The making of such arrangements as the Committee may deem advisable to invite those persons to be nominated by the Committee to visit The Diocese of West Tennessee;
- (6) The making of nominations of a small number of persons at the First Annual Convention, having notified the delegates on or about January 4, 1983, of the persons who will be nominated.

IT IS FURTHER RESOLVED that the following recommendations of the Episcopate Committee be adopted as procedures during the electing Convention:
- (1) Nominations shall remain open throughout the election, but no nominating speeches shall be allowed.
- (2) Any delegates making nominations from the floor shall be requested to be prepared to distribute biographical profiles of the nominee to all delegates at the Convention.
- (3) Voting shall follow Article XI of the Constitution of The Diocese of Tennessee (a two-thirds majority of each order on the same ballot required to elect).

CHAPTER 8

[1] *The Ordination of The Reverend Alex Dockery Dickson, Jr.*, April 9, 1983, Program on file

CHAPTER 9

[1] *The Order of Service for the Welcoming and Seating of the Right Reverend Alex Dockery Division in the Cathedral on the Occasion of the 125th Anniversary of St. Mary's*, Program on file.

CHAPTER 10

[1] Hymnal, p. 505
[2] Author unknown
Youth Service—See *Commercial Appeal*, Sunday, 7/31/1983.
Feature store—picture of the Rev. Don Mowery—by Mary Deibel, Washington, D.C. *"I can't help but believe we're being led,"* he says of his meetings with people at the pinnacle of American political, military and industrial power."
It is to be noted that in this volume the author has taken the privilege to quote freely from her previous books written on Episcopal Church history: *The Romance of the Episcopal Church in West Tennessee; The Holy Innocents* and *The Great Book, Calvary Protestant Episcopal Church, 1832-1972, Memphis, Tennessee*. All are named in the Author's Preface. In the experience of writing such is an author's prerogative!

BIBLIOGRAPHY

The Holy Bible, St. James Version
The Book of Common Prayer, 1928 and 1979.
Journals, Diocese of Tennessee; Diocese of West Tennessee 1983.
The Founding of Jamestown and the Church, by Jamestown 350th Anniversary Committee of the General Convention of the Protestant Episcopal Church. (A pamphlet, National Council of the Episcopal Church).
Old Churches and Families of Virginia, by William Meade, D.D. Bishop of Virginia 1854. Vol. 1
Virginia's Colonial Churches, by James Scott Rawlings, 1963.
Seventeenth Century Isle of Wright County, Virginia, by John Bennett Boddie, 1938.
Historical Magazine of the Protestant Episcopal Church (Bishop Seabury Sesquicentennial Edition 1784-1934), September 1934.
History of the Diocese of Tennessee, by Dr. Arthur Howard Noll, 1900.
History of Tennessee, by Stanley J. Folmsbee, Robert E. Corlew and Enoch L. Mitchell, 1960. Vol. 1.
Constitutional History of Tennessee, by Joshua W. Caldwell, 1907.
Commercial Appeal—Centennial Edition, January 1, 1940; Episcopal Church's Story in Tennessee for 110 Years, by the Rt. Rev. James M. Maxon.
The Tennessee Churchman, Gailor Memorial Edition, 1926.
The Chickasaw Nation, by James H. Malone, 1922.
Historic Madison, by Emma Inman Williams, 1946.
History of Tennessee (Shelby County), by Goodspeed, 1886.
Old Times in West Tennessee, by Joseph S. Williams, 1875.
Beginnings of West Tennessee, by Samuel Cole Williams, 1930.
St. Mary's Cathedral, by Dr. James H. Davis, 1958.
History of Memphis, by J. M. Keating, 1888. Vols. 1 and 2.
Sewanee Alumni News, Centennial Directory, Edited by Helen Adams Petry and Elizabeth Nickinson Chitty, 1957.
Some Memoirs, by Thomas F. Gailor, 1937.
The Episcopal Church, by George Hodges, 1892.
Preaching in American History, 1630-1967, by DeWitt Holland, 1969.
Three Hundred Years of the Episcopal Church in America, by George Bridges, 1906.
The Celebrant, by Charles E. Turner, 1982.
Created for Commitment, by A. Wetherell Johnson, 1982.

ACKNOWLEDGMENTS

In the writing of this book the splendid assistance received and so greatly appreciated has been extremely ecumenical. Persons of several faiths other than Episcopalians have given graciously toward my effort to produce this volume.

The listing of every name as an individual citation is quite impossible. However, the opportunity to include the names of several persons cannot be foregone.

Especial appreciation is expressed to Presiding Bishop John Maury Allin and to Bishop Dickson, of West Tennessee, for their Messages included in *Heirs Through Hope*. Also to Bishop William E. Sanders for having shared highlights from his sermons about the creation of the new Diocese of West Tennessee.

For the pictures used the author is indebted to Glenn Holliman, Dixie Photo Center, Britt T. Woodward and Nadia Price Bates.

Appreciation is expressed to all who wrote special sections for the book particularly, to Canon George Fox, M. Anderson Cobb, Jr., Gordon Bernard and Bishop Gates. Thanks to Flocene Strickland Murphy for having drawn the map of the West Tennessee Counties on which the thirty four Churches have been located and to Mrs. George Dando for having shared the history which she had written of the Episcopal Church Home.

To Alfred G. Millikan, Jr., god-son of the author, hearty thanks for research in Davieshire Library which greatly aided the effort. To Mrs. Malcolm (Rae) Savage, Librarian, Davieshire Library, and Mrs. Marc (Becky Berlin) Askew for help.

To Eva Webb (Mrs. Lester) Donaldson, my long-time Secretary, my gratefulness for typing and giving valuable assistance in editing the manuscript. Appreciation is also expressed to Mrs. Robert M. (Ann Welting) Ford, Mrs. Randolph (Kathy Ford) Drake, Miss Natalie Tooke and Mrs. Milton (Betty Farmer) Hatcher for their contribution by typing the manuscript.

A devoted family—two of my four foster-daughters—Sarah B and Frances Gandy for loving cooperation and many deeds of kindness which have provided more time for research and writing, for which appreciation is expressed.

To faithful household and plantation help,—Valerie Moss, Arthur Humphreys, Marion Chambers, Ophelia Smith, Shirley Perry, Willie Chambers, Ida Mae Moss—hearty thanks.

To Dr. Glyn O. Carroll, veterinarian and his son, Britt Carroll, for managing the plantation herd of Angus, cutting and baling hay, hearty thanks. To the Horne Brothers—Wylie and Billy for corn and wheat planting and growing cotton and soy beans, hearty thanks.

And a word of appreciation to Seawell J. Brandau and his firm, Brandau Craig Dickerson Co., of Nashville, for having given full cooperation in the manufacturing of *Heirs Through Hope*.

Many, many calls have been made to the West Tennessee Diocesan Office in the course of writing this book. The courtesy of each person is acknowledged—and in particular to Mrs. Becky Peeples is accorded abundant gratitude! Nor can the gracious help of Mrs. T. E. (Mabel Bennett) Mitchell, Jr., affectionately called "Miss Mimi" ever be forgotten as she served for twenty years as Diocesan Secretary.

In conclusion, to each and every person who in any way has so kindly given time and talent in the creation of this book, deep and enduring appreciation is sincerely expressed by the author.

The Author

THE AUTHOR

Ellen Davies-Rodgers (Mrs. Hillman Philip Rodgers), planter, author, historian, club woman, genealogist, and parliamentarian was born Davies Plantation, Brunswick, Shelby County, Tennessee, November 13, 1903, the daughter of Gillie Mertis and Frances Ina Stewart Davies. Married Hillman Philip Rodgers, December 21, 1932.

Degrees: Positions; B.S., George Peabody College, Nashville—Majors in English and Science, 1924; M.A., Columbia University, New York City—Majors in Early Childhood Education, Supervision, Child Psychology, 1927, Teacher of all levels of education from Nursery School, Kindergarten and College including: Critic Teacher Campus School, Memphis State University, 1924-1926; Principal, Arlington (Tenn.) High School, 1928-1929; Professor, Early Elementary Education, M.S.U., 1929-1938; State Supervisor, Elementary Education, West Tennessee, 1938-1940; Principal Lausanne School for Girls, June-December, 1954. Member, Shelby County Board of Education, 1961-1965; Director, Tennessee School Boards Association, 1963-1965.

Church: St. Philip Episcopal, Davieshire, Brunswick, Tennessee.

Among Offices held: President of the following—Tennessee Association for Childhood Education, 1936-1937; Memphis Quota Club, 1935-1936; Pleasant Hill Cemetery Association, Inc., 1937-; Memphis Branch A.A.U.W., 1940-1942; Memphis State University Alumni Association, 1944-1946; Memphis and Shelby County Council of Garden Clubs, 1947-1949; Tennessee Federation of Garden Clubs, 1949-1951; State Regent Tennessee Society N.S., DAR, 1956-1959; Hester Shortridge Chapter, Calvary Episcopal Church, 1948; National Awards Chairman, National Council of State Garden Clubs, 1951-1953; Personnel Chairman, Women of the Episcopal Church, Diocese of Tennessee, 1947-1948; First President Phi Mu House Corporation MSU, 1964; Vice-President (West Tennessee) Tennessee Historical Society, 1967-1968; National Parliamentarian, Southern Dames of America, 1965; Parliamentarian, First District, Tennessee Federation of Garden Clubs, 1971-1973. Shelby County Historian, appointed by Shelby County Quarterly Court, 1965—. Clerk St. Philip Episcopal Church, Davieshire, 1976-1983.

Citations: Special Diploma, Supervision of Nursery Schools, Kindergartens, Columbia University, 1927; National Achievement Award in Education, Community Service and American Heritage, Phi Mu Fraternity, 1954; Woman-of-the-Year, Memphis Kiwanis Club, 1965; Woman-of-the-Year, Memphis Phi Mu Chapter, 1966; Cited by *The Commercial Appeal*, Memphis, Tennessee as one of ten women of the Mid-South who had contributed most to the cultural, political and social progress of the nineteen sixties and who had set the pace for the nineteen seventies, December, 1969; "Tennessee Women", (one of nineteen), cited by Panhellenic Council, University of Tennessee, Knoxville 1974-1975, (representing Phi Mu Sorority). Memphis State University presented the first Distinguished Alumnus Award, September, 1977; Memphis Branch A.A.U.W., gave and named a national Fellowship Grant, 1982.

Gave to the Diocese of Tennessee ten acres of land from Davies Plantation as a site for Saint Philip Episcopal Church, Davieshire, 1974.

Gave Church-house for Saint Philip Episcopal Church, Davieshire, built 1980-1981. Consecrated by the Bishops of the Diocese of Tennessee on November 1, 1981.

Publications: A Three Year Program is Church Personnel, Christian Vocations, 1948; "Beautiful Plant Life in Tennessee" in volume, *Pioneer American Gardening*, published by National Council of State Garden Clubs, 1951; "Historic Homes of Tennessee DAR", *DAR Magazine*, August 1958; "The Voting Age", *Proceedings of the Tennessee Constitutional Conventions*, 1953 and 1959; "The President's Message", *Volunteer Gardener*, Tennessee Federation of Garden Clubs, 1949-1951; "State Regent's Messages", *Tennessee DAR News*, 1956-1959; *The Romance of the Episcopal Church in West Tennessee*, The Plantation Press, Brunswick, Memphis Tennessee, 1964; *The Holy Innocents*, The Plantation Press, 1966; *The Casket Case* (unbound booklet), written in cooperation with Staff of Pink Palace Museum, Memphis, Tennessee, 1970; *Education—Then, Now and Yon*, Human Development, The Plantation Press, 1971; *The Great Book*, Calvary Protestant Episcopal Church 1832-1972, Memphis, Tenn., The Plantation Press, 1973; *Heirs Through Hope*, The Episcopal Diocese of West Tennessee, The Plantation Press, 1983.

INDEX

A

Abbett, Wm. C.—183
Acknowledgments—313
Acting Dean of St. Mary's Cathedral—50, 59
Act of Parliament—27
Adair, Mrs. Hiram T.—107
Adcock, Frank—105
Aiken, Warwick—168
Alford, Joseph S.T.—285
Allen, Curtis T.—94, 183
Allen, Robert E—103, 201, 268, 270
Alley, Carson—240
Alley, Frances—240
Allin, John Maury—14, 141, 179, 258, 267, 269, 306
All Saints' Church, Memphis—171
Alston family—147
Alston, Mrs. Elizabeth Whitmel Williams Johnston—93
Alston Plantation—39
Alston, Philip W.W.—65, 150, 176
American Colonies—25
American Continent—23
American Episcopal Church—18, 24
American Revolution—28
Anderson, George—31, 147
Anderson, John—31, 33, 66, 80, 147, 149
Anderson, T.C.—42
Anglican Church in Western Hemisphere—24
Anglican Communion—24
Applegate, Mrs. Allan W.—103
Archbishop of Canterbury—27
Armstrong, William J.—110
Ashwood School—37
Association of Anglican Musicians—137
Ascension Day, Thursday, May 12—277
Atkins, Jarrette C.—190
Atkinson, Robert P.—19, 178, 179
Attending Presbyters—268
Awsumb, Richard N.—106
Aswumb, Wells—103, 173
Author's Preface—17
Author, The—314
Ayers, Robert M. Jr.—303

B

Babin, David E.—134
Bailey, Douglass M.—179
Baker, M. Clark—168, 182, 191, 253
Balch, Lee C.—233
Baltus, D. Barrington—197
Barrett, Harold—203
Barrett, Peggy Lucas-Memorial Library—204
Barth House—283
Barth, Theodore Nott— 53, (children) 54, 57, 62, 94, 155, 156, 167, 171, 178, 181, 189, 203
Bartusch, Robert—269
Batchlor, George H.—93
Baumgartner, Mrs. Louis (Isabel)—284
Bazaars, St. Philip, Davieshire—108
beacon of hope—34
Beaty, Jr., Abie Earle and Clara—109
Beatty, Daniel Troy—47, (children) 48, 62, 164, 304
Beatty, Thomas—177
Beatty, Jr., Troy—48
Beckett, George—65
Bedford, Helen Mangum—114
Bell, St. Philip, Davieshire—104
Benitez, Maurice M.—271
Bernard, Gordon—17, 101, 103, 173, 271
Bernard, Jayne Lewis (Mrs. Gordon)—105, 111
Bush, George H.—306
Bibliography—312
Bills, Leonidas—89
Bishop's Bible—24
Bishop and Council—256, 257, 285
Bishop's House—40, 44
Bishop is consecrated—265
Bishops of the Diocese of Tennessee—35
Bishop Otey Memorial Mission—35, 173
Black, Isaac Edgar—159, 185
Blacklock, Joseph H.—65
Blackwell, England—23
Blaisdell, Charles F.—178, 203
Blount, Margaret—109
Bodley, James O.—60
Boldt, Ed—228
Bolivar, Tennessee—75
Book of Common Prayer—24, 29, 265
Bowman, William H.—177
Boyd, James—103
Bradley, Edward—65
Branch, Eliza (Lyde)—233
Brandau, Craig, Dickerson—4
brass railings—109
breaking of ground—102
Brinkley, Robert Campbell—221, 222
British Duchess of Teck—142
Broer, Mrs. Richard C. (Jill Schaeffer)—118
Brough, Mrs. Augusta H.—105
Brownsville, Tennessee—75
Brunini, Joseph B.—269
Bruton Parish Church, Williamsburg, Virginia—216
Buckner, Walter D.—178
building endowment—287
Bull, John—141
Burford, Elisha Spruille—65, 114, 199
Burgess, Sr., Mrs. J.O. (Doris)—98
Butler, Frank N.—141, 144
Butler, Geoffrey—298

C

Calame, Paul Jr.—301
California—23
Calvary Church, Wadesboro, North Carolina—175
Calvary Episcopal Church, Memphis—39, 55, 61, 85, 101, 147, 148, 175, 186
Cambridge University, England—40
Camp Gailor Maxon—295
Campbell, Mr. and Mrs. Alexander—251
Canfield Orphan Asylum—194, 289
Canterbury Cathedral—122
caring adults—293
Carrier, Homer C.—197, 233
Carriere, Ann S.—199
Carruthers, Ewing—391
Catechism—307
Cathedra, the bishop's chair—58
Catmur, Mr. and Mrs. Eric—137
Celtic cross—23
Cemetery, St. John's—219
Centennial Celebration, Emmanuel, Memphis—185
Challenge of Tomorrow—281, 307
Chalmers, Vernon—185
Chambers, Arthur B.—208
Chavis, Charles L.—277
Cheney, Reynold S. II—203
Cherry, Robert—134
Chickasaw Country—71
Chickasaw Purchase—71
Chickasaw Treaty—71, 72, 79
Chilton, John—33, 65, 85, 97, 141, 148, 161
Chimes—211
Christ Church, Brownsville—97
Christ Church, Nashville—31, 32
Christ Church, Pennsylvania—24
Christ Church, Philadelphia—27, 33
Christ Church, (Whitehaven), Memphis—181
Christian services—23
Church Home—173
Church in Tennessee—29, 32
Church in the American Colonies—26
Church of England—23, 24
Church of The Good Shepherd, Memphis—193
Church of The Holy Communion, Memphis—201, 203
Church Mission of Help (Memphis)—304
Church, Roberta—191
Churches erected during Bishop Otey's Episcopate—37
churchmen—281
Churchmen of Scotland—26
churchwomen—281
Churchwomen United—293
Cisel, Meredith—295
Civil War—37, 39, 89, 93, 245, 302
Claiborne, Thomas—66
Clark, Charley—127
Clark, John—109
Clarke, Mrs. Charles L. (Jane Alvis)—277, 293
Clarke, George—292
Clay, Karen—295
Clergymen, St. Elisabeth's, Memphis—211
Clergymen, St. Matthew's, Covington—124
Clown Ministry—296
Cobb, M. Anderson, Jr.—263
Cochran, Fred—291
Cochran, John—159
Cochran, Morris Bartlett—188
Cochran, Priscilla Brown—159
Cockerham, Indie—217
Collins, Charles Francis—65, 161
Columbia Female Institute—36
Columbia, Tennessee—30
Comfort, Alexander—141
Commercial Appel—213
Communications Officer—285
Communications Outlook—285
Concelebrants—268
Confederate Soldiers—45
Consecration of St. Mary's Cathedral, 1951—52

315

consecration of three Bishops—27
Consecration of the Bishop, Cook Convention Center, April 9, 1983—272
Constitution of the United States of America—27
Constitutional Convention—28
Constitutional government—25
Contents—7, 8
Continental Congress—25
Convention, 1785—26
Convention, 1786—27
Convention, 1789—27
Convention, 1882—255
Convention, 1883—255
Convention of the Diocese of West Virginia—19
Cookbook by Women of Christ Church, Brownsville—98
Cook Convention Center—265
Cooke, C. Allen—135, 270
Cooper, Frank M. IV—223, 224, 266, 277
cornerstone of the Western District—76
cornerstone of Immanuel Church, LaGrange—150
Counties of the Western District—76
county parish—165
Covington, Tennessee—75
Cowgill, Nathaniel Newlin—251
Crane, William Croes—65
Cravens, C. Frazier—240
Cravens, Herman R., Memorial Library Fund—239
Creation of the Diocese, West Tennessee, The —255, 258, 298
Creech, Mrs. Robert W.—110
Crenshaw, Frank—213
Crenshaw, Mrs. Merritt H.—110
Crim, Sheppard—233
Crisman, C.C.—199
Crockroft, Robert—239
Crook, Mrs. Jere L.—110
Cross—103
"Crown Him with Many Crowns"—277
Crump, Charles M.—291
Crumrine, James R.—269, 296
Cubine, James W.—103, 136
Cumberland Plateau—301
Cuningham, Frances Seay (Mrs. William B.)—169
Cuningham, William B.—167

D

Dandridge, Edmund P (children) 51, 62, 114, 129, 181, 302
Dare, Virginia—23
Daughters of the King—304
Davenport, Frederick P.—65, 199
Davies Hall—109
Davies Manor—107
Davies Plantation—21, 101
Davis, Jefferson—66
Davis, Jr., John Paschall—177
Davis, John H.—221
Davis, Orion W.—211
Davis, Sheldon—94, 124, 166, 282
Dean, Robert Charles—115
deBirmingham, Therese—305
Declaration of Independence—25, 63
Dedication—11
Degen George Frederic—65
Demby, E. Thomas—187
Dent, Lucian Minor—216
Development Committee, West Tennessee—288
Development Office, The—287
Dial-a-Burger and carepackages—157
Dickenson, The Rev. and Mrs. Paul C.—110
Dickinson, William G.—33, 66
Dickson, Alex Dockery, Jr.,—11, 15, 18, 141, 258, 263, 265, 271, 277, 286, 288, 293, 302, 306
Diffee, James—141
Dilts, Nancy—295
Diocesan Book Society—34
Diocesan House—50, 55
Diocesan Journal, 1976, p. 44—102
Diocesan Journal 1983—281
"diocese"—64
Diocese of Mississippi—38
Diocese of North Carolina—29
Diocese of Tennessee—32, 33, 83, 101, 103, 171
Diocese of West Tennessee Endowment Corporation—19
Diocese of West Tennessee—18, 21, 85, 101, 257, 307
Donor of the land and of the church—103
Douglass, Col. and Mrs. Henry—233
Drake, Sir Francis—23
Drummond, John—161
DuBose Conference Center—56, 293
Dumbell, George William—47, 65
Dumbell, Howard Murray—163, 195

E

early clergymen, Christ Church, Brownsville—97
earthen jug—78, 81
East window of St. Luke's Chapel, Sewanee—53
Education for Ministry—303
Eggleston, Mrs. Joseph C. (Isabelle Ridley)—178
Election of the First Bishop of the Diocese of West Tennessee—259
Ellis, Sidney—135
Emmanuel Church, Memphis—185
Emmanual Church, Warrenton, North Carolina—30, 80, 147
English Church—26
English clergy—23
English domination—27
Episcopal Church Comes to West Tennessee, 1832—79
Episcopal Church Home—289, 293
Episcopal Church in America 1784-1789—25
Episcopal Church in Tennessee 1829—1834—28, 29
Episcopal Church in the United States—63
Episcopal Church of Jamestown, Virginia—23
Episcopal Churchmen of Tennessee—291
Episcopal Churchwomen—292
Episcopal Churchwomen, Diocese of West Tennessee (officers)—68
Episcopal clergy from other Dioceses—266
Episcopal Day School, Jackson—297
Episcopal Diocese of West Tennessee—3, 17 (creation) 85
Episcopal Schools—296, 298
Episcopal Shelby Planning Commission—101
Episcopal Young Churchmen—293
Episcopal Young Churchmen, St. Philip, Davieshire—107
Episcopal Youth—294
Episcopate Committee—259
Episcopate for the Colonies—25
Eppes, Robertson Jr.—152, 171
Ewell, Richard S.—66
Examination and Definition of the Office of Bishop—260
Eylau Plantation—243

F

Fagg, William—65
Fayette County—80
Fellowship of Episcopal Youth—294
few ladies of Calvary Church—221
first annual Convention, Diocese of West Tennessee—258
First Assistant Bishop (Bishop Coadjutor)—40
First Bishop of the Diocese of West Tennessee—265
first church building erected in the Western District—93
first Episcopal Church in Shelby County—179
First House of Bishops in the United States—27, 35
Fisher, William Dallas—109, 110
Fisk University, Nashville—40
Fletcher, Francis—23
Flynn, Richard M.—243
Fogg, Francis B.—33, 66, 301
Fogg, Godfrey M.—32, 33, 66
Font in St. Philip Episcopal Church, Davieshire—109
Forward in Tennessee—284
founders, St. Andrew's, Collierville—113
founders, St. John's, Martin—155
Founding Fathers—28
Fowler, Judge Morgan C.—103
Fox, George A.—197, 223, 258
Fraser, William Carson—115
Frayser, J.W.—227

G

Gailor, Frank M.—44
Gailor Industrial School—43, 159
Gailor Memorial—43, 46
Gailor, Thomas Frank—30, 40, 42, (children) 43, 45, 49 62, 97, 113, 114, 127, 128, 187, 188, 195, 196, 199, 207, 235, 237, 256, 289, 302, 305
Gaines, Edmund P.—177
Galbraith, Charles—201
Gallaway, Thomas S.—247
Gandy, Elba—105
Gandy, Frances—110
Gandy, Sarah B.—110
Gates, William Fred Jr.—61, (children) 62, 101, 103, 109, 178, 179, 191, 229, 258, 278, 299
Gayoso Hotel—46
Gehri, William G.—199
General Convention 1892—256
General Convention 1982—258
Gerber, Beatrice Scheibler—298
Gibbs, George—251
Givens, Bill—287
Gloster-Anderson family—79
Gloster, Arthur Brehon—80

INDEX

Gloster, Elizabeth Willis—80
Gloster, Mary Hayes Willis (Mrs. Thomas Benn)—31, 78, 80, 82, 85, 147
Gloster, Mrs. (horse-ride)—81
God's children—111
God's everlasting Kingdom—21
Gohn, Joseph M.H.—223
Golden Gate Park—23
Gorgas, Josiah—66
Gospel—111
Gotten, Dr. and Mrs. Henry B.—110
Grace Episcopal Church, Paris—235, (windows) 236
Grace-St. Luke's Church, Memphis—181, 199, 297
Grace-St. Luke's School—199
Grabau, Agnes—305
Graham, William—65
Graves, Carl—133
Gray, Charles McIlvaine—65
Gray, Duncan M. Jr.—269, 270, 296
Gray, Duncan M. III—203
Gray, William Crane—65, 89, 113
Green, Bruce—201
Green, William Mercer—30, 35, 64
Greenwood, Eric Sutcliffe—60, 201, 203
Griffin, J.B. Memorial Chapel—101
Griffin, Mrs. J.B.—110
Gundrum, James Richard—267
Gunn, Julien—213

H

Hackett, David R.—207, 304
Hale, Charles—199
Hale, George Bladgett Stuart—181
Hardeman, William—66
Harpeth Academy—31, 36
Harris, Adlai O.—66
Harris, George Carroll—65
Harrison, John A.—65
Haynes, Warren E.—129
Haywood, John—72
Hazlip, Mrs. Henry—115
Hebron, John Bell—133
heirs—19, 20, 34
Heirs in Service—35
Heirs Through Hope—3, 17, 18, 38
Henderson, Dr. and Mrs. William—233
Henning, Donald—182, 204, 227, 228
Henry, Gustavus A.—66
heritage house of worship—147
Hess, Cameron—156
Hines, John Elbridge—61
Hines, Richard—42, 65
History of Episcopal Churchwomen, Diocese of Tennessee—67
Hodgson, Telfair—65
Hoffman Hall—40
Holden, Anna—113
Holden, Kate—115
Holden, William R.—110
Holliman, Glenn N.—287, 304
Hollis, Samuel B.—13, 110, 211, 291
Holy Innocents, Arlington—165
Holy Scripture—17
Honesty, George W.—159, 186
Hooker, John—178, 266
Hoover, Edwin L.—283
hope—19, 20
Howard, Henry Ripley—65
Hughes, Leonard V., Jr.—137
Hughes, Nathaniel—204
Hulsey, Mrs. Chessley H.—105
Humes, Thomas W.—65
Humphrey, Herbert—217
Hunt, Blair T.—191
Hunt, Christopher—161
Hunt, George Henry—65
Hunt, Robert—24
Hutson, Tom—139, 229

I

Illustrations—9
Immanuel Church, LaGrange—85, 147, 148
Immanual, Ripley—243
Independence Hall—27
Ives, Levi Silliman—33, 83

J

Jackson, George J.—185
Jackson, Tennessee—75
Jamestown Church—24

Jamestown, 1607—79
Jefferson, Thomas—28
Jesus said—307
Jelt, John F.—162
Jenkins, Al Warren—67
Jenkins, Caroline—171
Johnson, James Aladubi—187
Johnston, Lloyd E.—253
Jones, E. Baget—199
Jones, George David—181
Jones, Ian—103
Jones, Martha Wharton—199
Joyner, Matthew Nevill—164
Joyner, Quintard—164
Juny, Edward deSeebach—163
Juny, Margaret—248

K

keel-boat—75
Kephart, Francis W.—182
Keese, Peter—233
Keese, Thomas M.—110
King, Mrs. Edward (Monica Scott)—110, 130
King James Bible—23, 24
King James I—24
Kirkhoffer, Richard—181
Klein, William—186
Knox Hall—229
Knox, Ira—227, 229
Knoxville, Tennessee—84
Kortecht, Charles—134
Kramer, Irma—213

L

LaGrange's incorporation, 1828—81
LaGrange, Tennessee—84
Lambeth Conference—40, 114, 302
Lambeth Palace—27
Lane, Vernon W.—196
Lannom, June Fearnside—131
Lauderdale County, Tennessee—243
Layman and Laywomen—66
Leacock, William Thomas—65
Leever, George—105
Lipford, Mrs. Henry F.—110
Little, Suzanne Trezevant—303
Litton, Samuel George—33, 65, 85, 148, 149, 161, 245
Loaring-Clark, Alfred—215
Loaring-Clark, William J.—143
Lockard, Robert—228
Lofton, Anita—105, 207
love of His people—19
Love, Mary G.—227
Love, Octavia—227
Luck, Mrs. Curtis—109

M

MacDonald, Malcolm Richard—199
Maclin, Henderson—159
Madison County, Tennessee—145
Maher, Billy—299
Maney, Thomas—33, 66
Mangum, Dorothy Brode—117
Mangum, J.H. Jr.—113
Manning, William Thomas—178
Map of Counties and Churches, 1983—79
Map, Diocese of West Tennessee—86
Marlar, Luther W.—103
Marsh, John Henry—90
Martin, Joseph A.—133
Martin, Joseph E.—65
Martin, Thomas Ferdinand—65
Masonic Hall, Columbia—32
Masonic Hall, Franklin—32
Masonic Hall, Nashville—32
Mason's Depot (new Episcopal church)—162
Maxon, James Matthew—(children) 49, 59, 62, 114, 237, 256, 289, 302
McCullough, J.W.—65
McKee, Lewis K.—203, 288, 300
McKnight, James Pope—199, 248
McNabb, Edward T. Jr.—199, 294
McNeal, A.T.—89, 302
McNeal, Ann—90
McNeal, E.P.—89
McNeilly, Robert—257
McRae, Bob—291
Meade, William—24, 32
Memorial Gifts to St. Mary's Dyersburg—130, 131
Memory of Bishop Otey—38
Memphis City Schools—290

Memphis Institute of Medicine and Religion—282
Memphis Sesquicentennial Commission—179
Memphis State University—283
Memphis, Tennessee—83
Memphis University School—171
men of Calvary—188
Men-of-the-Cloth—63, 64
Men of the Cope and Miter (Bishops)—35
Men's Loyalty League—178
Mercer Hall—37
Merchant's Hope Church—24
Message from Presiding Bishop of West Tennessee—14, 15
Miller, Mrs. Milton (Elizabeth Sudlow)—157
Miller, Pitser—90
Miller, W.B.—185
Millikan, A.G. Sr.—105
Millikan, Alfred Jr.—103, 104
Ministers who served Holy Trinity—207
Ministers who served Immanuel, LaGrange—152
Ministers, St. Thomas the Apostle, Humboldt—139
Mission Council, St. Philip, Davieshire—108
"Mission Investors"—211
Missions—19
Missions of Calvary—179
Mississippi—45
Mississippi River—29
Mitchell, Mrs. R.E.—304
Mitchell, Robert I.—121
Monroe, James—71
Moore, Francis—164
Moore, Mrs. W. Joe—107
Moore, Richard Channing—29, 64, 82
Moore, Rue I.—282
Moore, W. Joe—159, 168
Morgan, J.P.—235
Morning Sun, Tennessee—75
Morrow, Joe A.—223, 278
Morton, C. Brinkley—199
Mosby, J.D.—246
"Mount Prospect"—35
Mowery, Donald E.—223, 305, 307
Mulherin, Mary Jo Tate (Mrs. Joseph G.)—145
Murry, Ruth Neil—171
music at Calvary Church—178

N

Nash, Mr. and Mrs. Kenneth—105, 109
Nash, Rodney—103
Natchez Trace—29
National Council of the Episcopal Church in America—43, 46
Naval Air Station—305
Navigation Board—75
Nealon, Dan—239, 240
network of post and stage routes—74
new Diocese of West Tennessee—286
Newell, Richard N.—65
newly created Episcopal Diocese of West Tennessee—281
new nation across the seas—26
Newport, Rhode Island—26
Nichols, M.C.—56, 167
Noe, Israel Harding—213
Noe, Mrs. J.H.—304
Noll, Arthur Howard—29, 114, 162, 176, 194, 195, 196, 245
North Carolina—23, 79
Northrop, J.M.—196

O

oak bucket—291
Old Bruton Parish—24
Oldham, Samuel—243
Old Trinity-in-the-Field—159, 161
Olsen, Carl—105
one nation under God—28
organ, St. Philip, Davieshire—105
Orgill, Edmund—171, 188, 303
Orgill, Joseph III—288
Orgill, Kenneth—228
Otey, James Harvey—11, 30, 31, 32, 33, 35, (children) 36, 62, 85, 89, 97, 141, 142, 147, 148, 150, 162, 177, 179, 199, 221, 245, 277, 301
Owens, Sam Batt—199, 266
Oxford University (England)—44

P

Packard, Laurence K.—157
Page, David—65, 199
Palmer, Mrs. Hestyr Shortridge—181
Palmer, Robert E.—181

Parsons, Charles Carrol—65, 194
patent for Virginia—23
Patten, Joe—291
Patterson, George—65, 114
Pauley, W. Harold—238
Peaks of Otter—36
Pearson, Donald E.—197
Pennepacker, Frances Roome (Mrs. Wallace M.)—219
Pennepacker, Wallace M.—216, 219, 277
Perry, John James Patrick—165
Pettis, William Montrose—65
Phillips, John—29
Pickett, Isaiah—185
Pilgrims to Massachusetts—24
Pillow, Gideon J.—66
pioneer members, St. John's—215
Piper, James H.—66
Pise, David—65
Planned Giving—288
Planning Committee for Shelby County—52
Plantation Press, The—3
Plaque to Vicar and Mrs. Gordon Bernard—111
Pleasant Hill Cemetary—109
Plummer, Kemp—31, 147
Polk, Leonidas—50, 65, 150, 246, 301, 303
Pollard, John—185
Pope, Mary Elizabeth Foote (Mrs. LeRoy)—179
Poteet, Jack—230
Prayer Book—23
Prayer Book Cross—23
Prayer of Consecration—269
prelates of the South—35
Presenters, The—267
President of the first Convention of the Protestant Episocpal Church held September 27, 1785—64
Presidents of Tennessee's Episcopal Women—67
Primary Convention—258
Pritchartt, Paul—227
Protestant Episcopal (the name)—63
Protestant Episcopal Church in the Confederate States of America—246
Protestant Episcopal Church in the United States of America—27, 28
provisional vestry, Grace Church—199
Provost, Samuel—27, 35
Pugh, Prentice—51, 237

Q

Quintard, Charles Todd—34, 38, (children) 41, 42, 47, 62, 65, 113, 114, 122, 123, 127, 142, 150, 162, 178, 185, 186, 194, 196, 243, 246, 255, 256, 302
Quintard Foundation—282
Quintard Memorial Parish—39, 94, 124

R

Racine College—42
railroad—162
Raleigh, Tennessee—75, 211
Randolph, Tennessee—75
Ravenscroft Chapel—39, 93, 94
Ravenscroft, John Starke—29, 35, 64
Ravenscroft Male Academy—37
Ravenscroft Plantation—147
Rectors, Calvary Church 1838-1983—177
Rectors and Vicars of St. James, Bolivar—91
Reeves, Charles Edward Jr.—223, 277
Reference Notes—308
Refuge of the Good Shepherd—193
religious diversity—297
Rembert, Samuel—177
Revolutionary War—25
Ringgold, Samuel—65
Roberts, Thomas D.—91
Robertson, Ken—105
Robinson, James D.—219
Ridley, Joseph James—65
Ripley, Tennessee—243
Rock City Guard—39
Rodgers, Hillman Philip—102, 103, 104
Rogers, James W.—159, 161
Romance of the Episcopal Church, The—18
Root, Benjamin F.—165
Royce, Moses L.—65
Ruch, Bob—291
Rudder, Samuel D.—190

S

saddle bags—175
St. Andrew's—245
St. Andrew's Church, Collierville—113, 114
St. Anne's Church, Millington—233, 291
St. Augustine's Church—253

INDEX 319

St. Augustine's Guild—293
St. Columba Episcopal Conference Center—(altar) 292, (Retreat Center) 295, 298, 299
St. Edward's Chapel—207
St. Elisabeth Church, Memphis—211
St. George's Church, Germantown—133
St. George's Day School, Germantown—134, 297
St. James Church, Bolivar—89, 90
St. James Church, Memphis—213
St. James Church, Union City—251
St. James Church, Wilmington, North Carolina—82
St. John's, Ashwood—50
St. John's Church, Martin—155
St. John's Church, Memphis—215, (bell) 217
St. John's Church, Williamsboro, North Carolina—30
St. John's, Knoxville—32
St. Luke's Chapel, Sewanee—53
St. Luke's Church in Virginia—24
St. Luke's Episcopal Church, Jackson—85, 141, 148
St. Mary's Church, Dyersburg—127
St. Mary's Church or Cathedral, Memphis—40, 43, 45, 49, 50, 51, 56, 58, 204, 221, 277, 282, 295, 304
St. Mary's Episcopal School for Girls, Memphis—179, 297
St. Matthew's Church, Covington—121
St. Matthew's Church, Hillsboro—31
St. Matthew's (Grace), Paris—148
St. Paul's Cathedral—46
St. Paul's Church, Franklin—32, 148
St. Paul's Church, Frayser, Memphis—227
St. Paul's Episcopal Church, Chattanooga—47
St. Paul's Episcopal Church, Randolph—85, 94, 121, 122, 148
St. Paul's, Mason—159
St. Peter's Church, Columbia, Tennessee—32
St. Philip Protestant Episcopal Church, Davieshire—17, 19, (Mission Council) 101, (Convention Delegate) 102, (Organized Mission) 102, (Consecrated) 103, (Women) 106, (a mission venture) 111, 271
St. Theodore's Chapel—283
St. Thomas, Somerville—245, (Memorials) 247, (Ministers) 249
St. Thomas The Apostle Church, Humboldt—139
Salley, Dale—103
Salisbury, North Carolina—83, 97
Sandels, John—65
Sanders, William Evan—50, 59, (children) 60, 62, 64, 103, 179, 191, 211, 222, 257, 259, 268, 270, 284, 302
Sargent, Henry R.—114
Saunders, David M.—233
Scheibler, James E., Jr.—211, 298
Scheibler Lodge—299
Schetky, George—199
Schwrar, John Miller—65, 151, 247
Scruggs, John B.—133
Seabury, Samuel—26, 27, 35, 64
Seating of the Bishop—279
Seay, Nevill Rivers—166
second mission founded by Calvary Church—221
Sesquicentennial Celebration—141
Sessums, Davis—65, 178, 247
settlement of the Colony of Virginia—24
settlement of Covington—121
Seven Hills Plantation (The Rembert Place)—233
Sewanee Summer Music Center—303
Sharkey, William L.—230
Sharp, James A.—237
Sharp, James R—56
Shawhan, Ben H.—167
Shelby, John—66
shores of America—23
Shoup, Francis A.—65
Simpkins, Julian A.—188, 191
Sister Anne Christine—289
Sisters of St. Mary (Peekskill)—289
Sivley, John H.—94, 124
Sivley, Nevill Rivers—166
Skipwith, George C.—33, 66
Sloan, Fletcher—89
Sloan, Paul Earle—124, 165
Smith, Augustine—177
Smith, Edmund Kirby—66
Smith, Franklin G.—65
Smith, Frederick—215
Smith, Hugh—252
Smith, Laura Long—252
Smith, P.N.—66
Smith, Peyton J.—124
Smith, Ralph W.—233
Smith, William—63
Snowden, Brinkley—117
Snowden family (Memphis)—302
Somerville, Tennessee—75
Sparkman, Thorne—60
Stainback, Charles—249

Stamp Act—26
State Constitutional Convention, 1834—28
Steel, William M.—161, 245
Stelle, Warren H.—213
Stehl, Catherine—105
Stephens, Daniel—32, 65, 89, 90
Steuterman, Adolph—178
Steuterman, Harry J.—204
Stevens, Burnell—291
stewardship is time, talent, treasure—300
Stewart, Dean M.—153
Stonebridge Center—102
Stonebridge Country Club—101
Stidham family—173
Stith family—114
Strahl, Otho French—90
Sunday, Billy—45
Swoope, Mrs. J.K. (Lucille)—115

T

Talbot, James L.—142
"Talk It Out"—305
Talley, F.D.—207
Tappan, B.S.—33, 66
Tate, Shep—291
Taylor, George Tarry—159, 161, 162
Taylor, Mr. and Mrs. J.N.M.—168
Taylor, William—161
television coverage—266
Tennessee 1833-1834—33
Tennessee Churchman—284
Tennessee Episcopal Church—35
Tennessee's First Constitution—28
The Cathedral Chimes—223
The Centennial History, 1858-1958, St. Mary's Cathedral, Memphis—221
The Church of The Holy Apostles, Memphis—201
The Church of The Holy Trinity, Memphis—207
The Evangel—102
The Great Book, Calvary Protestant Episcopal Church, 1832-1972, Memphis, Tennessee—18, 101, 175, 179
The Holy Bible—29
The Holy Innocents—18, 163, 164
The Hymnal—29
theology of Christian stewardship—288
"The Philippians"—107
Thirty-Four Episcopal Churches in West Tennessee, 1983—89
Thomason, Mrs. J.N.—235
Thompson, Hale—302
Thompson, Jacob—66, 302
Thornton, Kathryn—191
three Dioceses in the State of Tennessee—257
Three giant scrapbooks—178
Time is Postlude—281, 307
Time is Prelude—23, 307
Tomes, Charles—65
Tracy, Sterling—166
Travelogue—83, 97, 148, 175
Trimble, William B., Jr.—199, 270
Trinity Episcopal Church, Mason—161
Trout, Irenaeus—164, 251
Turner, Marian—105
Turner, Dr. and Mrs. W.M.—252
Twenty-One Counties Formed 1819-1875—71
Twenty-Two Parishes—87

U

United States—38
University Interfaith Center—282
University Ministries in Memphis—282
University of North Carolina—30
University of the South, Sewanee—37, 39, 40, 43, 47, 48, 49, 52, 291, 301
University of Tennessee Center for the Health Sciences—282
Upchurch, Mrs. F.H.—235
Usher, Guy S.—133, 196

V

Vaden, Dr. and Mrs. James L.—110
Vander Horst, John—57, 58 (children), 62, 139, 167, 168, 182, 211, 233, 253, 256, 284
Vault in the Cathedral crypt—52, 55
Vaulx, James J.—65, 193, 197
Vaulz, Mrs. Eliza—141
Venice—162
Venture In Mission—157, 204
video tapes—266
volumes on Episcopal Church—17
Voorhies, Emma Denie—203

W

Waffle Shop—179
Wagner, Mr. and Mrs. Daniel F.—108, 110
Wagner, Peter—215
Walker, Noble R.—173
Ward, Letitia S.—233
Warren County, North Carolina—93
Warrenton Male Academy—30
Warrenton, North Carolina—30
Washington, Emery—191
Washington, George—27, 29
Watkins, Hennie—93
Watkins, Mary Ellen—94
Watson, Matthew—33
Watson, Robert M.—282, 283, 284
Webb School, Bell Buckle—287
Weddings at St. Philip, Davieshire—110
Welcoming and Seating of the Bishop—277
Weller, Charles K.—93, 133
Weller, George—32, 65, 149, 175
Western District—29, 72, 73, 74, 75, 76, 79, 80, 83, 84, 85, 93, 147, 152, 176, 177, 245
Westminster Abbey—44
West Tennessee—28, 245
West Tennessee Mission Program—19
West, Thomas—65
Wheat, John Thomas—65
Wheeler, Mrs. Richard H.—131
Wheelock John Ambrose—122, 161, 199
White, George—65, 113, 255
White, Kimberly—105
Whie, Richard T.—217
White, Mrs. Thomas P.—235
White, William—25, 26, 27, 33, 35, 64
Whitney, George L.—237
Widney, Charles L.—133
Williams, Joseph S.—73
Williams, Rembert—233
Williamson, Thomas—185
Wilmer, George T.—65
Wilson, George—66
Wilson, Morris K. III—125
Wilson, Paul P.—277
Winchester, James Ridout—65, 178
Winchester, Mrs. R. Lee, Jr.—269
windows in Calvary Church—179
Winston, William L.—240
Women of Calvary—178
Wood, W. Lewis—223, 277
Woodstock—233
Wormley, John C.—33, 66
Wright County, Virginia—24
Wright, Elmer Morton M.—188
Wright, Charles Thomas—163
Wright, Mary Hostler Green (Mrs. Thomas)—178
Wright, Thomas—65, 82, 83, 84, 97, 121, 141, 148, 175, 176, 179, 248

Y

Young at Heart—107
Young, Mrs. T. Rivers—107
Young, Thomas Rivers—108
Youth Service, Inc., Memphis—296, 304, 305

Z

Zahrndt, Mrs. Fred—139
Zion (Christ) Church, Brownsville—85, 97, 148
Zion Hall—185